love, altruism,
and world crisis:
the challenge of
Pitirim Sorokin

Joseph Allen Matter

love, altruism, and world crisis:

171.8
M429l

the challenge of
Pitirim Sorokin

Nelson-Hall Company Chicago

HIEBERT LIBRARY
PACIFIC COLLEGE - M. B. SEMINARY
FRESNO, CALIF. 93702
10081

ISBN 0-88229-114-9

Library of Congress Catalog Card No. 73-84209

Copyright © 1974 by Joseph Allen Matter

All rights reserved.
No part of this work covered by the copyrights hereon may be reproduced or used in any other form or by any means—graphic, electronic, or mechanical, including photocopying, recording, taping, or information storage and retrieval systems—without written permission of the publisher.
For information address
Nelson-Hall Company, Publishers, 325 W. Jackson Blvd., Chicago, Ill. 60606.

Manufactured in the United States of America

contents

	foreword **vii**	
	introduction: why this book was written	**xi**
1	the need **1**	
2	Sorokin: the man and his work **13**	
3	can our existing institutions prevent war and revolt? **23**	
4	what love is **35**	
5	the manifold aspects of love **45**	
6	love in world religions **59**	
7	the unity of creation and everything in it **69**	
8	love as creative power **79**	
9	what is altruism? **89**	
10	biological factors in the creation of altruism **113**	
11	altruistic love and the supraconscious **143**	
12	self-help, polarization, and avatars **157**	
13	brotherly love for mankind **169**	
14	altruistic love in organized brotherhoods **181**	
15	earlier studies and experiments **193**	
16	what can be done: general considerations **205**	
17	what can be done: specific techniques **215**	

18	what can be done: additional techniques	**227**
19	what can be done: infant and child care and education **241**	
20	Sorokin's challenge **263**	
	notes **269**	
	bibliography **285**	
	index **303**	

foreword

This precious volume of Pitirim Sorokin is a lucid exposition of the prophetic vision of one of the master minds of our time. It is very timely, deeply inspiring, thought-provocative, and amply suggestive of practical measures. A call to man's creative intelligence to meet the challenge of history!

I had the good fortune of personally knowing Dr. Sorokin, whose warmth of heart was as extraordinary as his breadth of vision. A front-rank creative genius, he combined the broad historical perspective of a brilliant social scientist with profound philosophic insight into the timeless dimension of the universe. The ultimate meaning of human life and evolution, which emerged from this combination, inspired him to engage in sustained research at Harvard University with a view to discovering the key to the solution of our contemporary crisis.

Sorokin found that key in the magic of love hidden in the human heart. It sounds, of course, all too familiar, but it is truly an eternal mystery, ever baffling to reason's cold calculation, although readily yielding to the soul's inward vision. Like Mahatma Gandhi in recent times, Sorokin perceived the omnipotence of love in solving all human problems. Love in its true essence is what Sorokin called altruistic love. Spiritual masters and mystics of all ages called it divine love—pure, egoless, unconditional love—which expresses itself as the spontaneous self-giving of total concern. Altruistic love is that alchemy which can turn ordinary metal into gold and transform any crisis into a stirring opportunity for manifesting the glory of truth and beauty and righteousness.

On the basis of his morphological study of the great cultures of mankind, Sorokin discovers, like Vico and Spengler, a cyclical pattern in social dynamics. Every great culture starts, in his view, with the inspiration of an exalted, all-unifying, supersensory idea, e.g. God or Supreme Spirit or Being. This is what Sorokin calls the Ideational stage of the culture cycle. Having reached the zenith of its glory, the shining sun of this culture pattern begins to decline. During this period of decline, characterized as the Idealistic phase, objects and phenomena of sense experience begin to assume increasing importance. The motivation of unconditional devotion to the Supreme, the hallmark of the Ideational phase, begins to be replaced by the spirit of compromise between the Supreme Being on the one hand, and the factual or empirical realities of sense experience on the other. This compromise, known as synthesis, is achieved with the aid of metaphysical ideas, essences, laws, etc.

The Idealistic phase is followed by the final Sensate phase, in which we are living today. In the Sensate era, metaphysical ideas as well as the Supreme Being as the source of all intrinsic values fade into insignificance. Sensory objects and phenomena usurp men's field of vision as the ultimate reality. Purely utilitarian motives take over as the chief determinant of human behavior.

Gone are the days of both lofty idealism and creative inspiration!

But, fortunately, the end of a particular culture cycle is also the beginning of a new, glorious culture cycle. "The night is darkest before the dawn, but the dawn is sure to come," as another great sage of our time, Sri Aurobindo, has said. Like Sri Aurobindo in the East and Teilhard de Chardin in the West, Pitirim Sorokin beholds the dawn of a new culture epoch in the stirrings of a new spiritual awakening slowly sweeping the world today. He calls the New Age looming on the horizon the era of creative altruism. He recognizes a superconscious factor of human personality as the psychological root of pure altruistic love. It is on the basis of a new renaissance of man, resulting from the full flowering of his superconscious level of personality, that a new kingdom of heaven on earth is likely to be established.

It was probably no accident that my contact with Pitirim Sorokin was followed within a brief span of time by my acquaintance with the author of this book, Joseph Allen Matter. I was profoundly impressed with his unassuming manner, quiet devotion to humanitarian service, and active interest in the work of inter-cultural understanding between East and West. We found in him a unique combination: a successful lawyer, an affectionate family man, a competent executive officer, an imaginative writer, and an ardent philanthropist. Actively interested in community development and quality education, he combines appreciation of life's intrinsic values with perfect acquaintance with the ways of the world. His own life seems to be a practical application of Sorokin's concept of creative altruism.

x LOVE, ALTRUISM, AND WORLD CRISIS

So this precious volume is indeed a spontaneous outpouring of the author's deep personal conviction. I have no doubt in my mind that it is going to be a source of inspiration to all those concerned over the crisis of our age and motivated to do something about it.

> Haridas Chaudhuri
> Professor Philosophy and
> President, California Institute of
> Asian Studies

San Francisco
July 1973

introduction:
why this book was written

In November, 1948, Reginald de Courcy, an Englishman with worldwide sources of international information, spoke at the Union League Club of Chicago. His audience knew that Russia was developing an atomic bomb, but assumed that it could not be perfected for many years. It came as a shock to hear de Courcy say that there was strong reason to believe that between June 1 and June 15 of the next year, Soviet Russia would have completed production of its first atom bomb. "The child's play of the German war," he continued, "and the monstrous difficulties of politics at home and abroad, are nothing to compare with this single, all-powerful, transcendent issue. We shall have no time, no opportunity of setting our political philosophies in order, of bringing about the renaissance in religion which we also desire, and the other great things which we have in mind, if we allow the next year or so to drift on, as we are allowing things to drift now."

De Courcy's talk, repeated on many platforms, convinced many of us that we must speed up current efforts for a world government to supplant the impotent United Nations. Right or wrong, America regarded Russia as an enemy, restrained only by respect for our atomic arsenal. Obviously, when two nations possessed nuclear weapons, others would soon succeed in joining the club; we shuddered at the idea of a hundred-odd antagonistic, war-prone nations in possession of the means to destroy much or all of the world and everything in it.

Several organizations here and abroad were already formulating and seeking support for systems of world union, but the country as a whole showed little interest in doing anything, some of the organizations began to dispute with others, and little was accomplished. Many persons thought that world government could come only through world conquest by one nation or a group of nations.

On almost exactly the date predicted by de Courcy, Russia exploded its first atomic device. Hope that that might get the world government movement off dead center proved vain; the apathy continued. If anything, national belligerence, racial fanaticism, and internal strife and disorder steadily increased. City dwellers were afraid to walk their streets at night. Senseless killings were becoming commonplace. Rioting, burning and looting were taken for granted. The words "law and order" were no longer meaningful. Too many persons, discouraged by these and other depressing conditions over which they had no control, began to feel as did Littlechap, the small, likeable fellow in the Broadway musical whose good intentions were continually frustrated, and who would periodically shout out when things became too much for him, "Stop the World—I want to get off!"

Not everyone was indifferent to the peril of our situation. Many professional people were deeply concerned. Article after article and book after book were published, each emphasizing the deterioration of national and international order, analyzing and discussing causes, and in some instances proposing solutions. Among these writers was the man recognized as the world's leading sociologist, Pitirim Sorokin, organizer and Chairman of the Sociology Department at Harvard. Sorokin's lifetime of study and observation had convinced him that the only solution of the world crisis and the avoidance of catastrophic nuclear warfare is a purposeful, persistent and intelligently directed effort to develop in the people of the world a sufficient measure of brotherly love for their fellow beings and to increase in the world what he called creative altruism. Although I mentally scoffed at such an impractical hope when I first heard of it, I was interested enough in it and its advocate to want to pursue the subject. No other preventative of the impending cataclysm seemed to be in sight, and Sorokin's reputation as a brilliant scholar was well-established; why not at least give him a reasonable hearing?

Sorokin had retired from active work in the Sociology Department he had set up in order to organize and direct the *Harvard Research Center in Creative Altruism*. According to the Center's introductory pamphlet, the main task of the Center was "to study the chief properties and functions of creative, altruistic love and, especially, to investigate and invent efficient techniques for the creative altruization of persons and groups, or find efficient ways for the production, accumulation and circulation of creative love in the human universe." A preliminary exploration of the phenomenon of altruistic love, the pamphlet continued, as carried on by the Center, had well confirmed the age-old belief in love's enormous creative and therapeutic potentialities. The existing evidence was analyzed and factors affecting love and its power set forth. The meagerness of our knowledge of creative love and of techniques for its production and accumulation was recognized, and the importance of increased knowledge of the subject and the invention of more efficient techniques for the creative altruization of human beings was stated.

The Center, financed principally by Eli Lilly and the Lilly Endowment, had been opened in February, 1949. The pamphlet outlined the preliminary work done by the Center, listed the Center's publications and researches, and described the work the Center hoped to do. In spite of the ambitious scope and idealistic nature of his program, Sorokin appeared to have his feet on the ground; it seemed worthwhile to read his books on creative altruism and such books and articles as could be found appraising the value and accuracy of his work and findings.

This excerpt from his autobiography tells much of the man and helps explain his later consuming interest in altruistic love (he was born and educated in Russia):

> In 1918 I was hunted from pillar to post by the Russian Communist Government. At last I was imprisoned and condemned to death. Daily during six weeks I expected to be shot, and witnessed the shooting of my friends and fellow prisoners. During the subsequent four years of my stay in Communist Russia I underwent other painful experiences and observed, to the heartbreaking point, endless horrors of human bestiality, death, and destruction. Exactly in these conditions I jotted down in my diary the following "observations of a cold intellect and plaintive murmurs of a saddened heart":

"Whatever may happen in the future, I know that I have learned three things which will remain forever convictions of my heart as well as my mind. Life, even the hardest life, is the most beautiful, wonderful, and miraculous treasure in the world. Fulfillment of duty is another marvelous thing, making life happy and giving to the soul the unconquerable force to sustain ideals—this is my second conviction. And my third is that cruelty, hatred, violence, and injustice never can and never will be able to create a mental, moral or material millennium. The only way toward it is the royal road of all-giving creative love, not only preached but consistently practiced."

Hate begets hate, violence engenders violence, hypocrisy is answered by hypocrisy, war generates war, and love creates love. Unselfish love has enormous creative and therapeutic potentialities, far greater than most people think. Love is a life-giving force, necessary for physical, mental, and moral health.[1]

Writing 35 years later, Sorokin said he was more convinced than ever of the truth of those words he had written. Reading the above excerpt, one could not but feel that a man of these convictions, backed by a tremendous intellect and life-long study of the subject, must be given a respectful hearing.

National and international crises are nothing new; they have existed since the beginning of written history and doubtless before. It seemed important to find out whether brotherly love, altruistic love or creative altruism (Sorokin tended to use the terms interchangeably) had not been considered as a solution to problems in other times and realms. No doubt learned men of other cultures had discussed the subject; what were their arguments and what conclusions did they reach? Could we not to some extent measure the value of Sorokin's work and conclusions by using such previous studies as a yardstick?

When Erich Fromm wrote his book *The Revolution of Hope Toward a Humanized Technology*, he stated his purpose in writing the book in words that express equally well my purpose in writing this one. He told his readers that his book was written as a response to America's situation in 1968; that he was convinced we are at a crossroads in which one road may lead to destruction by thermonuclear war and the other to a renaissance of humanism and hope; that the book was meant to clarify the issues as well as to be an appeal to action, and was based on his conviction that solutions can be found only through reason and passionate love for life—never through irrationality and hate.[2]

In this book we will not go into the wide range of Sorokin's writings, but will confine our attention to his studies of altruism. Basically, we will be delving into sociology and anthropology, but we will from time to time be impinging on some of the other behavioral sciences. It is the intention to: first, emphasize again the extreme gravity and urgency of the problems that confront us all today; second, review and summarize in nontechnical language Sorokin's studies in and conclusions about altruistic love as a remedy for those problems; and third, appraise that remedy (and perhaps suggest others) in the light of conclusions reached by authorities and other leaders of varying cultures and times. And now to the book.

love, altruism,
and world crisis:
the challenge of
Pitirim Sorokin

1
the need

There is no problem in getting together analyses of the critical condition of the world today and of what needs changing—such analyses are legion. However, if we are to study a possible cure we need to know what we are to cure. We will look first at Sorokin's analysis and then briefly at several others.

In his prologue to *The Reconstruction of Humanity* Sorokin saw a humanity frightened by the atomic Frankensteins of destruction, desperately looking for a way out of the deathtrap, craving life instead of death, wanting peace in place of war, hungry for love in lieu of hate, aspiring for order to displace disorder, and dreaming of a better and wiser humanity. Moreover, during this century of catastrophes no leader and no plan has delivered to humanity the promised goods; the blunders of man's leaders must be corrected before it is too late, since otherwise humanity is doomed to deviate towards an inglorious and painful Calvary devoid of either redemption or transfiguration.[1]

In *Social Philosophies of an Age of Crisis* Sorokin examines the significant modern philosophies of history: those of Danilevsky, Spengler, Toynbee, Schubart, Berdyaev, Northrop, Kroeber and Schweitzer. Sorokin calls the twentieth century a period of the greatest crisis, the end of an era and a catastrophic transition to a new culture. Many of the philosophers whose theories he reviews agree with his conclusion, but not always on the same reasoning. Walter Schubart saw the century as an apocalyptic period in which various seers had foreseen the ending of something important: the post-Atlantis humanity (Merejkovsky); Christianity (Unamuno); The Thousand-year-long Western culture (Spengler); capitalism (Marx); the epoch of the Renaissance (Berdyaev).

Sorokin says in summary that with the possible exception of Spengler all the writers so examined agree that the great crisis of our age is not necessarily tantamount to the fatal last act in the drama of human history. In spite of its apocalyptic character, its further development can be stopped and eventually replaced by a new, constructive era. If humanity mobilizes all its wisdom, knowledge, beauty, and especially the all-giving and all-forgiving love or reverence for life, and if a strenuous and sustaining effort of this kind is made by everyone—an effort deriving its strength from that love and reverence for life—then the crisis will certainly be ended and a most magnificent new era of human history ushered in. It is up to mankind itself to decide what it will do with its future life course.[2]

Sorokin devotes the first part of *S.O.S.: The Meaning Of Our Crisis* to a rather unimpressive attempt to depict the pending crisis more dramatically, intentionally abandoning (as he put it) dry, scientific description in favor of a dramatic, impressionistic portraiture. The section consists of an appeal to God and "Supplications of the Little Mortals to the Big Immortals," in which Sorokin sets forth for the edification of God and the Big Immortals all the complaints, problems and troubles of the world, somewhat as preachers frequently use a long prayer to God in the pulpit as a means of emphasizing the points made or to be made in the sermon.

Sorokin was fully aware of the defects of Western culture in what he calls its declining sensate phase: newspapers and magazines devoted largely to sensation, with little emphasis on positive good; fiction ditto; cinemas and plays, operas and songs, painting and sculpture, radio and TV, also ditto. He avers that sex, insanity and crime constitute roughly from 80 to 90 percent of the topics in these fields of contemporary Western culture. Concentration on the pathological manifests itself even in our social sciences. We study crime, insanity and perversion and develop special disciplines for the purpose, but neglect the *positive* aspects of humanity and human living. In *Altruistic Love* Sorokin proposed and began the study of saints, altruists, creative geniuses and just plain "good neighbors," as one kind of study to stress the positive.[3]

Sorokin frequently uses the terms *sensate*, *ideational*, and *idealistic*, usually in regard to types of cultures, and we must understand what they mean to him. As Parsons has put it, Sorokin's *ideational* culture gives primacy to transcendental and other-worldly interests in the religious sense, and prescribes a goal of life in closest possible accord with the nature of transcendent reality, renouncing all worldly interests. Asceticism and mysticism might be paths to it. The ethical component so prominent in Christianity would take the form of altruistic love—pure, personal, selfless acts of love by individuals.

In a *sensate* culture we would go to the opposite extreme and accept the "material" aspect of reality as the real or predominant. The thing to do would be to make the most of the opportunities of the here and now, making our goals worldly success, power and hedonistic gratifications. In an *idealistic* culture we would take an intermediate position and strive for a synthesis achieving a harmonious balance between the other two.

In *Reconstruction* Sorokin gets down to some fairly brassy tacks in discussing what needs to be changed in contemporary culture, in our social institutions, in our family, school and religious institutions, and in our political, economic and other (meaning press, TV, movies, etc.) institutions, and explains why. He throws in for good measure a discussion of what is pathological in the main compartments of our culture. He tells us to recognize that although man is composed of electrons and protons and is an organism with biological drives, he is nevertheless an incarnation of the conscious mind and supraconscious essence of God; we must believe with Kant that man must always be regarded as an end in himself, and never a mere means to an end. Our existing norms must be replaced by a set of fundamental norms universally valid and unconditionally binding on everyone; many negative and empty values and norms must be discarded. What these new norms must be we shall discuss later.[4]

In suggesting needed reforms in our social institutions, Sorokin stresses our overemphasis on competition among men and recommends a reduction of this emphasis, thinking that this is possible without any corresponding reduction of man's industry and creativeness.[5] Reading his argument, one may be reminded of the ruined handball-courts in Mexico where a type of handball was played centuries ago by teams of young Mayan men. Each season ended with a championship game, the victors in which became great heroes and were feted and given the best of everything for the ensuing year. The members of the defeated team were executed—surely an example par excellence of overemphasis on competition!

Sorokin finds the family less subject to criticism than other social institutions; the good family has possibly been the most effective agency of altruism. Nevertheless, he says that because of the growing transformation of the family from a family union of husband and wife into an egoistic contractual association of male and female in the interest of pleasure and utility, the family has increasingly generated the force of egoism and demoralization. He suggests technical means of rebuilding the family into something that can become the cornerstone of a new creative social order. We will come back later to this and to his suggested improvement in school, religious, economic and political institutions.

That some of the problems confronting us are far from recent is no ground for comfort, since under today's surrounding circumstances they are far more perilous. India has, after a fashion, survived some of them for many centuries. We read this complaint in the ten centuries and more old Matsya Purana: "There is no one any more in whom enlightening goodness (*sattva*) prevails; no real wise man, no saint, no one uttering truth and standing by his sacred word. . . . Old people, destitute of the true wisdom of old age, try to behave like the young, and the young lack the candor of youth. The social classes have lost their distinguishing, dignifying virtue; teachers, princes, tradespeople and servants sprawl alike in a general vulgarity. The will to rise to supreme heights has failed; the bonds of sympathy and love have dissolved; narrow egotism rules. Indistinguishable ninnies conglomerate to form a sticky, unpalatable dough. When this calamity has befallen the once harmoniously ordered City of Man, the substance of the world organism has deteriorated beyond salvage, and the universe is ripe for dissolution."[6] Sounds pretty contemporary, doesn't it? Sorokin might have written it.

P. D. Ouspensky was a great Russian scholar and scientist whose *Tertium Organum* received wide scholarly approval. In *A New Model of the Universe*, first published in 1931, he wrote this indictment of contemporary mankind, strikingly like Sorokin's appraisal set out above:

> Man lives in the satisfaction of his appetites, in fears, in struggle, in vanity, in distraction and amusements, in stupid sports, in games of skill and chance, in greed of gain, in sensuality, in dull daily work, in cares and anxieties of the day. . . . He is infinitely remote from anything that is not connected directly with the interests of the day or with the worries of the day, from anything which is a little above the material level of his life.[7]

Although Ouspensky wrote before nuclear weapons were dreamed of, he predicted with striking prescience that there must come a period when the growth of the technique of destruction will begin to proceed so swiftly that it will destroy the source of its origin, namely, civilization.

Producing and consuming, says another writer, have become Western man's main preoccupation; means have been transformed into ends. We manufacture machines which are like men and we produce men who are like machines. As Emerson put it, "Things are in the saddle and ride mankind. . . . We need to love what we are for instead of hating what we are against."

Philosopher Charles Peirce wrote that the great attention paid to economic questions during our time has induced an exaggeration of the beneficial effects of greed and of the unfortunate results of sentiment, until there has resulted a philosophy which comes unwittingly to this, that greed is the great agent in the elevation of the human race and in the evolution of the universe. One wonders what he would have thought had he lived until today with its powerful advertising campaigns designed to constantly increase human wants and desires. Peirce predicted that the twentieth century in its latter half would surely see the deluge-tempest burst upon a world deep in ruin which that greed-philosophy had long plunged into guilt. Peirce recognized three modes of evolution—fortuitous variation, mechanical necessity and evolution by creative love (anticipating Sorokin?)—but was not very hopeful that any of the three could avoid the revolution he saw coming.[8]

Forty years ago historian Charles Beard foresaw a coming cataclysm, and warned us that rampant nationalism and the certainty of each culture of its own moral superiority might well cause the nations of a machine civilization to destroy each other. He illustrated his statement about self-righteous nationalism with a story from long ago in which a Wahhabee preacher, while praising the people of Riad, of whom he was one, remarked that the followers of Mohammed were to be divided into 73 sects—72 being destined to hellfire and only one to Heaven—and then added in solemn measure: "And that, by the mercy of God, are we, the people of Riad."[9]

Anthony Storr, a London psychiatrist, calls it a tragic paradox that the very qualities which have led to man's extraordinary success are those most likely to destroy him; he fears that since man now possesses weapons which can totally eliminate all men from this globe but lacks the inhibitions which prevent most animals from killing others of their own kind, it just may happen. Storr emphasizes the necessity for giving psychological research equal consideration with political, economic and other subjects of study.[10]

These examples of appraisals and warnings by men of stature and wisdom could be continued indefinitely, but would add detail rather than weight to those already quoted. We will consider specific weaknesses and suggest remedies in more detail under appropriate classifications further along in this book. We can perhaps best conclude this chapter by turning again to Sorokin and his own appraisal of our problem and what he hopes to accomplish through his study of, and books on, altruistic love:

> An exuberant blossoming of ethical creativity seems to be the most desperate need of humanity today. Mankind will survive if there are no great scientific or philosophical or artistic or technological achievements during the next hundred years. But

this survival becomes doubtful if the egotism of individuals and groups remains undiminished; if it is not transcended by a creative love . . . —love as a dynamic force effectively transfiguring individuals, ennobling social institutions, inspiring culture, and making the whole world a warm, friendly, and beautiful cosmos.

From the tragic experience of the last few decades we have begun to learn that without a minimum of love no social harmony, no peace of mind, no freedom and no happiness are possible. Partly in this book [*Altruistic Love*], but more fully in a series of forthcoming studies of the Harvard Research Center in Altruistic Integration and Creativity, it will be shown that love is literally a life-giving force; that altruistic persons have on the average a far greater duration of life than ordinary, and especially egotistic, persons; . . . that love is goodness itself; that love is freedom at its loftiest; that love is fearless and is the best remedy for any fear; that love is a most creative power; that it is an accessible and effective means to a real peace of mind and a supreme happiness; that it is the best therapy against hate, insanity, misery, death, and destruction; that, finally, it is the only means of transcending the narrow limits of our Lilliputian egos and of making our true self coextensive with the richest Manifold Infinity.

Even from a purely utilitarian and hedonistic standpoint, these verities are so significant that an intensive study of love—of its how and why, of the techniques of its "production," "accumulation," and "circulation"—can no longer be neglected if humanity wants to survive and to continue its creative mission."[11]

Sorokin's study of the history of cultures and civilizations had convinced him that today's Western culture is in a period of transition and that wars tend to explode in such periods. In such transitional periods the old crumbled system ceases to control groups and individuals, and since a new system of social control has yet to emerge, the result is utter confusion, atomization of all values, and moral anarchy.

At the end of the 1920's he had with near prescience predicted the coming gigantic explosions of wars, bloody revolutions, destructiveness and bestiality. The explosion came even sooner than he had expected. Some time ago the twentieth century had already become the most turbulent in revolutions and the bloodiest century in wars of all twenty-five centuries of Greco-Roman and Western history. He believed the reason had been not so much incompatibility of systems of values and norms in various countries, as, among other things, destruction of values, demoralization, extreme inflation of individual and collective egos, and emergence of rude force and fraud as the supreme controlling arbiters of persons and societies. He concludes the passage by reiterating his opinion that mankind has entered possibly the greatest and most dangerous transition from dying orders to a new—largely unknown and unbuilt as yet—order. Reading this, we might remember that Sorokin's fears, at least initially, were principally of international conflicts, but that now we must fear as much another force of destruction—internal hatreds.

With this brief look at Sorokin and his work and theories, it is now in order to review his life and the opinions of others about the man and his work so that we may appraise and make our further survey in the light of that background.[12]

2
Sorokin:
the man and his work

Pitirim Alexandrovich Sorokin (in deference to his request to his students to call him simply "Sorokin," we are doing likewise) was born on January 21, 1889. He has left three accounts of his life: *Leaves From a Russian Diary,* *A Long Journey,* and *Sociology of My Mental Life,* the last appearing as the first chapter in *Pitirim A. Sorokin in Review.*

To the age of 11 he lived among the Komi people, a Finnic ethnic group in extreme Northern Russia. His father was an itinerant "master of gilding, silvering, and ikon-making," and his mother, who died when Sorokin was three, was a Komi peasant. His Russian father, when sober, was a loving and admirable man, but during his frequent periods of extreme drunkenness, was depressed, irritable, and sometimes violent. Pitirim assisted his father and later traveled with an older brother, following the same trade. After his mother's death, his father, older brother and Sorokin lived together "as a good and harmonious team bound together by warm, mutual love, community of joy and suffering, and by a modestly creative work," until the death of his father.

Sorokin had little, if any, formal schooling until he was about 12, when he enrolled in a grade school. His only home life was with his aunt and her husband, with whom he frequently lived. He wrote, and considered it important, "I had in my early (and also later) life abundance of a true, pure, and warm love granted to me by my family, relatives, and many others." His family was Russian Orthodox; Sorokin was sincerely religious. "The moral precepts of Christianity," he wrote, "especially of the Sermon on the Mount and the Beatitudes, decisively conditioned my moral values, not only in youth but for the rest of my life."

From grade school Sorokin entered a teachers' college. In 1906 he was arrested and imprisoned for political activities. Upon release he became "a starving and hunted revolutionary, and a student of a night school, of the Psycho-Neurological Institute, and of the University of St. Petersburg.... Two more imprisonments gave me a firsthand experience in criminology and penology—the field of my graduate study and then of my first professorship. Besides several papers, in my junior year I published my first volume on crime." While in prison he joined other prisoners in reading and discussing Marx, Engels, Tolstoy and other exponents of socialism. He says in *A Long Journey* that he entered the university to avoid an army draft, that he mastered many fields there and graduated in 1914, and that after another imprisonment, he studied for his "magister" degree, which he considered more difficult to get than an American Ph.D. degree. He was an active participant in the 1917 revolution and became successively one of the founders of the Russian Peasant Soviet, a newspaper editor, secretary to Prime Minister Kerensky, and a leading member of the Constituent Assembly, vigorously opposing Lenin, Trotsky and other Communist leaders. On May 26, 1917, he married Elena Baratynskaya.

When, not long after his marriage, the Bolsheviks overthrew Kerensky, Sorokin was arrested and imprisoned in the Fortress of Peter and Paul. Tourists going through the old Winter Palace in Leningrad today are shown the room in which Kerensky and his cabinet were arrested by the Bolsheviks; Sorokin was one of the group. He was imprisoned, escaped, and was rearrested and sentenced to be shot. Each day he expected the list of executions fixed for that day to include his name but, probably in part by reason of his academic reputation, Lenin had him freed after six weeks and he returned to the university, where he founded the Department of Sociology.

During the years 1920 to 1922, Sorokin published five volumes on law and sociology, one of which blamed Communist agricultural policies for years of famine and millions of deaths from starvation. This book was the last straw; he was again arrested, but fortunately Lenin agreed to his banishment in lieu of execution. President Masaryk of Czechoslovakia invited him to Prague, where he lectured, studied and wrote for a year while partially recovering his health.

In October, 1923, Sorokin came to the United States. After a year of lecturing at Vassar, Illinois and Wisconsin and improving his command of English, he was offered a professorship at the University of Minnesota, where he says he spent six years of happy work. The year's work on his English must have been needed. Charles Loomis, in introducing Sorokin to an audience some years ago, warned his listeners that Sorokin learned English while reading Mark Twain's *Tom Sawyer* in a Russian prison and that it might have been better had he been reading some other book! He became a naturalized American citizen in 1930 and in that year was made a professor at Harvard and requested to organize and become Chairman of that University's first Department of Sociology.

Sorokin speaks in *A Long Journey* of his happy years at Harvard. He and his wife were close friends of the Serge Koussevitzkys. He loved the outdoors and with his wife enjoyed many camping trips and visits to national parks. The extensive azalea garden he planted on the high slope next to his home in Winchester is still known today for its beauty. He would frequently resort there and to the woods next to his home for thought and meditation. He enjoyed friendly relationships with many of Harvard's top scholars but was criticized by some members of other "cliques," as he called them. He was not surprised at opposition to some of his theories since, as he said, he believed politically in his own "conservative Christian anarchism," which he hoped would usher in an era to be animated by altruistic love. This view owed much to the influence of Tolstoy, whom Sorokin loved, as he did most things Russian.

There was nothing modest or shy about Sorokin's belief in himself; when after 12 years as chairman of his department he was released at his own request, he felt the department not as good thereafter. However, he magnanimously gave "anyone complete liberty to dismiss these remarks as the biased grumblings of an old man." It is good to know that in spite of his confessed lack of interest in sports and "passing social fads and fashions" he was reputed to have a better wine cellar than any member of the Harvard faculty.

During his last 10 years at Harvard he continued to give half his time to courses and seminars, and after full retirement continued to write, to attend occasional congresses and meetings, and to give papers as an "itinerant lecturer," as he put it. He refused many offers of positions; his principal interest during that period was the Harvard Research Center in Creative Altruism mentioned previously. Sorokin wrote that the Center grew naturally out of theories expounded in his *Social and Cultural Dynamics* about the existing world crisis, "its causes, consequences, and ways to overcome it."

Impressed with Sorokin's work and studies in creative altruism, Eli Lilly, through the Lilly Foundation, unexpectedly contributed $20,000 to Sorokin to advance his work. After the publication of his *Reconstruction of Humanity* in six languages, Lilly urged Sorokin to "put more steam into it," and contributed $100,000 more. The Center was then created; additional money was later supplied by the Foundation. Sorokin's forthcoming books on altruistic love were variously published in 20 languages. After his retirement as Emeritus at Harvard, the Center was almost without money and it became necessary to transfer it to the American Academy of Arts and Sciences.

Of his 10 years of work on altruistic love, Sorokin said: "If the results are more modest than I might have wished, my excuse can be expressed by an old adage: *Feci quod potui faciant meliora potentes* (I did what I could, let those more capable do better)." Despite the virtual cessation of the work of the Center, the impact of the work it did and the books Sorokin wrote are continuing to have ever-widening circles of influence. The Kraus-Thomson organization announced in 1968 that it was about to publish reprints of seven of Sorokin's books. Significantly, of the books so chosen five are those relating to altruistic love.

Carle Zimmerman says that Sorokin always wanted to go back to Russia and be received in his home university. The idea grew on him; after the death of Stalin he hoped he could safely make the trip but thought he would not dare unless Khrushchev himself guaranteed his safety. He did send his books and publications to the Library of his University but his gesture was unproductive. Later at a meeting of sociologists held in West Germany arrangements were made for a week's conducted tour through East Germany to West Berlin, but Sorokin felt he dared not even cross over Russian-occupied territory, since his banishment had been an alternative to death.

In *Sociology of My Mental Life* Sorokin comments frequently on events and things in his life that affected his ultimate views and his belief in the power of altruistic love. His work as a boy on icons and church decoration strengthened his religious faith, and its influence became so strong that after reading the *Lives of the Saints*, he tried to become an ascetic-hermit, but instead became a good preacher-teacher at neighborhood gatherings of peasants. His feeling for the power and importance of brotherly love originated in the morality and mores of the Komi peasant communities, which were based on the Ten Commandments and emphasized mutual help.

Sorokin's literary output was staggering. In addition

to 30 books, some running to four volumes, published in 17 languages, he published hundreds of papers in numerous journals in America, Europe and Asia and delivered hundreds of lectures in American universities and colleges and at professional meetings.

Sorokin died on February 10, 1968, at the age of 79. The bulk of his papers and memorabilia are now in the Shortt Library at the University of Saskatchewan, where they are available to scholars. That university has established an annual Sorokin Lecture.

The honors and offices bestowed on him were many. Cabinet members frequently invited him to Washington for conferences. Universities conferred on him honorary degrees, he was elected president of the Society for Creative Study of Civilizations and president of the American Sociological Association, he participated in the World Congress of Sociologists, and the government of Austria invited him to lecture at an International Diplomatic Seminar. He was elected to many foreign learned societies, including the Belgian Royal Academy. Indonesia asked him to organize sociology departments in its universities, his own university (Leningrad) has organized a Sorokin Archive, university chairs are being endowed in his name, and annual lecture series are being given in his honor.

So much has been written praising and appraising the work of Sorokin that it is a temptation to devote too much space to the subject. We are interested primarily in weighing the value of his theories and prescriptions in the light of the opinions of qualified critics. Perhaps the best single source for this purpose is the book *Pitirim A. Sorokin in Review* (Durham, 1963), which contains 15 critical articles by historians and behavioral scientists, and in addition a rebuttal by Sorokin and his *Sociology of My Mental Life* mentioned above.

Charles Loomis of Michigan State University, writing in *Modern Social Theories*, recognizes Sorokin as one of the most prominent of the analysts and theoreticians of the social system, calls his work monumental, discusses it in considerable detail, but finds it necessary to add, "He frequently reveals his own set of beliefs concerning the age of which he is a part; to the extent that his works are action-oriented, he appears to be the judge as well as the theoretician. Sorokin the scientist and Sorokin the man, as revealed by his works, are often inextricably blended."

Although Sorokin undeniably had a penchant for making enemies, on balance the testimony of his many students and colleagues is that his influence was predominantly creative and positively stimulating. Loomis relates a well-known passage written by Sorokin long before nuclear weapons, and apparently repeated to his classes, in which he said: "Suppose someone should discover a simple but terrific explosive which could easily destroy a considerable part of our planet . . . out of 1,800,000,000 human beings there certainly would be a few individuals who, being 'scientifically minded,' would have to test the explosive," and as a result would destroy the planet. Merton and Barber say, "No one who sat in Sorokin's classes during the 1930's is apt to forget that annual impassioned lecture."

After citing the works which made him one of the world's greatest sociologists, Loomis mentioned in a short memorial article about him written after his death, that in an informal poll Loomis took among the past-presidents of the American Sociological Association the year before Sorokin died, the consensus was that only two others had equalled his contribution to sociology.

With his background now in mind, let us look at Sorokin's analysis of the remedial efforts to solve the critical perils of the world that have been made in the past, and the reasons why they have not been successful.

3
can our existing institutions prevent war and revolt?

The first of the series of Sorokin's books on altruistic love, *Reconstruction of Humanity*, was published in 1948, and was subsequently published in Japanese, German, Norwegian and Hindi. It is an analysis of things in today's world that must be changed if wars are to be ended, and of methods that might be effective to that end; one of these is the increase of altruistic love. Sorokin first discusses the failure of various political, economic, scientific, educational, religious and other "institutions" to end or even diminish internal or external wars and strife.

He treats democracy, the United Nations and world government as political institutions, and says they are among the most popular nostrums for eliminating war. Of the plans offered by a legion of social doctors, the most frequent is democracy. Sorokin analyzes statistics covering much of recorded history and concludes that republican and democratic nations have been no less belligerent or more peaceful than monarchic and autocratic ones. After World War I democratic nations dominated the West, but were able to preserve peace for only 20 years before the most terrific explosion in human history. In civil wars and internal disturbances also, democratic nations have been no less turbulent than the autocratic nations.

Most of us will probably agree with Sorokin that democracies as they exist today are no preventative of war. This need not mean that democracy cannot be so improved that it can bring about a war-free world. Northrop says in his *Meeting of East and West* that two conditions are necessary if democracy is to function: The first is universal education, and the second is that this education must concern itself not merely with science, literature and practical matters but also with man's basic beliefs concerning the nature of himself and his universe.[1] Sorokin would add that that education must be such as to instill an adequate degree of brotherly love in the members of the democracy. It is the man more than the form of government that is important. That crusty old Scot, Carlyle, summed it up well in a single sentence: "Get *him* [a hero as Carlyle used the term] for Governor, all is got; fail to get him, though you had constitutions plentiful as blackberries, and a parliament in every village, there is nothing yet got!"[2]

Having concluded that democracy as it exists today is not in itself sufficient to prevent war and revolt, Sorokin examines the world government possibility, with particular attention to the United Nations. He acknowledges that belief in such remedies had grown rapidly during the preceding few years (we must remember that he wrote *Reconstruction* in 1948) and that for millions the United Nations was the only hope for a lasting peace, but he fears it a false hope. He recalls that the League of Nations, launched in an atmosphere of the highest hopes and expectations, died after 20 years, impotent and relegated to oblivion. His analysis of the United Nations, although made only two years after it was created, is remarkably like subsequent analyses made by others, and is a prescient recognition of the weaknesses that have brought it to almost the state of impotence reached by the League of Nations. Those weaknesses are too well-known to need recounting here. Writing when he did, Sorokin hoped that in a modified form, and as part of a much vaster system of social, cultural and personality changes, the United Nations might play an important role in the realization of its great mission. Some 20 years later we see little trend in this direction.[3]

Sarvepalli Radhakrishnan, professor of philosophy, ambassador to Russia, vice-president and then president of India, combines in his writings a deep understanding of religion, philosophy and practical government. He too has been deeply concerned over failure of the United Nations to fulfill expectations. In *The Concept of Man*, written some 10 years after Sorokin's book, Radhakrishnan says, as did Sorokin, that the victory of any particular nation, group, religion or ideology, is no longer a basic issue. Our choice now is the survival or suicide of man—extinction or human brotherhood. Not the size of a nation's armament, but the depth of its concern for the human community as a whole will decide its right to survival.[4]

Our loyalty, both agree, must now be to the world community. Democracy if it is to survive must be born again, must unlearn its national idolatries and cease to be self-seeking. It is not a written constitution that can create a commonwealth of humanity; it is a community of ideals, freedom and dignity of the individual, rule of law, economic opportunity for all citizens and love of peace.[5] Gandhi's principle of truth and love must be practiced. Radhakrishnan does not despair of the attainment of these goals—he only hopes that the commonwealth of man can produce leaders of sufficient understanding, courage and conviction to bring it about. The great Indian sage, Sri Aurobindo, also believed that political endeavor can succeed only if predicated on "the animating ideal of an all-comprehending international unity, the ideal of one family of free, self-determining nations, brought together by the spirit of universal brotherhood."[6]

Sorokin does not discount world government per se as a remedy. He calls world government indispensable as part of a vast ensemble of social and cultural changes necessary for the elimination of war, but ineffective without such changes. The "One World" government as advocated by many, he calls simply a camouflaged imperialism of nations and groups bent on promoting their special interests and without any willingness for genuine sacrifices. The egoism of contemporary individuals and groups makes it hardly possible under existing social and cultural conditions to create a real world government. He recognizes as common and very old the belief that the cause of wars is the existence of a multitude of sovereign states, but he cites 967 international wars in Europe between 500 B.C. and A.D. 1925, as against almost twice that many (1623) *civil* wars in the same countries within the same period, as sufficient proof that a purely external unification of all mankind under the sovereign rule of a world government would merely substitute civil wars for international wars without decreasing their total number, their frequency and destructiveness or their bloodiness and inhumanity.[7]

Recent suggestions for the creation of international corporations for control of the international seas and their wealth of resources, or to supply all countries with weather information, offer interesting possibilities. Either, if successful, might result in such acceptance by its member nations as would make them willing to give it broader governmental powers. Neil Jacoby suggests that future expansion of the huge corporations that own and operate international businesses throughout the world in countries other than their home base might serve the same purpose. These multinational corporations, he says, are beyond doubt the most powerful agency for regional and global economic unity that our century has produced and might ultimately succeed in doing what the awful threat of nuclear destruction has so far failed to accomplish—to bring unity to mankind. Perhaps, but shall we be given the time to wait?

Let's turn to a Russian view of the need for a universal state. Dostoevski inserted in his novel *The Brothers Karamazov* a long parable called *The Grand Inquisitor*. In it, Christ has returned to earth, and in Seville in the terrible time of the Inquisition has resurrected a dead child. The Grand Inquisitor of the Inquisition sees the incident, arrests Christ, puts him in jail, and threatens to burn him at the stake. A long monologue follows in which although Christ listens without comment, the Grand Inquisitor is really seeking to justify himself in his own eyes. He reproaches Christ for not having accepted all the kingdoms of the earth when the offer was made to him by Satan, since had Christ done so, he could have taken even the sword of Caesar and "accomplished all that man seeks on earth—that is, someone to worship, someone to keep his conscience, and some means of uniting all in one unanimous and harmonious ant heap, for the craving for universal unity is the third and last anguish of man. Mankind as a whole has always striven to organize a universal state. There have been many great nations with great histories, but the more highly they were developed the more unhappy they were, for they felt more acutely than other people the craving for world-wide union. . . . Hadst Thou taken the world and Caesar's purple, Thou wouldst have founded the universal state and have given universal peace."[8]

The views of a Russian of today may be more valuable to us. Andrei D. Sakharov is an outstanding Russian scientist and physicist, a member of the Soviet Academy of Sciences, the winner of many state honors, and even more important, in Russia is called "the father of the hydrogen bomb." His patriotism cannot be questioned, but he has become convinced that unless the great nations act promptly and in unison there will be nothing left for Russia or for any other nation to rule.

Hoping to do what he could to prevent the world's destruction, he wrote in 1968 *Progress, Coexistence and Intellectual Freedom*, a sharp criticism of Russian policy. His stature and prominence are such as, at least until now, to preserve him from government retribution. The book circulated in typewritten form, among Russian scientists and intellectuals; when it reached this country the manuscript was translated and published by the *New York Times*.

Sakharov makes no bones about his conviction that the division of mankind threatens it with destruction and that civilization is imperiled by universal thermonuclear war, fed by the narcotic of "mass culture," bureaucratized dogmatism, a spreading of mass myths that put entire peoples and continents under the power of cruel and treacherous demagogues. Any action increasing that division and any preaching of the incompatibility of world ideologies and nations are madness and crime. Only universal cooperation under conditions of intellectual freedom and the lofty moral ideals of socialism and labor, accompanied by the elimination of dogmatism and pressures of the concealed interests of ruling classes, he continues, will preserve civilization.[9]

Sakharov presents what he terms a four-stage plan for cooperation which he thinks by the year 2000 can lead to creation of a world government under which the people of the world, due in part to scientific achievements, can live in fruitful, peaceful happiness. He concludes his essay by summing up eight concrete proposals addressed to the leadership of the Russian government. The little book is important to us not for the merit or finality of Sakharov's proposals, but because he so recognizes the frightfulness of the situation that confronts us that he is willing, in hope of mitigating it, to risk his position and his life itself.[10]

In Chapter 2 of *Reconstruction* Sorokin argues that no economic system has been a factor for world peace. In reaching that conclusion, he examines capitalism and the communist, fascist, socialist and other totalitarian economic systems existing in the world back to the time of the Pharaohs; he finds them all either wholly belligerent or at least utterly unable either to reduce or eliminate war. We can hardly quarrel with that conclusion and there is no advantage in going into his arguments in detail. Few persons would expect any form of economic system to be able per se to stamp out war.

Sorokin in *Reconstruction* next takes up the failure of schooling, scientific discoveries, technological inventions and religion to preserve peace. His statistics show that in each century from the twelfth century on, whatever increase there may have been in schools, scientific institutions and discoveries and technological inventions, that increase was exceeded by the increase in wars and internal disturbances. He does not deny the *potentiality* of both education and religion to increase the amount of altruism and brotherly love in the world; rather, he censures the educational methods that have been used, and the failure of religions to convert their teachings into practice.[11]

The remaining preventatives of (or cures for) war and riots Sorokin tries and finds wanting he classifies as "legal and ethical" cures. "What has been said of religion," he says, "applies to law and ethics as inhibitors of war and other conflicts. Even if legal and moral norms prescribe altruistic conduct and prohibit war, they can be effective factors of peace only if they indeed influence the overt actions of persons and groups; that is, if they are practiced and enforced. Otherwise they remain simply impotent speech reactions."[12]

Sorokin treats both law and ethics in the same discussion because he believes that in general a law will be ineffective, no matter how rigorous its external enforcement, if the ethical norm which it embodies is not deeply rooted in a person's convictions and in his emotional and volitional nature, becoming a potent inner mentor and guide to his actions. He does not mean only that a law is impossible to enforce if it is out of line with a people's mores or ethical convictions—the impossibility of enforcing national prohibition in this country sufficiently evidenced that. For Sorokin, law is a *part* of ethics, along with morals.[13]

I think Sorokin would have felt that a passage in one of Northrop's books shows his agreement with him. In it, Northrop refers to our disputes with Mexico, Peru and other Latin-American countries over the "confiscation" of American properties in those countries for use in alleviating poverty and distress. He points out that the Lockean principle of primacy of property rights over human, social or economic needs on which the American constitution was predicated is not recognized there. He recognizes a growing body of public opinion there and elsewhere that accepts the assumption that human rights may under at least some circumstances, be superior in value to property rights. The policy of the United States which has insisted upon recognition of the sacredness of property rights as a minimum standard of international law has done much to persuade Mexicans and Latin-Americans that it is impossible to extend democracy in their countries from the political to the economic sphere without replacing the Lockean with the Marxian philosophy.[14]

To illustrate his point Northrop cites Orozco's fresco at Dartmouth College in which a school teacher and her blank-faced self and pupils are entitled, "Anglo-American Soul." The painter's criticism is that a philosophy of life which shuts its eyes to the creative fire in man's nature, so cuts man's soul off from the fresh, warm, bodily, earthy feeling of life that one becomes artificial and stereotyped, afraid of one's emotions, tense, and often colorless or neurotic.[15]

Sorokin thought it unfortunate that intellectually sophisticated, modern men apply their altruistic ideologies much less consistently than primitive tribes, unsophisticated children, or simple persons in general. This brings to mind the principal character in Dostoevski's *The Idiot*, a young man acute of mind, yet so full of love and unselfishness towards all humanity as to be regarded by some as less than bright. Dostoevski himself felt this same love for and oneness with humanity. He once said that each of us is responsible *for* everything and *to* every human being, and refers to an old Russian proverb that says: "Love me black as I am; when I am white everyone will love me."

Sorokin comments wryly that in spite of millions of sermons on Christian love and invocations of the name of Jesus, and in spite of powerful forces directed against anti-Semitism and other racial and religious discrimination, overt Christian altruism has shown no tangible increase nor have anti-Semitism and racial and religious tensions perceptibly decreased. Had he been writing today, we can be sure he would have referred to a tangible *increase* in racial antagonism.[16]

Sorokin concludes that none of the foregoing "institutions" can assure peace, that taken alone they are either fallacious or inadequate, and that their principal defect is that they neglect the decisive factor of altruism and love, without which war cannot be eliminated, and are unable to make the overt behavior of persons and groups, with their social and cultural institutions, more altruistic than they are now. Whatever the other prerequisites of a creative and lasting peace may be, he was convinced it cannot be achieved without a substantial increase of love, sympathy and free cooperation in the overt relationships of persons and groups.[17]

If we agree with Sorokin that law or laws alone, as well as the other "institutions" discussed in this chapter, cannot alone assure peace, and that it may well be that only the development and spread of altruism and love can assure internal and external peace and save the world from impending disaster, we should now investigate the conditions and means through which human beings, groups and social and cultural institutions can become altruistic.

4
what love is

In summary, the need for a new means of preserving world peace is clear; Sorokin after a lifetime of thought and study concluded that a studied and planned increase in altruistic love is the only possible, although admittedly difficult, solution; Sorokin's life, professional background and acknowledged stature give weight to his conclusions and recommendations, and his reasons for feeling that no remedy or solution heretofore attempted can by itself be effective are plausible. It is now in order to take up in at least a preliminary way the subject of love itself and its many ramifications. What is love? What are its attributes? What are its values? More specifically, what did Sorokin mean by his phrases "altruistic love" and "creative altruism"?

Strangely, Sorokin did not attempt a concise definition of love. He perhaps explains his reason in the opening passage of *The Ways and Power of Love*. "Love," he says, "is like an iceberg: only a small part of it is visible, and even this visible part is little known. . . . Love appears to be a universe inexhaustible qualitatively and quantitatively." He adds that Paul Tillich well expressed this infinity of love when he wrote: "I have given no definition of love. This is impossible, because there is no higher principle by which it could be defined. It is life itself in its actual unity. The forms and structures in which love embodies itself are the forms and structures in which life overcomes its self-destructive forces."[1]

Of necessity, dictionaries must attempt greater conciseness, but the many different meanings they give the word serve principally to evidence its diversity of use. It will help to look at what a few writers have said in describing it.

Any approach to a discussion of love and its powers should begin with a reading of what Ralph De Bit, in a fine passage unfortunately too long to quote here, correctly calls the words of St. Paul in I Corinthians 13 (which see) the finest exposition of love ever given to the world. De Bit testifies that in all the experiences of a life devoted to philosophical research and to internalizing the awareness of his own being, never had he discovered a secret law for attaining superior power except one of conscious cooperation with the marvelous force of love that is within each of us. "Let love," he says, "be the predominant thought, motive, impulse of your life, and all other qualities and conditions will fall into place harmoniously. When you manifest love, you manifest God, for God *is* Love."[2]

Isadore Schneider in his introduction to *The World of Love*, recognizes the specialized terminology needed for various approaches to love, yet notes that all see it as a principle in which forces are exerted for unification and growth against opposing forces of hatred and disintegration. He refers to the classic terms for the three kinds of love: Eros, Agape and Philia, the first to denote love in which the self and its demands are predominant, the second that in which others are acknowledged and their needs and demands made important, and the third in the sense of a fusion and fulfillment of the two. Schneider suggests simplifying the terms to "need-love," "gift-love" and "mature love."[3]

Eberhard Arnold, a man of whose work we shall read later, wrote: "Love is simply life itself, life in every sense, entire and eternal life. Hence the love that is Agape. . . . knows no limit in time and space. . . . It is strong enough for any task because of its persistent faithfulness. . . . It seeks and demands nothing for itself because its whole life is in the object of its love. It knows nothing about rights; its nature is to discard and forget the standpoint of rights and to find its happiness in giving."[4]

Anders Nygren summarizes the content of the Christian idea of divine love as follows: Agape is spontaneous and unmotivated, is indifferent to value, is creative, is the initiator of fellowship with God and, in summary, is God's way to man.[5] His point, which he appears to consider new but which has been the tenet of more than one Eastern religious philosophy, is that while fellowship with God has always been understood to involve the question of the way by which men can come to God, there is in reality from man's side no way at all that leads to God; there is only a way from God to man—the way of Divine forgiveness and love.

Sorokin agrees with Nygren that Agape comes down from above while Eros is man's effort to ascend, but he wants it clear that Agape in no way excludes Eros-Love, which he says is nothing but falling in love with love and trying to be more perfect in love, with all the mental, moral, aesthetic and physical ennoblement such perfection implies; he does not want to play down man's ability to perfect himself by his own efforts. If the transfiguration can be achieved only by way of Nygren's Agape, Sorokin says all effort to achieve the goodness of love would be of no avail; it might shine equally upon the virtuous and the sinful.[6]

The Indian sage-poet, Tagore, in his book *The Religion of Man*, mentions some songs which he had often heard from wandering village singers belonging to a popular sect of Bengal, called Bauls, who have no images, temples, sculptures or ceremonials, but who declare in their songs the divinity of Man and express for him an intense feeling of love. Coming from a people unsophisticated and living a simple life in obscurity, Tagore feels this a clue to the inner meaning of all religions, for it suggests that these religions are never about a God of cosmic force, but rather about a God of love.[7]

An important factor in the increase of love in the individual is the ability of that individual to identify himself with others. This has been particularly emphasized in Eastern philosophies, where that identification is extended not only to other humans but to all living and sometimes inanimate things. George Palmer divides love into three levels, the third of which is mutuality, which he defines as recognition of two persons as inseparable elements of one another, each being essential to the welfare of each. The attitude of each must be that of identification with the other. Mutuality must have love to be truly ideal, and as a necessary corollary, altruism attains its fullest and steadiest expression in a super-personal love, identified by dedication to others and to society in general.[8] Tagore put it:

> However, whatever name our logic may give to the truth of human unity, the fact can never be ignored that we have our greatest delight when we realize ourselves in others, and this is the definition of love. This love gives us the testimony of the great whole, which is the complete and final truth of man. .... The Spirit of Love, dwelling in the boundless realm of the surplus, emancipates our consciousness from the illusory bond of the separateness of self; it is ever trying to spread its illumination in the human world.[9]

The Hindu view is expounded with less beauty but more directness in one of the Upanishads, where the writer explains human love according to the enlightenment received in his meditations: human beings and natural things cannot be direct objects of love. Our love is directed through them—we embrace the Self in another. Although in one sense this might be called self-love, it is not selfish love. Complete union between individuals may be had only in recognition by each of the true Self in the other. "Verily, a husband is not dear, that you may love the husband, but that you may love the Self through the husband. . . . Verily creatures are not dear, that you may love the creatures; but that you may love the Self through the creatures." The important point made here is one Plato made later, that love is the pursuit of the whole, not important in itself but in its revealing a more eternal or fundamental love, realized through this love of Self through everything.[10]

Psychologist Jean Mandler, after reading these last few paragraphs, commented that although "identification" as used above, is a major Freudian concept, it is given little emphasis in the West. She suggested that perhaps the difficulty of our society is not so much increase in crime, violence and such dramatic things, as such, as it is the total unwillingness of most people to identify in this sense with others.

Even Schopenhauer says that loving-kindness is the real cardinal virtue; it was reserved for Christianity to formulate and expressly advance it as the queen of all virtues and to extend it even to enemies, although in Asia a thousand years before, the boundless love of one's neighbor had been taught and practiced. Not to be denied his reputation for pessimism, however, Schopenhauer goes ahead to question whether altruism is worthwhile, since one's happiness and service of the human race are a relative illusion and the conclusion of the whole matter is thus: All is vanity.[11]

Erich Fromm in the preface to his *Art of Loving* warns his readers that his book wants to show that love is not a sentiment that can be easily indulged in by anyone. All one's attempts for love are bound to fail unless he tries most actively to develop his total personality; satisfaction in individual love cannot be attained without the capacity to love one's neighbor, or without true humility, courage, faith, and discipline.[12] His book is based on the premise that love is an art and requires knowledge and effort. Most people see the problem of love primarily as that of being loved rather than that of loving, of one's capacity to love. To the same effect, Haridas Chaudhuri says there can be no substitute for *genuine* love and sympathy; one must be in warm rapport with fellow beings—love begets deep understanding and transforms it from cool calculation into warm-hearted participation and transforms knowledge from vainglorious self-seeking into compassionate self-giving.[13]

We should not leave this general topic of love and its various forms without further mention of self-love. It is a common saying that self-love is no love, but this is not true. Charles Peirce makes the statement, but later qualifies its abruptness.[14] Fromm would seem to agree, but what he really does is set up narcissism, Freud's term for self-love, as something that must be overcome to achieve pure love. To do this requires the development of humility, objectivity and reason.[15] Fromm has devoted much space in his writing to showing that you *must* first love yourself if you want to love others. Probably the theory is now pretty well accepted—we must love *everything*, including ourselves.

Because they teach that one's first duty is to develop his own spiritual potentialities, Buddhism and Vedantism are sometimes criticized as given to self-love rather than to love of others. Christopher Isherwood explains the fallacy of this view in an imaginary dialogue between himself and some Indian sages running somewhat like this: Being advised what he is to do for his spiritual development he is told to judge every thought and action from this standpoint: "Does it make me freer, less egotistical, more aware of the Reality; or does it attach me more tightly to the illusion of individual separateness?" When he objected that this selfishness would disregard his obligation to others, he was told that his duty towards the community would be far better done because his motives would be less mixed with vanity: "You think you love some of your neighbors now. You cannot dream how you will love them all, when you begin to see the Reality within each human being, and to understand his absolute identity with yourself."[16]

With correct knowledge of self-love, we can no longer think of it and selfishness as synonyms. We are not told by religion not to love ourselves, but rather to love our neighbors *as* ourselves. If we do not love ourselves, the rule is meaningless. The point is the one made in the Isherwood dialogue.

Isadore Schneider has a hopeful thought for us in his *World of Love*. He says that although classical culture contained intimations of what was to come, it was the development of Christianity with its commands to love that enlarged the awareness of societal and spiritual love; that in the religious community, the craft guilds and other groupings, a greater range of individual choice appeared and new communal attachments evolved; and that hence today the slow but perceptible consciousness of universal unity is no longer seen as an ideal, but rather as a realizable aspiration in the first attempts at supernational organization of the human community.[17] The current phenomenon called the "hippies," and their emphasis on loving, perhaps furnishes an example of the point Schneider makes. The foundation of social sciences to study and report on lesser known world cultures has also enlarged the understanding of the basics of human relationships.

What has been written in this chapter well illustrates the nebulous character of love and the frustration involved in trying to pin it down to definite and concrete attributes. Serving to add a bit of realism which is nevertheless pertinent is this ad recently appearing in a Madrid newspaper: "Use this automatic washer: less work, more time for love."

5
the manifold aspects of love

To this point, our look at what has been written about love has been pretty general in nature. In *Ways and Power*, Sorokin gets into the heart of his discussion. Love, he says, has seven main aspects. Its religious aspect was briefly touched upon in Chapter Four. On its second —the ethical—aspect he pauses only briefly. Ethically, love is the essence of goodness inseparable from truth and beauty. All three are unified aspects of the Absolute Value or God. Real goodness is always true and beautiful; pure truth is always good and beautiful; and genuine beauty is invariably true and good.

The third aspect of love he calls the ontological aspect, and treats at some length.

"Ontologically," he says, "love is, side by side with truth and beauty, one of the highest forms of a unifying, integrating, harmonizing, creative energy or power. Empedocles correctly noted the unifying creativity of love as its ontological essence. . . . Subsequent thinkers viewed even the unifying physical forces of gravitation, of the unification of electrons and protons in the atom, of chemical affinity, of magnetism and so on, as the manifestation of love energy acting in the *physical* world; the 'instincts' of sociality or gregariousness, biological mutual aid and cooperation, as the manifestation of love energy in the *organic* world; [and] conscious love, sympathy, friendship, solidarity, as its manifestation in the *psychosocial* world. . . . Love raises man as a biological organism to the level of divinity, infinitely enriches the human self, and empowers humanity with a mastery over the inorganic, organic, and sociocultural forces, up to the potential rescue of an individual and mankind from even biological death. Dostoevski well expressed this ontological power of love in his *Brothers Karamazov*: 'Seeing the sins of men, one sometimes wonders whether one should react to them by force or by humble love. Always decide to fight them by humble love. If it is carried through, the whole world can be conquered. Loving humbleness is the most effective force, the most terrific, the most powerful, unequaled by any other force in the world.' . . . A person who becomes a real incarnation of love will yield an influence greater than that of the sceptered monarch, testifies Gandhi. 'Love is basically not an emotional but an ontological power, it is the essence of life itself, namely, the dynamic reunion of that which is separated' [Tillich]."[1]

Sorokin mentions two Russian philosophers (Federov and Solovyev) who have shown that only through love can man realize his true nature and fulfill his mission.[2] According to Solovyev love replaces the struggle for existence by harmonious unity and mutual aid, tending to make the universe one harmonious cosmos

the manifold aspects of love

in which each particle is not fighting all the others but harmoniously working with the rest of the world. So far in the natural world we have only a partial realization of this creative work of love energy.[3]

Sorokin's exaltation of the power of love may at first blush seem overdone, but there is nothing new in what he asserts—he merely echoes the substance of what philosophers and mystics have been saying through the ages. For example, Boethius after his term as actual, although not titular, ruler of the Eastern Roman Empire, was falsely betrayed by a rival and put in jail to await execution. While there he wrote the great book *The Consolation of Philosophy*, and in it (probably having in mind the theory of Empedocles mentioned above) says:

> Through Love the universe with constancy makes changes all without discord: earth's elements, though contrary, abide in treaty bound: Phoebus in his golden car leads up the glowing day; his sister rules the night that Hesperus brought: the greedy sea confines its waves in bounds, lest the earth's borders be changed by its beating on them: all these are firmly bound by Love, which rules both earth and sea, and has its empire in the heavens too. . . . O happy race of mortals, if your hearts are ruled as is the universe, by Love![4]

The fourth—the physical—aspect of love Sorokin explains in a single sentence, possibly because the explanation has been foreshadowed in his discussion of the ontological aspect: "According to Solovyev and others, the physical counterpart of love in the inorganic world is shown in all physical forces that unite, integrate, and maintain the whole inorganic cosmos in endless unities, beginning with the smallest unity of the atom and ending with the whole physical universe as one unified, orderly cosmos."[5]

Of the fifth—the biological—aspect of love, Sorokin says, citing 10 authorities, that the biological counterpart of love energy manifests itself in the very nature and basic processes of life. This energy, still little known, and often called the "vital energy" that mysteriously unites various inorganic energies into a startling unity of a living organism, is the first biological manifestation of the Empedoclean energy of love. The generation of practically all unicellular organisms from a parent cell, by fission of the parent cell, is another manifestation of biological love energy: the two are for a time bound together in an interactive association and the life of either one or the other is at some time dependent upon the potential or actual being of the other. Without such interaction the appearance of a new organism is impossible; the very continuity of life itself becomes impossible. Cooperation of two organisms in sexual reproduction of multicellular organisms, accompanied by the passion of biological attraction between them, is a visible form of this "biological love" necessary for the maintenance of all such species and, through that, of life itself.[6]

The sixth—the psychological—aspect of love is less technical. According to Sorokin, the experience of love is psychologically a complex consisting of emotional, affective, volitional, and intellectual elements. In any genuine psychological experience of love, the ego or I of the loving individual tends to merge with and to identify itself with the loved Thee. The joy or sorrow of the loved person becomes joy and sorrow to the loving person. Genuine sharing of all the values of life follows.

Sacrifice for the loved person becomes a sacrifice for the sacrificing person himself.[7] In other words, love as psychological experience is "altruistic" by its very nature. In a genuine love the loved person is experienced always as the end value; in the egoistic experience the other person is always only the means value (Kant's "categorical imperative" ethic).

Sorokin quotes Solovyev as saying love is the justification and deliverance of individuality through the sacrifice of egoism; it rescues us from the inevitability of death, fills our existence with an absolute content, annuls our individual loneliness, fills the emptiness of our isolation with the richest value, breaks and transcends the narrow walls of our little egos and makes us coparticipants in the highest life of humanity and in the whole cosmos. Sorokin adds on his own that love is marked by a feeling of fearlessness and power and is hence the best and most scientific remedy for fear, and that the love experience is equivalent to the highest peace of mind and happiness.[8]

Much of the foregoing has the support of psychologists. Erich Fromm also says that the "I" of love tends to merge with and identify itself with the "Thee." The deepest need of man, he says, is the need to overcome his separateness, to leave the prison of his aloneness. The absolute failure to achieve this can mean insanity. The desire for interpersonal fusion is the most powerful striving in man; it is the most fundamental passion and the force which keeps together the human race and its sub-groups.[9] This reference to "I" and "Thee" may remind us of the Jewish philosopher Martin Buber and his best known work *I and Thou*, in which he perceives love as the unique quality of the I-Thou relationship.

"Love," he says, "is responsibility of an I for a Thou. In this lies the likeness . . . of all who love, from the smallest to the greatest and from the blessedly protected man . . . to him who is all his life nailed to the cross of the world, and who ventures to bring himself to the dreadful point—*to love all men.*"[10] Mere charity or solicitude will not do, . . . for in them one offers one's assistance but not one's self to the other person. There must be love.*

Closely allied to the psychological aspect of love is its seventh—the social—aspect. Sorokin says love on the social plane is a meaningful interaction or relationship between two or more persons where the aspirations and aims of one are shared and helped by other persons. It is the joy of giving and the joy of receiving, fulfilling oneself in others and by others; its highest forms are magnificently defined in the Sermon on the Mount.[11]

Fromm says of the social aspect of love that one of its principles is the solidarity of all men and the loyalty to life and to humanity which must always take precedence over the loyalty to any particular group; any true love for another person has a particular quality, for I love in that person not only the person but humanity itself, or, as a Christian or Jewish believer would say: God.[12]

---

*This sounds much like Christianity, and Buber was never anti-Christian. He once came up with an unforgettable comparison when, in a famous address to an audience of Dutch clergymen, he gave this succinct account of the difference between Jewish and Christian attitudes towards the central conviction about Christ as the Messiah in the Christian Faith: "To the Christian, the Jew is a stubborn fellow, who in an unredeemed world, is still waiting for the Messiah. To the Jew, a Christian is a heedless fellow, who in an unredeemed world, affirms that salvation has, somehow or other, taken place."

There is almost complete unanimity on this aspect. De Chardin words the thought: "Only love can bring individual beings to their perfect completion, as individuals, by uniting them one with another, because only love takes possession of them and unites them by what lies deepest within them."[13]

Reinhold Niebuhr says that man is an individual but he is not self-sufficing. The law of his nature is love, a harmonious relation of life to life in obedience to the divine center and source of his life; this law is violated when man seeks to make himself the center and source of his own life.[14] In one of his stories Dostoevski has an Elder advise a doubting woman that there is in religious matters nothing to prove; she will become convinced of God's reality and the immortal state of her soul to the degree that she progresses in practicing love.[15] We find in so many of the Russian novelists this same outpouring of spiritual and humanistic love.

There seems to be a simplicity in the Russian nature that has lent itself to unquestioning acceptance of daily living and love as an alleviation of hardships. Tolstoy's story *What Men Live By* is another example.[16] In it an angel being punished for disobeying God is deprived of his wings and dropped naked in the churchyard of a poverty-stricken Russian village. He is rescued from freezing to death by a poor cobbler who puts on the naked man some of his own clothing, takes him home, shares with him the bit of food available and keeps him on as an apprentice cobbler. Various charitable things happen under the influence of the mysterious stranger. After about six years, during which the stranger has smiled three times with so wondrous and illuminating a light that it dawns on the cobbler that his apprentice is more than human, he asks him why he smiled three times and why light had streamed from him.

The angel explains that in exiling him the Lord had said to him, "Thou shalt learn three lessons: Thou shalt learn what is in men, and what is not given unto men, and what men live by. When thou shalt have learned these three lessons, then return to Heaven." A long explanation of various incidents which had occurred during the story follows, after which the angel's body becomes manifest and he tells the three things he has learned and which have earned him his right to return to Heaven. He says, "I have learned that every man lives, not through care of *himself*, but by love. . . . When I became a man, I was kept alive, not by what thought I took for myself but because a stranger and his wife had love in their hearts, and pitied and loved me. The orphans were kept alive [referring to one of the incidents in the story] not because other people deliberated about what was to be done with them but because a strange woman had love for them in her heart, and pitied them and loved them. And all men are kept alive, not by their own forethought, but because there is *love in men*. . . . I have learned that God does not wish men to live each for himself, and therefore He has not revealed to them what they each need for themselves, but He wishes them to live in union, and therefore He has revealed to them what is necessary for each and for all together. I have now learned that it is only in appearance that they are kept alive through care for themselves, but that in reality they are kept alive through love. *He who dwelleth in love, dwelleth in God, and God in him, for God is Love.*" Whereupon the angel sings a hymn of praise to God, the ceiling parts, a column of fire reaches from the earth to heaven, and with the cobbler and his wife and the children prostrate on the ground, pinions appear on the angel's shoulders and he soars away to heaven. It is too bad that space does not permit printing in full this remarkable parable.

The Yoga aphorisms expounded by Patanjali near the time of Christ set forth spiritual disciplines intended to aid man in fulfilling his life. One aphorism reiterates the principle we are examining: "We are to live so that no harm or pain is caused by our thoughts, words or deeds to any other being. In a positive sense, this means that we must cultivate love for all, and try to see the one Atman [real Self—the Divine existing within the person] within everybody. We must think of ourselves as the servants of mankind, and be ready to put ourselves at the disposal of those who need us." (Prabhavananda translation.)[17]

The importance Sorokin attaches to this seventh —the social—aspect of love receives support in one of the most popular Indian religious festivals. The festival is celebrated by the tying of a sacred thread around the wrist of every person among the Hindus throughout India, without regard to caste or creed. This thread symbolizes the spiritual binding of its wearer to all others and sacrifice of his personal, family and caste interests for the realization of the well-being of all in the nation, which according to the Indian viewpoint takes in all of humanity.[18]

A. J. Heschel finds a basis for the view not dependent on religious belief. He reasons that man is social by nature and needs society not only to survive but to satisfy other basic needs of his nature. Unlike animals, who are content when their needs are satisfied, man insists on not only *having* but on *being needed*. There is no man who has not been moved by anxiety as to whether he is needed; man is not sufficient to himself and life is not meaningful to him unless he is serving an end beyond itself and which is of value to someone else.[19]

The British philosopher, Francis Bradley, also argues from a nonreligious viewpoint. He holds that the moral end is self-realization—not the isolated self as with the utilitarians nor the abstract self acting for the sake of duty as with the Kantians, but a self having a relation to other selves in a community. Only individuals are real, but they become real through relations with other individuals in families, states and nations. Man has a place in a system of selves which requires that he act in certain ways in relation to the whole and to the other selves which are parts. "In short, man is a social being; he is real only because he is social, and can realize himself only because it is as social that he realizes himself."[20]

Chaudhuri of the American Academy of Asian Studies has summarized well the necessity of love of others to one's own development:

> But even in the process of spiritual fulfillment and constructive self-development of an individual, human relations play a very dominant role. This is so because relations enter into the essential structure of the individual self. Apart from relations to the social environment, the individual self is a mere abstraction . . . . Relations are essential to the growth of the individual soul, because the individual in his essence is not an isolated entity. He is not like a Lucretian atom, solid in singleness

and enclosed within itself. He exists in close interdependence and interrelationship with his fellow beings. He grows through constant social intercourse with others. He belongs inseparably to a community and a country. He belongs in a larger perspective to the international human family. From a still broader standpoint, he belongs to the cosmic whole, to the entire universe. Relatedness to the social context or cosmic whole is then an essential ingredient of the individual. So the development of an individual as an individual requires increasing skill in the adjustment of his relations to others. It consists in joining hands with others in constructive cooperation without loss of inner freedom and sense of value.[21]

As would be expected in view of the purpose of Sorokin's study in this field, he says, as he concludes this preliminary analysis of love's seven aspects, that we will now concentrate mainly on the psychological and social planes of love (which in combination he terms "psychosocial")—love as a "visible" empirical psychosocial phenomenon.[22] That sentence is rather formidable. Just what does Sorokin mean? His discussion might be summarized as follows.[23]

He says first that even as an empirical psychological phenomenon, love remains a many-dimensional cosmos having at least five "dimensions": its intensity, extensity, duration, purity and the adequacy of its objective manifestation in overt actions and material vehicles in relation to its subjective purpose. We might say more simply, that in considering and measuring love we must take into consideration its degree of intensity, the scope and breadth of the objects of the love, the length of time it lasts, the extent to which it is influenced by selfish motives, and the efficiency with which it effects its benefits to the creatures or things to which it is directed.

Intensity can be illustrated by two examples. When we observe a person who preaches love but does not practice it, we know that the intensity of his love is near the zero point; at the other pole, actions by which a person freely gives to others greatest values—health, life, "soul," hedonistic or utilitarian happiness—are love actions of the highest possible intensity.

Extensity of love may range from the zero point of love of oneself only, up to the love of all mankind, all living creatures, and the whole universe, including even inanimate objects, as did St. Francis, who loved his "dear brother—earth" and thus "reverently and lovingly walked the earth."

Duration refers only to the length of time the love continues.

Purity of love may range from that without the taint of a "soiling motive" of utility, pleasure, advantage, or profit, down to the "soiled love" where love is but a means to a utilitarian or hedonistic or other end—love that is only the thinnest trickle in a muddy current of selfish aspirations and purposes. The statements of saints that they love God and would love him even if He were to condemn them to an eternal hell for such love, are perhaps the most striking expressions of the purest love.

As to the *adequacy* of love, we might say simply that the test of its adequacy is, "does it work?" Sorokin says that love may be subjectively genuine in the loving person but that the objective consequences of his love actions may be very different from, even opposite to, the love goal. For example, a mother who loves her children intensely and, wanting to make them "lovable" and good, pampers and fails to discipline them, thus often making them capricious, irresponsible, weak, lazy or dishonest.

Because it is manageable and not too complex, this five-dimensional classification can serve us in many ways. It allows us to grade the magnitude of love, that is, how much of each of the five dimensions is included in any specific instance of love. We shall make use of it in some of the following chapters.

6
love in world religions

In his discussion of religion as a remedy, Sorokin says that if Christianity and its norms of conduct as they are enunciated in the Sermon on the Mount were really practiced by Christians, and if Confucianism and Taoism, Hinduism and Buddhism, Judaism and Jainism, Mohammedanism and other religions, with their moral commandments, were actually realized in the overt behavior of their followers, they would exert a decisive influence upon the inhibition of war. Through the universal practice of love, hatred and injustice would be eliminated and abiding harmony would prevail throughout the entire human universe.[1]

With Sorokin's statement that universal practice of the basic teachings of almost any of the major world religions would probably solve our problem, few of us would disagree. The "Golden Rule" is to be found in nearly every religion, largely almost identical in language. In Christianity, Jesus's second law of love, "Thou shalt love thy neighbor as thyself," follows tautologically from His first law of love, "Thou shalt love the Lord thy God with all thy heart, with all thy soul, and with all thy mind." (Luke 10:27 and Matthew 22:37, 39.) Love of neighbor flows from and *is* love of God.

Eberhard Arnold, founder of the Brotherhood about which we shall hear more later, was a convinced and forceful advocate of the Sermon on the Mount and all that it stands for. He, too, equated love of God with love of one's neighbor. Although a highly educated man, his published works are written with simplicity and understanding and are imbued throughout with a spirit of warm love for humanity. Recognizing that Christianity has tended to emphasize the redemption of the individual, Arnold considered that emphasis a grave misunderstanding of the historical Jesus, who taught that there is no reconciliation with God without reconciliation with *all* men. There is no subjective Christianity in the sense of exclusive attention to one's own little individuality in its isolated relationship to its personal God, because there is no such thing as an isolated individuality, and God does not see a man out of the context of his relationship to other men. Arnold correctly understood the Christian teaching of how to love your fellow-men—love Jesus, and *through* Him and His love, love of fellow-men will come.[2]

"Love God, mankind and everything" seems pretty well to sum up the spirit of the Sermon on the Mount. The emphasis placed today on the importance of love by those we call the "hippies," merely follows that biblical injunction. The hippies in their effort to shake themselves loose from the hidebound conventions that control most of us, may have hit upon a fundamental truth the rest of us tend to discount or forget. We need not condone the bad habits of some of them, but in a few years we may find that the hippy phenomenon has been good for us.

Christianity is only one of the three major religions whose foundation stone is the Old Testament; Judaism and Mohammedanism (Moslemism) are the others. Although Christianity grew directly out of Judaism the teachings of the two religions about love are the same only in part. The duty of the people of Moses and his Judaic successors was to obey Jehovah, not to love him. Judaism's traditional admonition to love is a law to be obeyed, rather than something to be done out of love for God, and embraces all Jews rather than all men.[3] However, this narrow conception is no longer accepted by all Jews, and there are passages in the Old Testament and in the Torah that seems to dissent from it. For example, love of one's fellow-man is enjoined not only towards Jews (Lev. 19:18) but also the stranger (compare Lev. 19:34 and Deut. 10:19). Judaism also differs from Christianity in that by orthodox Christian doctrine love of one's fellow-man grows out of and is really part of love of God or love of Jesus as the son of God. Love of God and love as a pure and important natural force or quality are less important in Judaism than in Christianity.

The Mohammedan bible, the Koran, treats law and morals as identical; every commandment, including those related to morality, is from Allah. Very little emphasis is placed on love of man for his fellow-man. Charity is required, but this is to be extended only to other Moslems. Only true believers are to be considered as brothers; this must be remembered when we consider the Mohammedan version of the Golden Rule: "No one of you is a believer until he loves for his brother what he loves for himself."[4]

The Koran has always been considered so final that no book is needed; nevertheless good Moslems accept and obey, in addition to precepts of the Koran, many of the precepts and traditions that had grown up and were reduced to writing in 870. Christian influence seems to have molded many of these traditions, and here we find love toward one's enemies advocated, although Mohammed had held sterner views.

Since Buddhism, like Hinduism, originated in India, was an outgrowth of Hinduism, and so far as our present interest in it is concerned, embodies substantially the same principles as Hinduism, their precepts on altruistic love may be considered together.

There is really no such thing as a single unified religion which can be called Hinduism, but the teachings of its various branches about brotherly and universal love for all men and even all creatures, are much the same. The teachings of Krishna, the Hindu counterpart of the Christian Jesus, established the fatherhood of one omnipotent personal god who taught peace, charity, love for human beings and all creatures, kindness to all, unselfish and disinterested work for the good of humanity, and faith in the inexhaustible goodness of the supreme Lord of the Universe; he forbade revenge and taught his followers to return good for evil and love for hatred. He truly taught a religion of love and devotion.[5]

Turning to the Buddhist development of Hinduism, we find that the *Sutra of the Golden Light*, a masterpiece of Mahayana Buddhist literature enjoying undiminished influence for centuries, declares that Buddha exists as the saviour possessed of an all-embracing love. Since

Buddha is omnipresent, everything that exists is subject to his eternal vigilance of boundless compassion. The climax of the sutra is a parable in which Buddha, because of his great love for all living creatures, gives himself up as a meal for a hungry lion. Universal Brotherhood born of the love of all beings is the basis of the Buddha's moral principles: there can be no love greater than the love of man, and there can be no service greater than the service of man.

Two of the world's great religions still alive today originated in China—Taoism and, if it can be properly classed as a religion, Confucianism. Of religion in the narrow sense of the word, Lao-tse, the founder of Taoism, said nothing. He did not believe in the gods and opposed all forms of worship. Some of the verses in the Tao Te King of Lao-tse might be translated to advocate love or compassion for others but the religion definitely did not emphasize it. Much of the genuine Taoism became incorporated and continued to live in Confucianism. Later Taoism became corrupt and holds no interest for us.

In determining the attitude of Confucianism towards love, the key word is *jen*. Like so many Chinese characters, *jen* can be translated in several ways; it is best translated as love, and has been oftenest used in that sense. Confucius did not define the word, but when he was asked its meaning he replied, "It is to love man." On that basis the early Chinese philosophers, whether Confucian, Taoist, Mohist or Legalist, have equated *jen* and love. In referring to love the philosophers have meant love for all and Confucius said, "love all men comprehensively."

Jen was the foundation of Confucian ethics because it stands for the ideal relationship among human beings.

Confucius considered *jen* to be the perfect virtue of a human being and the only road to a peaceful and harmonious society. Not only will he who embraces *jen* treat people gently and humanly but he will practice courtesy, magnanimity, good faith and kindness everywhere and at all times.[6] Robert Merton has well said that Confucianism is not just a collection of formalistic devotions, but was meant to give full expression to that natural and humane love which is the only genuine guarantee of peace and unity in society and which produces that unity not by imposing it from without but by bringing it out from within men themselves.[7] To practice *jen* is to love mankind universally. In illustration, there was once told to Confucius a story about the King of Chu, who lost a precious hunting bow and looked for it for days. After a while he gave up and said, "What does it matter? A man of Chu lost it and another man of Chu found it." When Confucius heard the story he said, "He should have left out the words 'of Chu'."

The writings of K'ang Yu-Wei, a Chinese philosopher and reformer born in 1858, are so startlingly pertinent to our subject that they must be mentioned, even though this drastically abridged account can give not much more than a hint of his full prediction.

K'ang revived the very ancient theory that China (meaning the world) would go through three ages—those of Disorder, Small Tranquillity and Great Unity. K'ang thought it now apparent that the Age of Disorder was that of the time of Confucius, the Age of Small Tranquillity was that of his own day, and the Age of Great Unity was yet to come. Not only China, K'ang wrote, but the entire human race has been steadily moving from Disorder, through Approaching Peace or Small Tranquillity, and towards the common goal of Universal Peace, which will be reached in two or three more centuries hence. (Wright.)

K'ang believed with Confucius and Mencius that all men possess minds which cannot bear to see others suffer, and that it is the existence of this kind of mind that will make the achievement of the Great Unity possible.

After naming nine steps to be taken to achieve the goal, K'ang says: "The future world state will emerge within two or three centuries as the final result of a gradual process of amalgamation, stimulated both by wars and by disarmament conferences. [One wonders if K'ang would have been so certain of his timetable had he known that within less than a century there would exist in man's hands the means of destroying all living things on earth. With the final achievement of unity, ... the world commonwealth will have a universal language, calendar, and system of weights and measures, and will be governed by a people's world assembly, elected through universal suffrage. Migration and intermarriage will gradually merge the existing races into a single uniform world race, and class distinctions will likewise disappear. Women will enjoy the same rights, perform the same tasks, and wear the same clothes as men. Marriage contracts will be valid for one year only, renewable after that time according to the wishes of the partners. The family will vanish, its functions being performed by state-operated nurseries, schools, hospitals, old age homes and similar institutions. There will be no private ownership of agricultural, industrial or commercial enterprises, all of which will be communized."

K'ang further predicted that in the new society

people will live in huge air-conditioned public apartments and that great airships will transport them rapidly to all parts of the globe, propelled either by electricity or by power produced through the refining of some new substance—a prophetic allusion either to gasoline or to something like atomic energy? In addition, there would be mercy killings, synthetic foods, and chemicals to check the spread of harmful insects. Inasmuch as love would be taken for granted in the Great Unity, religions like Christianity and Islam would no longer be needed and would gradually wither away. At the least we have here food for thought![8]

Over most of its history Japan has had four major religious movements: Shinto, Buddhism, Confucianism and Christianity; the Japanese practice of the last three is substantially that followed in other countries. Shinto existed in prehistoric times as a primitive animism and Emperor-worship. In very early times it was combined with Buddhism. When they were later separated, Shinto became largely a state ceremonial religion primarily intended to unify and deepen national sentiment and is not important to our discussion.[9]

Religion in Japan during the past 50 years has undergone more major changes than that in any other country. Japan emerged from World War II so shaken and with its beliefs and faith in its history and destiny so destroyed that it offered fertile soil for new religions. Those registered with the Minister of Education in 1963 numbered 171 and boasted a total membership of perhaps 18 million. Most of the new religions do not depart greatly from traditional teachings except that practically all are now working to attain or establish the Kingdom of God on earth, and now, not later. For such a kingdom world peace is necessary, so this is emphasized in the official writings of most of the new religions; the necessity of living the religion in daily life is also emphasized. Most recognize the validity of other religions. The traditional Japanese attitude towards plural religions is illustrated in the saying: "We are all climbing Mt. Fuji, some from one starting place, some from others, so we cannot see each other now because the mountain is between us, but we will all see the same moon when we finally arrive at the top." Many of these new religions mix the old Shinto and Buddhist doctrines with Christian teachings and biblical events. There are versions of the Sermon on the Mount and the Lord's Prayer, and Christian terminology is used extensively.[10]

Would it seem trivial to end this rather serious chapter by repeating here Leigh Hunt's *Abou Ben Adhem*, which many of us first read in grade school? Perhaps the fact that love of God is love of one's fellow-men has never been more beautifully explained than in that poem. Many of you will remember it:

Abou Ben Adhem (may his tribe increase!)
Awoke one night from a deep dream of peace,
And saw, within the moonlight in his room,
Making it rich, and like a lily in bloom,
An Angel writing in a book of gold:
Exceeding peace had made Ben Adhem bold,
And to the Presence in the room he said,
"What writest thou?" The Vision raised its head,
And with a look made of all sweet accord
Answered, "The names of those who love the Lord."
"And is mine one?" said Abou. "Nay, not so,"
Replied the Angel. Abou spoke more low,

But cheerily still; and said, "I pray thee, then,
Write me as one that loves his fellow-men."
The Angel wrote, and vanished. The next night
It came again with a great wakening light,
And showed the names whom love of God had
    blessed,
And, lo! Ben Adhem's name led all the rest!

7
the unity of creation and everything in it

As Sorokin frequently points out in his books, one of the most difficult obstacles encountered in increasing in man love for his fellow-man is his egotism. That it is already strong in us at an early age is illustrated in this anecdote telling of a conversation between four-year-old Gunda and her mother:

"Mommie, am I *one*?"

"Yes."

"Is Taddy (the next younger) one?"

"Yes."

"Is Dusty (the youngest) one?"

"Yes."

After a long silence: "I don't want to be one."

"But why, Gunda?"

"I want to be *two*."[1]

It must be recognized that if man could be convinced that each man is not a separate organism living independently of all others but is in fact an undifferentiated, tiny yet integral part of the universe his egotism could be more easily overcome. Philosophers and scientists have long studied and written on the subject; most have reached an identical conclusion. Touched on briefly in Chapter Four, we can now look more closely at some of the arguments adduced and the conclusions reached.

Since the Hindus in India have probably been debating religious problems longest, that will be a good place to start. Hindu thought penetrated more deeply than that of European philosophers because Hindu interpretation of the world was internal and intuitive rather than external and intellectual. Will Durant has well said that while intellect divides everything, intuition unites everything. The Hindus saw that "I" is a delusion, that the individual is merely a phenomenon, and that the only reality is the Infinite One. As Schopenhauer put it, "Whoever is able to say this to himself, with regard to every being with whom he comes in contact"—whoever is clear-eyed and clear-souled enough to see that we are all members of one organism, all of us little currents in an ocean of will—he "is certain of all virtue and blessedness, and is on the direct road to salvation."[2]

Vivekananda, a great expounder of Hindu Vedantism in simple terms, says: "If you take away the two differences of name and form, the whole universe is one; there are no two, but one everywhere. You and I are one. There is neither Nature nor God nor the Universe, only the One Infinite Existence, out of which through name and form, all these are manufactured. . . . When man has seen himself as one with the Infinite Being of the Universe, . . . then will sorrow disappear. What can cause sorrow? I am the One Existence of the universe.

Then all jealousies will disappear; of whom to be jealous? Of myself? Then all bad feelings disappear. Against whom can I have bad feelings? Against myself? There is none in the universe but me."

If once it is established that the individual self is ultimately identical with the universal self (Brahman), it goes without saying that the aim of life is not self-interest in the sense of seeking satisfaction of individual desires but self-realization, which lifts the aspirant from the lower level of renunciation to the heights where he rises above all contradictions, and hence above narrow-mindedness and selfishness. The person who has attained the true experience of the universal self must constantly be devoted to the well-being not only of human beings but of all the living creatures. The Bhagavadgita, which is rightly regarded as the quintessence of the Upanishads, calls a person the seer if he considers all living creatures his equal.[3] Coleridge has said in the same strain: "He prayeth well who loveth well both man and bird and beast."

In interpreting the Bhagavadgita, Sri Aurobindo says that real self-knowledge can only come when man perceives that the self in him and the self in others are one being, and this self is something higher than the ego—an infinite, an impersonal, a universal existence in whom all move and have their being.[4] "When one discovers the spirit within him, he realizes that he is one with God and all other fellow human beings, and that is the solid spiritual basis of human unity. Only then, and not before, can love become the law of life and peace, and harmony be established permanently on earth. Only then the religion of humanity will find its firm and true basis and justification, for that essentially must be the aim of the religion of humanity, as it must be the earthly aim of all human religion, love, mutual recognition of human brotherhood, a living sense of human oneness and practice of human oneness in thought, feeling and life.[5] There would [then] be no question of selfishness or altruism, of oneself and others, since all are seen and felt as the one self."[6] An Indian psychologist suggests that the doctrine affords a simple explanation of the great commandment of love one's neighbor as oneself—one's neighbor *is* oneself.

As we would expect, since Buddhism originated in India, it has embraced this Hindu doctrine. In the early Japanese school of Kegon Buddhism, one of the realizations which must be attained by the Buddhist aspirant is that of *jiji suge hokkai*—the realm in which all things together form one complete and total whole by means of harmonious and unobstructed penetration, interconvertibility, and identification with each other. In Kegon Buddhism the symbol for illustrating *jiji suge hokkai* is known as Indra's Net. It is described as being a great net extending throughout the universe, vertically to represent time, horizontally to represent space. At each point where the threads of the net cross one another is a crystal bead, the symbol of a single existence. Each crystal bead reflects on its shining surface not only every other bead in the net but every reflection of every reflection of every other bead upon each individual bead—countless, endless reflections of one another.[7]

Evans-Wentz in his exposition of Tibetan Buddhism has written: "Not until mankind shall transcend dualism and phenomenal appearances, and realize the natural at-one-ment of all living creatures, will they be able to formulate a sound standard of morality. Such a standard will be based entirely, not partially, as are prevailing standards of morality, up on world-wide Bodhisattvic altruism."[8] The Tibetan lama Govinda warns us that we should not force our good deeds upon others from a sense of moral superiority, but should act spontaneously from that natural kind of selflessness which flows from the knowledge of the solidarity of all life and from the indescribable experience of oneness, gained in meditation.[9]

Chinese Taoism taught that not only are the distinctions which men make relative, but also the respective natures of all things are relative. So also relative is the difference between the "I" of me and other things. As Hui Shih put it more simply, "Love all things equally, for heaven-and-earth is one body."[10] Mencius, the great disciple of Confucianism, taught that all that is necessary is to realize that we are originally one with all things, and, having comprehended this truth, to remember it unceasingly. Our every act should be motivated by this one thought.

The Neo-Confucian school taught that the man of *jen* (the meaning of which is mentioned in Chapter Six) forms one body with all things comprehensively and regards the Universe and all things, including Heaven and Earth, as one body. "The great man . . . regards the world as one family and the country as one person. As to those who make cleavage between objects and distinguish between the self and others, they are small men. That the great man can regard Heaven, Earth, and the myriad things as one body is not because he deliberately wants to do so, but it is natural with the loving nature of his mind that he forms a unity with Heaven, Earth, and the myriad things."[11]

This illustration of the doctrine is by Wei Wu Wei,

a modern Chinaman: "When you give a shilling to a beggar, do you realize that you are giving it to yourself? When you help a lame dog over a stile, do you realize that you yourself are being helped? When you kick a man when he is down, do you realize that you are kicking yourself? Give him another kick—if you deserve it!"

It will not do to say that only Eastern mystics espouse this theory of identification. Eighteen hundred years ago the hardheaded Roman administrator Marcus Aurelius wrote in his *Meditations*:

> No matter whether the universe is a confusion of atoms or a natural growth, let my first conviction be that I am part of a Whole which is under Nature's governance; and my second, that a bond of kinship exists between myself and all other similar parts. If I bear these two thoughts in mind, then in the first place, being a part, I shall not feel aggrieved by any dispensation assigned to me from the Whole; since nothing which is beneficial for any Whole can ever be harmful to a part, and in this case there is nothing contained in this Whole which is not beneficial to itself. . . . In the remembrance, then, that I am a part of such Whole, I shall cheerfully accept whatever may be my lot. In the second place, inasmuch as there is this bond of kinship between myself and my fellow-parts, I shall do nothing that might injure their common welfare, but keep those kindred parts always purposefully in view, directing every impulse towards their good and away from anything that runs counter to it.[12]

The English poet John Donne phrased the idea nicely in the quaint English of his time (1624): "No man is an Iland, intire of itselfe. . . . any man's death diminishes me, because I am involved in Mankinde; and therefore never send to know for whom the bell tolls; it tolls for thee."

Many hardheaded thinkers in addition to Marcus Aurelius have believed in the truth of the doctrine under discussion. Harvard's philosopher, William Hocking, considered it important to remind ourselves that the distinctions and divisions which our concepts make in the world of objects are misleading, since in reality all things are one. We must deny the boundaries which separate thing from thing, person from person, level from level, race from race, nation from nation.[13] The skeptical French philosopher, Jean Paul Sartre, should receive our prize for the briefest exposition: "One and one are one." Goethe was also brief: "Only man*kind* is the true man, and the individual can be joyous and happy only when he has the courage to feel himself in the whole."

Ouspensky was a firm believer in mysticism yet, as has been mentioned, his *Tertium Organum* when published in 1920 was hailed as one of the great scientific writings of its time. In a later book he says that once in a "strange state of consciousness" he suddenly received a conception of the world in which each thing appeared not as a separate whole, but as a part of another whole, in most cases incomprehensible and unknown to us. Nothing existed separately. He felt that the separate existence of anything, including himself, was a fiction, something nonexistent, impossible. This terrified and oppressed him at first, but later was to him the most joyous and radiant sensation that could exist. Sorokin would have accepted this experience of Ouspensky's without question.[14]

This is part of an item Norman Cousins wrote for the *Saturday Review*:

> I am a single cell in a body of 3 billion cells. The body is mankind. I glory in the individuality of self, but my individuality does not separate me from my universal self—the oneness of man. My memory is personal and finite, but my substance is boundless and infinite. . . . My dedication, therefore, is to the cause of man in the attainment of that which is within the reach of man. I will work for human unity under a purposeful peace. I will work for the growth of a moral order that is in keeping with the universal order. In this way do I affirm faith in life and life in faith.

Alan Watts, in his tongue-in-cheek *The Book*, has spelled out in his usual amusing style what he considers the "taboos against knowing who you are." His thesis is that what he considers the prevalent sensation of oneself as a separate ego enclosed in a bag of skin, is a hallucination underlying the misuse of technology for the violent subjection of man's natural environment and, consequently, its eventual destruction. He thinks our problem today is not simply that of growth in technical powers without corresponding spiritual growth but rather our mistaken belief in our individual existence and identity. Each of us is wrong in feeling that he is a separate center of feeling and action within a physical body that confronts an external world of people and things contacted through the senses.[15]

Using modern scientific terms as a means of explaining the theory, Watts refers to us as clusters of electrons and asks us to remember that our bodily cells and their

the unity of creation and everything in it 77

smallest components appear and disappear much as light waves vibrate and as people go from birth to death. Consequently, since at death we leave no more trace of ourselves in the universe than a system of electronic patterns, this should not worry us because that is no more nor less than what we are when "alive." Our ego sensation is really a memory record (somewhat like a photographic film or magnetic tape) which gives one the impression of oneself as something that remains while life goes by, perhaps as if oneself were a mirror reflecting a passing procession.[16]

8
love as creative power

We may now look further into Sorokin's *The Ways and Power of Love*, in which he goes into his subject of altruistic love more deeply and from a more scientific base than had been possible in his earlier writings. His two chapters on "the aspects of love" we have already reviewed. His third chapter deals with "the production, accumulation and distribution of love energy."

In beginning his discussion, Sorokin accepts the theory he develops more completely elsewhere: that love is one of the highest energies known; and therefore, at least in theory, we can talk about its generation, accumulation (or loss), and transmission. As of today, he says, this talk must be largely theoretical and speculative, but even now it has practical possibilities. Until now we have collected and used love-energy only insofar as it is "naturally" produced in our societies. So little effort is made to produce it deliberately that we are hardly aware that there is a process of love-generation that goes on wherever social harmony and peace exist.[1]

Sorokin's terms "accumulation and transmission" of love-energy are possibly not too well chosen, but their use becomes clearer in his discussion. We must assume he uses the word "energy" in its classical meaning of power by which things act to change other things, rather than a force in terms of modern physics; perhaps in one aspect at least we could think of its "energy" as a powerful method of behavioral control. Like other forms of energy, he continues, love-energy can be accumulated or stored in individuals and in social institutions. The "storing" of love-energy in individuals means making their love-actions and reactions spontaneously habitual, rooted to such an extent that they become second nature. As such it flows spontaneously, not hindered by internal friction nor demanding any special effort—it pours itself out whenever needed. If such storing of energy were begun during earliest childhood and continuously practiced thereafter, it could amount to a great accumulation of love-energy in individuals and through them in humanity as a whole. The productive capacity of this accumulated energy of love is potentially unlimited. If humanity and its leaders earnestly set out to accomplish this task, much love-energy can be produced and accumulated even with the human world in its present stage.[2] Sorokin seems overly optimistic here, but in this area who can be sure?

As to creative love, Sorokin says: In the atmosphere of our sensate culture we are prone to believe in the power of the struggle for existence, selfish interests, egoistic competition, hate, the fighting instinct, sex drives, the instinct of death and destruction, all-powerful economic factors, rude coercion and other negativistic forces. Yet we are highly skeptical in regard to the power

love as creative power 81

of creative love, disinterested service, unprofitable sacrifice, mutual aid, the call of pure duty and other positive forces. Marxism and the economic interpretation of history; Freudianism and its libidinal-destructive explanation of human behavior; instinctivist and behaviorist theories of personality and culture; Darwinistic and biological theories of the struggle for existence as the main factor of biological, mental, and moral evolution —these and similar theories dominate contemporary sociology, psychology, anthropology, political science and other social and humanistic disciplines.

To support his opposing belief in the power of love Sorokin summons up "a vast body of evidence in favor of the enormous power of creative love, friendship, and nonviolent, nonaggressive conduct in human affairs and social life." He relates 50 supporting incidents, citing the authority for each. The first is typical. In it he tells of an elderly woman who, on entering her hotel room, found a burglar rifling her bureau drawers. Disregarding the gun he brandished, she told him to go ahead and help himself to anything she had, since he obviously needed it more than she did, and even told him some places to look where there were valuables he had overlooked. Suddenly the man let out a low cry and ran from the room, taking nothing. She later received a letter from him in which he said, "I'm not afraid of hate. But you showed love and kindness."

As other evidence of the power of love, Sorokin cites actual experiments showing that unselfish love influences human behavior in others as tangibly as does hate. His examples cover experiments with patients in hospitals, with Harvard and Radcliffe students, and with children; they are pertinent, and support his case.[3]

An important element of the power of love is the

unanticipated personal reward flowing to individuals and groups who cultivate the power. Sorokin's experiment with "good neighbors" convinced him that most of them enjoy above average creative love. Their altruistic "ego-transcendence" turned out to be beneficial to themselves, even though their sacrifices for others were not made with such end in view.[4]

In his similar study of the lives of saints, Sorokin found an extraordinary longevity which he thought indicated that saintly life is an important factor in longevity—still another personal reward and perhaps also evidence of the power of love. Through the deep peace of mind and integration of personality which it produces, altruistic loving becomes a therapy.[5]

Reading these writings about unselfish love as the only way to genuine happiness recalls the story of the ruler of one of the Arab dynasties in Spain who was as powerful as any ruler of his time, but who said near the end of his life: "I have now reigned above 50 years in victory or peace . . . riches and honors, powers and pleasures have waited on my call; nor does any earthly blessing appear to have been wanting to my felicity. In this situation I have diligently numbered the days of pure and genuine happiness which have fallen on my lot; they amount to 14. O man! place not thy confidence in this present world!"[6]

In his exposition of love as a creative power in social movements, Sorokin is easy to follow. He says:

> With the exception of love as the mainspring of life and of biological evolution, we have dealt so far mainly with the influence of love upon individuals and interindividual relationships. For-

love as creative power   **83**

tunately, the power of love is not limited by this influence. It goes far beyond individual relationships and cases; it affects the whole social and cultural life of humanity. It operates as the driving force of mankind's creative progress towards ever-fuller truth, ever-nobler goodness, ever-purer beauty, ever-richer freedom, and ever-finer forms of social life and institutions. Throughout human history each positive step in this direction has been inspired and "powered" by love, while any regressive step away from these values has been moved by hate.

Let us begin with a few cases of love's influence upon vast social movements. We can start with concrete questions: Can the nonviolent power of love stop war and give peace? Can the peaceful power of love achieve important social reforms and constructive changes? Can it compete with the social reconstructions inspired by hate and carried on by means of violent and bloody struggle of clashing parties?[7]

As the first of many examples from history he adduces to support a "yes" answer to his questions, Sorokin uses Asoka, who became ruler of a kingdom in India in 273 B.C. The first 12 years of his reign he spent in wars of conquest building a large empire. His inscriptions tell us that the horrors and miseries of war aroused in him such deep remorse, shame and understanding of the utter futility of war as a means of pacification or social improvement that he was converted to Buddhism. After a short period spent as a Buddhist monk, he completely transformed his policies and became a zealous apostle of peace, love, compassion and good works. The resulting internal and external peace in his empire lasted not only for the remainder of his life but for an additional 30 or 40 years. Many of the stone pillars engraved with Buddhist commandments which he erected all over his empire for the edification of his people still remain. Sorokin contrasts this period of 70 years of peace, growing from Asoka's practice of love, with the history of the world's nations as a whole, in which the average time between wars is much shorter.[8]

After concluding his examples, Sorokin in summing up says the love relationship is not only the supreme form of social relations but is an absolute necessity for the harmonious existence and survival of any social group. Without it no good social life is possible. Plato and Aristotle were quite right in their statement that true friendship or love is the most vital stuff of all true social relationships. Often overlooked, this function of love shows its unique power in social life and in man's historical process.[9]

A hundred years ago Emerson preceded Sorokin in the belief in the power of love to reform and lift up our society. He wrote that love is the one remedy for all ills, the panacea of nature. If we love, he said, the impossible becomes possible. Our history has not been the history of kindness, but of selfishness. He might have been writing today when he said that we make, by distrust, the thief and the incendiary, and by our courts and jails keep him so. Furthermore, love would put a new face on this world in which we dwell as pagans and enemies, and it would warm the heart to see how fast the vain diplomacy of statesmen and the impotence of armies and navies would be superseded. "Love will creep where it cannot go, will accomplish that by imperceptible methods—being its own lever, fulcrum, and power—which force could never achieve."[10]

His belief that love can be made a life-giving, therapeutic force was very important to Sorokin. He says:

> Other conditions being equal, of two persons with identical biological organisms, the kind and friendly person tends to live longer and to have better health than the unkind and especially the hate-possessed individual. Love in its various forms proves to be one of the most important factors of longevity and good health; being loved by others and loving others seems to be as important a single factor of vitality as any other.... This conclusion that love has curative power is corroborated by a vast body of evidence which demonstrates the tangible curative power of love in regard to certain physical and mental disorders. Modern psychosomatic medicine correctly views the strong emotional disturbances, especially of an aggressive, inimical, hateful, and antagonistic kind, as one of the basic factors of cardiovascular, respiratory, gastrointestinal, eliminative, skin, endocrine, genito-urinary disturbances, and others such as epilepsy and headache."[11]

Some psychologists in discussing this statement agree that hate can shorten life, but back away from Sorokin's added conclusion that love is an affirmative force which can lengthen it. In support of his theory Sorokin quotes statements by a number of recognized authorities. His excerpts do support him, but are for the most part limited to the relation between psychotherapists and their patients.

Since World War II a growing number of scientists have been studying what appears to be a primal energy (at least one psychiatrist calls it the "energy of love") in which the universe is immersed and which operates through the minds of men, an energy that can be tapped by mental concentration, that relates man to man, and that operates most commonly through the emotion of love. Parapsychological phenomenon is no longer considered a subject not suitable for scientific research. William James in his *Energies of Men* foreshadowed the study, citing various types of concentration—among them the will, yogic discipline and prayer—as openers of deeper and deeper levels of energy. Einstein predicted that the greatest progress in the next 50 years will be in the mental realm, and Edison is said to have predicted that the next great discoveries would be in the realm of "so-called spirit."[12]

In a little different vein, Sorokin says that love furnishes driving force to the total power of each of the highest values of human life: to the power of truth, knowledge, beauty, freedom, goodness and happiness. Each of these end values, he contends, has its own power that tangibly affects, enriches and ennobles the lives of individuals and groups, and the course of human history. Love of freedom has been instrumental in all movements for the realization of freedom in human history. Even more, love experience *is* freedom at its loftiest and best. In this sense, therefore, love and true freedom are synonymous.[13]

Pertinent to this last statement is an interview had by a reporter for *Réalités* with Lawrence Durell, author of *The Alexandria Quartet*. The reporter said to Durell, "In *Tunc*, you claim that 'free' is the most important word. In *Justine*, it was 'love.' How do you explain this development?" In reply Durell asked, "Where is the development? How can you free yourself other than through love? And I don't mean love only in the biological sense of the term, but love in all its forms. This is what all the religions offer you to empty and purify yourself—but at the price of what efforts? We are all twisted with hate, meanness, stupidity—hardly able even to live like vegetables. To start with, love is binding, but it changes as you make progress within yourself."

Sorokin closes his chapter with this quotation from Dostoevski: "Love all God's creation, the whole and every grain of sand in it. Love every leaf, every ray of God's light. Love the animals, love the plants. Love everything. If you love everything, you will perceive the divine mystery in things. Once you perceive it, you will begin to comprehend it better every day, and you will come at last to love the whole world with an all-embracing love."[14]

Lewis Mumford expressed somewhat the same idea when he wrote that "everyone realizes, at least in words, that only through a vast increase of effective love can the mischievous hostilities that now undermine our civilization be overcome. The means are plain enough, but the method of application is lacking. Though love could bring regeneration, we have still to discover how to generate love: as with peace, those who call for it loudest often express it least. To make ourselves capable of loving, and ready to receive love, is the paramount problem of integration. . . . Not a day [must pass] without nurturing or furthering life: without repairing some deficiency of love in our homes, our villages, our cities: without caring for a child, visiting the sick, tending a garden, or making at least some token payment of good manners on this common debt. But likewise not a day without some more smiling expression of the delights of love: . . . love, conscious and unconscious, is the daily food of all living creatures: the means of living, the proof of their capacity to live, the ultimate blessing of their life. . . . to open the way to love, by a score of daily acts, is the first step toward integration."[15]

A comment by Roberto Agramonte on this work of Sorokin's on the creative powers of love is perhaps of value: "Although we know very little about this creative love," he says, "it represents nonetheless a tremendous power if only we knew how to disseminate it widely. It is the highest form of energy and one with the greatest therapeutic possibility. Sorokin in the Research Center in Creative Altruism, which he founded at Harvard, made investigations of that unknown and vital theme. . . . . Consequently he does not treat it as a mere philosophical speculation, a dream or a utopia, . . . but as a genuine scientific investigation which begins as a hypothesis to be verified. With his collaborators, the brilliant sociologist studied the whole range from the mathematical theory of egoism and altruism to the psychology of love and hate, including psychotherapeutic aspects of altruism, encephalographic aspects of abnormal, homicidal, and amicable personalities, problems of labor harmony, and other areas."[16]

9
what is altruism?

We have to this point considered, albeit sketchily, Sorokin's life and work and his analysis of the deficiencies that make existing institutions and procedures ineffective to develop brotherly love in humanity. We have also examined definitions and general statements regarding love, the forms and aspects of love, love in world religions and the importance, if we are to understand love, of our recognizing the unity of creation and everything in it. We are now ready to move on to the subject of altruism itself.

After first pointing out the imperative necessity for altruism if we are to have peace or even survival, Sorokin begins his discussion by saying that without any pedantic definition, through our own direct experience we know what constitutes love or altruism. He probably does not mean the two words as alternates for each other—he probably means that altruism is unselfish service to others actuated by love rather than by other motives. An elaborate definition of altruism did not appeal to him as important, since in most cases we can unerringly point out what kind of conduct is altruistic or egoistic and can usually distinguish it as selfish or unselfish.

The Roman formula for minimum altruistic conduct was: "Do good to others, harm no one, and render to each his own." Such conduct would not necessarily contain any element of love or generosity. Real altruism begins, Sorokin says, only when this minimum is transcended: when an individual freely sacrifices his rightful interests in favor of the well-being of another, refraining from harming him even though his legal right entitles him to do so, and helping him in ways not demanded by law. Altruistic conduct is always free from external compulsion and is freely chosen. An additional element, the necessity for which, as we shall see, has been much disputed, would require an altruistic act to be pure in its motivation and performed solely for its own sake, quite apart from any considerations of pleasure or utility.[1]

We have already seen that Sorokin regarded the most sublime form of love and altruism to be that formulated in the Sermon on the Mount, a part of which, as it appears in the *New English Bible*, reads: "Love your enemies; do good to those who hate you; bless those who curse you; pray for those who treat you spitefully. When a man hits you on the cheek, offer him the other cheek too; when a man takes your coat, let him have your shirt as well. Give to everyone who asks you; when a man takes what is yours, do not demand it back. Treat others as you would like them to treat you. . . . Be compassionate as your Father is compassionate."[2]

Louis Budd,[3] in a paper entitled *Altruism Arrives in America*, analyzes the meaning of the word. Although little more than a hundred years old, he says, it yet once served as a banner in a continuing campaign to persuade man to submerge himself in the welfare of others. Budd credits Comte with having coined the word to denote the supreme virtue in the religion of humanity he was attempting to establish as a rival to Christianity in France. The word is rooted in the Italian *altrui*, which in turn follows from the Latin *alter*. Both simply mean "other." To Comte the word meant the discipline and eradication of self-centered desire and a life devoted to the good of others; more particularly, selfless love and devotion to society.

Herbert Spencer did much to spread the use of the word. Budd thinks Comte would not have liked the religious approval his new word won in America, but that approval did aid altruism in popular esteem. John Fiske even argued that the "fundamental characteristic of social progress . . . is a gradual supplanting of egoism by altruism." So popular did "altruism" become that in the 1880's a philanthropist (Alcander Longley), wishing to find a more palatable label for his communistic schemes, created what he called the Altruistic Society and published a paper called *The Altruist*, later continued in Chicago as *The Altruistic Review*, which sponsored almost every kind of movement for the ultimate good of mankind. William Dean Howells threw his prestigious reputation in support of the word, sometimes making it a carryall for a wide assortment of notions on improving man's lot. Small communities based on common ownership of property and on brotherly love sprang up; several were called Altruria, a named coined by Howells.

Budd adds that with John Dewey and his criticism of attempts to establish any fixed lines between egoism and altruism the word began to go out of style until "the most eminent Pitirim A. Sorokin refurbished the altruism—egoism dichotomy to preach the desperate need for Christian service." Today the admirable endeavors which were grouped together under the term of altruism are being separated into various classifications. Montagu, for instance, prefers to call for "cooperation." In the United States it has slowly been absorbed by social Christianity.

In its psychological sense, altruism is said to mean "the disposition of an individual to further the welfare or happiness of other individuals or groups; egoism is the contrary disposition to further one's own welfare or happiness."[4] The ethical theory of altruism assumes that the altruistic disposition is at least of coordinate psychological standing with egoism and that as a matter of ethics it should prevail over egoism in cases of conflict.

Midlarsky suggests we say that altruism refers to that behavior which involves some cost to the actor, while gain received in return is disproportionately low when one considers the magnitude of the investment, the two major manifestations of such behavior being the helping of others at risk to oneself and the sacrificing of a reward in order to benefit others. She comments that there has been a notable lack of scientific investigation into what is altruistic behavior and that, although in recent years there has been a notable increase in both theoretical and empirical work in this area, the long failure by psychologists to focus systematic efforts upon the study of altruism may serve as an interesting illustration of the *Zeitgeist*.[5]

Ruth Leeds proposes three criteria for judging whether an act is altruistic: (1) The person who engages in giving treats it as an end in itself, anticipating no other satisfaction or gain than the pleasure of contributing to the welfare of others; (2) the person gives voluntarily and is acting beyond the call of duty—not fulfilling stipulated role obligations; (3) on balance, the person "doing good" is not harming others or incurring costs out of proportion to his act. These criteria admit of practical application, and Leeds is approaching the question of "values," but they omit one requirement frequently made: namely, that a loss or disadvantage to the self is necessary to true altruism.[6]

In examining acts to determine their altruistic nature, we must remember that altruism does not consist of the giving only of material things. The most important sphere of giving lies in the human realm in which one person gives to another of himself, of the most precious thing he has—his life. This does not mean necessarily sacrificing his life, but rather giving a part of his life measured by time, or giving of that which is alive in him.[7]

Jack Sawyer made a cogent remark when he observed that the few previous attempts to measure altruism objectively in individuals have all approached it as a stable, general characteristic, whereas a better approach might conceive of altruism as a characteristic that may vary, within individuals, as a function of the object of the altruism and of the commodity and situation in which it is expressed. For example, one may be altruistic towards his equals but not towards subordinates, or may be altruistic with prestige but not with money, or vice versa.[8] This is becoming a more usual and doubtless more practical approach to the subject.

Altruism and egoism are not necessarily antithetic. There are three possibilities: man is essentially good by nature; man is essentially evil by nature; or man is neither essentially good nor evil, but has tendencies for both egoism and altruism. As H. W. Stuart says, "So long as the problem is stated in the traditional terms of separate groups of impulses set side by side in rivalry in human nature, solutions must, as history shows, be ambiguous and inconclusive. However, a strictly self-seeking egoist, with no disinterested thought whatever for any other persons besides himself, is a monstrosity.... Egoism is in fact not so much the preferring of one's own well-being to that of others as refusing to widen the scope of one's interest in other persons in order to include claimants who think themselves wrongfully ignored."[9] Whether man is born with an inherent tendency towards either altruism or egoism will be considered in Chapter Ten.

The ethical basis for true altruism is too important to our subject for us to give it too brief mention. Why must we be altruistic? Or even otherwise good? Will it bring any reward? If so, who gets it? What answers to these questions have been given by recognized thinkers of past and recent times? Sorokin suggests a partial analysis of the subject, simplified for his purposes, which does not follow very closely any of the analyses usually proposed.

We have already noted his characterization of what constitutes altruism. He now suggests making five divisions of altruism, based on its forms and gradations. His names for the divisions are: anti- or egoistic altruism (conduct opposed to altruistic conduct, including hatred, enmity and the like); non-altruism (conduct not contradicting altruism but devoid of its characteristics—for example, an exercise of strictly legal rights which nevertheless cause harm); pseudo-altruism (altruism preached but not practiced); impure altruism (altruistic acts performed for pleasure or utility, but the term not to include altruistic actions only incidentally resulting in a degree of pleasure or utility as a by-product); wise and creative altruism (distinguished from blind altruistic passion which may prove harmful to the recipient, as a fond mother spoiling her child).[10]

Sorokin says altruistic conduct may vary widely in respect to the *extensity* of the field to which it is applied and the *intensity* of the altruism itself, here using the two words as he does in analyzing the "dimensions of love" in Chapter Five. One may be altruistic to only a few persons and non-altruistic towards all the rest, or one may be altruistic towards many persons, even the whole of mankind and all living creatures. Intensity can vary from a minor act of sympathy to the boundless giving and all-forgiving love formulated in the Sermon on the Mount. Between these poles, the intensity assumes many specific forms, as is suggested by the following terms: friendliness, kindness, benevolence, compassion, loyalty, devotion, respect, admiration, reverence, adoration and infatuation. The duration of altruism may vary from a very short time to an indefinitely long period.[11]

It is hard to discuss the ethical phases of altruism and egoism without getting into the question of "values," yet we should if possible avoid going into the technical arguments on that subject; many thousands of pages have been devoted to it by the social scientists without much success at agreement. Sorokin approaches it in a preliminary way in saying that altruism is a special kind of creativeness in the field of goodness, entailing principally ethical values, in distinction to the cognitive values of truth, realized primarily by science, philosophy and religion, and the values of beauty, realized predominately by the fine arts. Famous altruists such as St. Francis of Assisi are as truly creative giants in the field of goodness as are the foremost scientists, philosophers, founders of religions and artists in their own particular fields.[12]

Joseph Ford in his article *Sorokin as Philosopher* commends Sorokin's contribution to ethics—to the philosophy as well as sociology of value. He agrees about the difficulty of using those terms; without entering into a discussion of their meaning and implication, Ford says merely that ethics has always dealt with the concepts of value in one form or another: the Good, the Ought, the Right. He continues:

> Sorokin has recognized the role of values and meanings *directly*. He has not tried to redefine them as something else, or reduce them to something less than they are, or change them to something different from that which marks them as what they are. . . . He has held to consistent concepts of "meaning" and "value" on a sociocultural level, and yet has urged and demonstrated their use in widely varying empirical fields. . . . Sorokin has exploited his tremendous knowledge of the historic social theories as well as the empirical studies of the day, to demonstrate to value-free and meaning-free scholastics in social science that their paths are variously blind or circular, and their hopes of avoiding the crucial issues are illusory. . . .
>
> Like many another notable thinker before him, Sorokin has sought a practical outcome in action for his theories of value. . . . [Some people may

criticize his later investigations of and reports on altruism and his hopes for the use of] "creative altruism" in reconstructing humanity, but few would doubt today the depth and seriousness of the "crisis of our age," as so many did when his earlier works used this phrase.[13]

Perhaps a simpler way of expressing what we are looking for is to ask what it is that causes us to behave ourselves and to act altruistically towards others. Sorokin's answer is, of course, "love," but generations of social scientists in probing the question have come up with other answers, many of them, as was to be expected, in disagreement. One of the least complicated statements of the problem and its ramifications is that of Lecky in his *History of European Morals*:

> The two rival theories of morals are known by many names, and are subdivided into many groups. One of them is generally described as the Stoical, the Intuitive, the Independent or the Sentimental [or the Pure]; the other as the Epicurean, the Inductive, the Utilitarian or the Selfish. The . . . [former argues] that we have a natural power of perceiving that some qualities, such as benevolence, chastity, or veracity, are better than others, and that we ought to cultivate them and to repress their opposites. In other words, they contend that by the constitution of our nature, the notion of right carries with it a feeling of obligation; that to say a course of conduct is our duty, is in itself and apart from all consequences, an intelligible and sufficient reason for practicing it; and that we derive the first principles of our duties

from intuition [virtue for its own sake]. The moralist of the opposite school denies that we have any such natural perception. He maintains that we have by nature absolutely no knowledge of merit and demerit, of the comparative excellence of our feelings and actions, and that we derive these notions solely from an observation of the course of life which is conducive to human happiness. That which makes actions good is that they increase the happiness or diminish the pains of mankind. That which constitutes their demerit is their opposite tendency. To procure "the greatest happiness for the greatest number" is therefore the highest aim of the moralist, the supreme type and expression of virtue ["virtue because it pays"—the tenet of the British Empiricist or Utilitarian School].[14]

Henry Sidgwick was a utilitarian. As he explained the doctrine, "ethics" (what Lecky called "morals") has to do with the reasons men use in deciding between two courses of action; the study of ethics is the attempt to bring these reasons together in a coherent system. Modern man uses three different ways of answering the question: "Why should I do such and such?" He may reason with a view to self-interest, or he may ask what his duty is, or he may try to estimate the effect of the action in question on the general well-being. Sidgwick thought that the ordinary man does not find it necessary to choose between these methods. On some occasions he uses one and on other occasions another. He called the three methods, for brevity, egoism, intuitionism and utilitarianism. British ethical opinion can be pretty well summed up in these three positions. Jeremy Bentham was perhaps the best known exponent of utilitarianism. That each of us in our own ethical decisions probably pretty much intermixes the three methods proposed by Sidgwick is perhaps now fairly well accepted. The "power complex" we think we see in our neighbor's desire to dominate and impress his fellow-men is latent in each one of us, and much that masquerades as altruism and a desire to help humanity is really only an expression of the same desire in ourselves.[15]

According to G. W. Cunningham's analysis of ethical altruism, there are two views as to the nature of goodness, depending on whether the standard of goodness is external to the mind or inherent in it. One, the intuitional theory, holds that certain general laws or principles of goodness exist in their own right without reference to particular experiences; these are absolute and unchangeable. Under one form of this view the standard is external to the nature of mind but exists outside it. The question then arises, where? One group answers, "in the nature of things"; another answers, "in the will of God." Under the other form, it is held that the standard is inherent in the mind: Good is good, Evil is evil, as man wills. By "mind" is meant not the mind of any individual man, but of humanity, the mind of *man*. Kant's categorical imperative (with which we shall deal later) is given as an example of this formulation. A man's will is good not because the consequences that flow from it are good, nor because it is capable of attaining the end it seeks, but it is good in itself, because it *wills* the good.

The second view of the nature of goodness Cunningham calls the teleological theory; it insists that the consequences of an act are of moral significance and are alone of ultimate moral value. The standard of the goodness of the act is to be found in its results. This view has three main forms, according to the nature of the ends or results used as the standard. The first, of which the utilitarian philosophy is an example, is *hedonism*—the theory that pleasures (using the word in its broadest sense) are the end in terms of which goodness is to be measured. A second Cunningham calls *energism*, accepting as the end measurement the full expression and development of the capacity of human beings; that act is ethically best which results in the fullest expression and development of human capacities. There are two kinds of energism. One is altruistic energism, which uses social significance as the primary end factor, and regards the self to be developed as the self having its being only in a society of selves. The other kind is egoistic energism, in which the accepted standard is the fullest expression of the individual's capacity, with only secondary regard to social consequences. The struggle for existence and survival of the fittest might offer an example of egoistic energism—we must strive to be the fittest. The third kind of teleological view is *asceticism*, which looks upon desires as ignoble and advocates the elimination, or at least the curbing, of all but our most unfleshly desires.[16]

Looking back over these theories it is easy to criticize some of the subforms. Either the intuitional view or the teleological view is perhaps the most sound, but since neither contains the complete truth and is not completely satisfactory on its own we cannot afford to neglect the other.

For support for the intuitive (pure) theory of good, we can go back as far as the early Chinese philosophers. Mencius opposed the idea of utility as the standard for the goodness of an act. He believed firmly that all men possess fundamental feelings which if developed become the four virtues of human-heartedness, righteousness, propriety, and wisdom. These virtues are not to be practiced merely because they are materially beneficial, although their practice will in fact automatically produce a result beneficial to society.[17] "There is no greater delight," Mencius said, "than to be conscious of right within us. If one strives to treat others as he would be treated by them, he shall not fail to come near the perfect life."[18] Mencius was possibly the first to propose the argument that if a man suddenly sees a child about to fall into a well, he will without exception experience a feeling of alarm and distress and will rush to save the child from falling, with no thought of reward.

In later Chinese philosophy, pure goodness known intuitively began to be linked with the sense of unity and with love. Some 2,000 years after Confucius, Wang-Ming, a leading Chinese philosopher of his period, wrote that it is through love of man that virtue is revealed. The attainment of the highest good is the exercise of love for men. The nature with which Heaven has endowed man is perfectly good and cannot be entirely dimmed. With this expression of the highest good it is intuitively known that the right is right and the wrong is wrong.

Intuitive or pure goodness was also important in the ethical philosophies of India. Sharma says, "There is no doubt that good will is central to morality. Kant has remarked, 'There is nothing good in the world and even out of it that can be regarded good without qualification, but good will. . . . A good will is good not because of what it performs or effects, not by its aptness for the attainment of some proposed end, but simply by virtue of the volition.'"[19]

Marcus Aurelius added to the theory the element of social instinct. To him, as unequivocal as man's duty to himself is his duty to others; since all men are manifestations of the one creative Mind-Fire, the doctrine of universal brotherhood played a leading part in the Stoic system. The rational and social instinct is something that is inherent in the constitution of man. Kindness to his fellow creatures is therefore at all times incumbent upon him; he must school himself to be tolerant of their feelings, make allowance for their ignorance, forgive their misdoings, help them in their need.[20]

Tagore was speaking for mankind as well as India when he wrote that from the time when Man became truly conscious of his own self he also became conscious of a mysterious spirit of unity which found its manifestation through him in his society. It is a subtle medium of relationship between individuals which is not for any utilitarian purpose but for its own ultimate truth. Somehow Man has felt that this comprehensive spirit of unity has a divine character which could claim the sacrifice of all that is individual in him, that in it dwells his highest meaning—transcending his limited self, representing his best freedom.[21] In a sense, Tagore's philosophy as here expressed might be tabbed as energism under the Cunningham classification previously set forth in this chapter.

Kant recognized two kinds of "imperatives" (formulas in which practical principles of reason are expressed): hypothetical and categorical. If the action dealt with in the imperative is good or necessary only as a means to the attainment of something else, the imperative is hypothetical, but if the action dealt with

what is altruism? 103

is good in itself or absolutely necessary, it is categorical. "If you want to have a prosperous old age, you must work hard in your youth," is a hypothetical imperative. But, "You ought never to tell lies," is a categorical imperative. Morality, Kant is saying, cannot be regarded as a set of rules which prescribe the means necessary to the achievement of a given end, whether the end be the general happiness, human perfection, or anything else; its rules must be obeyed without consideration of the consequences.

On this foundation Kant formulated his general categorical imperative to be used as a guide to moral action. It took two forms: "Act so that the maxim of thy will can always hold good as a principle of universal legislation [in other words, act in such a way that if all others should act like you, everything would be well]; so act as you treat humanity, whether in thine own person or in that of any other, in every case as an end, never as a means."[22]

Hocking calls this imperative one of the most impressive formulations of our moral common sense that has ever been made. The categorical imperative means that we must cease making exceptions in our favor; eliminate those modes of action which would show themselves self-contradictory if they became general. Do not allow yourself to lie, when the whole effect of the lie depends on that general habit of truthfulness which allows your language to be received at its face value. Do not allow yourself to steal, when the whole advantage of your theft depends upon having your stolen goods respected as your property. Do not kill when the only value of your deed requires the continued protection of your own life by the standards of the community.[23]

Some philosophers, while recognizing the value of

virtue as represented by altruism and vice as represented by egoism, have argued these two opposites are necessary and cannot be unequivocally regarded as evils to mankind. Browne in his *Religio Medici* wrote: "They that endeavour to abolish Vice, destroy also Virtue; for contraries, though they destroy one another, are yet the life of one another. Thus Virtue (abolish vice), is an Idea. Again, the community of sin doth not disparage goodness; for when Vice gains upon the major part, Virtue, in whom it remains, becomes more excellent; and being lost in some, multiplies its goodness in others which remain untouched and persist entire in the general inundation."[24]

Moving forward over the centuries, we find the same idea expressed by Alan Watts like this: "The real goodness of human nature is its peculiar balance of love and selfishness, . . . in which the positive pole has always a slight edge over the negative. . . . It is not for man to be either an angel or a devil, and the would-be angels should realize that, as their ambition succeeds, they evoke hordes of devils to keep the balance. This was the lesson of Prohibition, as of all other attempts to enforce purely angelic behavior, or to pluck out evil root and branch. . . . No species, or party to a game, can survive without its natural antagonists, its beloved enemies, its indispensable opponents. For to love your enemies is to love them *as* enemies; it is not necessarily a clever device for winning them over to your side." Watts expands in several different ways this theory that likes and opposites are both necessary to comprise a part of everything that exists, including mental processes. To light, for example, alternating waves of light and darkness are essential.[25]

what is altruism? 105

Not all world philosophies, religious or otherwise, have agreed on the value of altruism as such. The Hindu Sri Aurobindo thought that unless it is actuated by universal Divine Love, altruistic acts are "not truly liberative from ego-sense, they widen it at most and give it a higher and larger satisfaction; impotent in practice to change man's vital life and nature, they only modify and palliate its action and daub over its unchanged egoistic essence."[26]

The most ancient Japanese scriptures contain no admonition about altruism or neighborly love, or for that matter, any moral code at all. Even the later revivalists of the Kojiki and other early scriptures considered that morals are the invention of wicked people like the Chinese, while the ancient Japanese were pure in thought and act. To revere the Gods and obey the Mikado was the chief end of man. The conception of sin is wanting, or nearly so, in Japanese teaching and thought and history.[27] They seem to have retained in some measure a real incapacity to discern, or reluctance to grapple with, a problem of evil. Much that baffles us in Japanese history becomes clearer if we remember that the Japanese have never been tortured by the sense of sin.[28]

Such are the arguments in support of altruistic love as a form of "goodness" not dependent on considerations other than benefit, either personal or universal. We have already had a brief look at the other side of the coin and at some of the philosophers who believed benefit to be the only acceptable explanation. Jeremy Bentham and his predecessors and followers who followed that "utilitarian" school of thought (the "virtue because it pays" school) would probably argue in opposition to the "virtue for its own sake" idea that whether honesty is the best policy depends very much upon the condition of the police force, that the highest nature is rarely the happiest and, cynically, that Petronius Arbiter was very probably a happier man than Marcus Aurelius. Exponents of the utilitarian theory are to be found throughout history.

In an article by S. J. Holmes published in 1945 in the *Psychological Review*, he wrote that "certain skeptical or cynical philosophers such as Mandeville, La Mettrie, d'Holbach, Helvetius and La Rochefoucauld would give man no credit for being actuated by any motive higher than enlightened self-interest. With the exposure of the errors of associationism and the development of a more adequate psychological analysis, the conceptions of human motivation that were entertained by the philosophers referred to have largely given way to views which are less derogatory to man's nature." By way of support of his statement Holmes adds, "Our outlook on human nature is very different from what it was a century ago. Macaulay expressed a not uncommon opinion in his day when in answer to the question, 'What proposition is there respecting human nature which is absolutely and universally true?' he replied, 'We know of only one; and that is not only true, but identical: that men always act from self-interest.' It is now quite clear that the one general statement about human nature that Macaulay felt certain about is wrong. And many other opinions about human nature accepted by Macaulay's contemporaries are also wrong. Yes, man is truly altruistic; but there are curious features of his altruism that we can properly understand only by following the long and singular course of its evolution."[29]

Alan Isaacs has less quarrel than Holmes with self-

what is altruism? 107

interest as a basis for altruistic behavior. He says the religious inducements to moral behavior are almost always linked to self-interest, since they promise personal salvation. It is true that a few exceptional people are induced to behave morally for supernatural reasons that are devoid of self-interest—fulfilling God's purpose, or seeking to glorify Him—but this is probably much rarer than secular altruism. Isaacs recognizes how difficult it is to say how much human behavior is genuinely altruistic and suggests there are probably as many reasons for altruism as there are altruists. He makes the psychologist's argument that man's concept-forming ability allows him to imagine himself in the plight of others, so that sometimes the benevolent compassion he feels for his fellows may be a reflection of the compassion he would feel for himself in the same predicament, but the connection with self-interest here is rather remote. There is also the possibility that some aspects of both secular and religious altruism may be a disguised attempt to redeem an oppressive sense of sin, or simply a convenient way of achieving self-satisfaction.[30]

    Christian altruism does not fall within the scope of any classification thus far examined. The Christian admonition towards altruism is so completely identified with love that what has been already said in Chapter Six about the Christian teaching on love is applicable here as well. However, one really ought not to refer to anything as "the Christian teaching," since nearly 2,000 years of interpretations of the teachings of Christ and the Old Testament by a hierarchical church establishment, theologians, reformers and mystics have varied widely. Nevertheless, on this subject of neighborly love there has been fairly general agreement.

"Charity" is merely a narrower form of altruism, measured from the viewpoint of the recipient rather than the motive of the giver. The word translated in the English Bible for centuries as "charity," is now thought better translated as "love." Accordingly, for the particular purposes of the present discussion, we may accept the two words as having been used in the same general sense.

The Christian admonitions on brotherly love are many but much alike and are in general those set forth in the Sermon on the Mount. St. Augustine called charity (love) the law of God. For Martin Luther the love which is Christian faith in action must be part of the divine love given to man by God in order that man may pass it on to his fellow-men. He considered man merely the tube or channel through which God's love flows. "Faith brings you to Christ and makes Him your own with all that He has; love gives you to your neighbor with all that you have," he said. To Luther love is not a means to an end but is the ethical end itself. Francis de Sales, St. Teresa, St. Bernard of Clairvaux, and countless followers have concurred in Luther's explanation.[31]

When he takes up his analysis of the varieties and methods of creative altruists, to which we turn next, Sorokin begins with the Hindu system of Yoga. This phase of our review of Sorokin will be to some extent concerned with such things as Yoga, mysticism, supernatural powers and kindred subjects, and it will be important to maintain open minds. The tendency of many people is to scoff when they see or hear allusions to these things and to consider the speaker or writer who evidences his belief in the possibilities involved either a crackpot or a charlatan. It is true that certain phases of Yoga, mysticism and other Eastern religious

what is altruism? 109

philosophies have been carried to extremes by some communicants, have had claims made in their behalf by others which are patently impossible, and have been utilized by still others as excuses for undesirable behavior and as means of mulcting the public. These things have also been true of Christianity and other religions, yet are no reason for refusing to give serious thought to the possibilities afforded by these religions which have been honored and practiced for so many hundreds of years.

As Watts puts it: "The combination of our unfamiliarity with Eastern cultures and their sophistication gives them an aura of mystery into which we project fantasies of our own making. Yet the basic aim of these ways of life is something of quite astonishing simplicity, beside which all the complications of reincarnation and psychic powers, of superhuman mahatmas, and of schools for occult technology, are a smoke screen in which the credulous inquirer can lose himself indefinitely. . . . Although the ancient cultures of Asia never attained the rigorously exact physical knowledge of the modern West, they grasped in principle many things which are only now occurring to us."[32]

Today's scientists are the first to recognize the potentialities inherent in forces which are yet little understood. Charles P. Steinmetz, the great electrical engineer, was once asked by Roger W. Babson: "What line of research will see the greatest development during the next 50 years?" "I think the greatest discovery will be made along spiritual lines," Steinmetz replied. "Here is a force which history clearly teaches has been the greatest power in the development of men. Yet we have merely been playing with it and have never seriously studied it as we have the physical forces. Someday . . . the scientists of the world will turn their laboratories over to the study of God and prayer and the spiritual forces which as yet have hardly been scratched. When this day comes, the world will see more advancement in one generation than it has seen in the past four."[33] Sorokin was no credulous child and accepted nothing on faith, but ended his long years of study and experimentation firm in the belief that there are some so-called mystic or supernatural forces which could be of assistance in solving today's problems—problems that seem to be almost insoluble without such assistance. The least we can do is give him a fair hearing.

This chapter has been rather wide in scope and has covered a good many things. Perhaps we can sum it up by saying that it is concluded that the principles and theories applicable to ethics and to altruism are largely the same, that the two principal opposing theories are the utilitarian, which holds that whether an act is ethical depends on its results, and the intuitive or pure ethics school, which holds that the ethical character of an act must be judged by a standard which exists as an absolute and which has no relationship to the results of the act; modern philosophy seems to tend more and more away from the utilitarian theory. Jean Mandler has suggested, and with some pertinence, that utilitarianism, despite its limited understanding, is nevertheless a part of our national inheritance from Britain, as such is one of the bases of American capitalism and the American theory of democracy and that this tradition may well be a reason why our society does not understand love very deeply.

One likes to think that most of the words that have been expended by philosophers in arguing the matters discussed in this chapter could have been avoided by using and following the few words of St. Augustine: "Love wholeheartedly, then do what you like." If followed as St. Augustine meant it, we could forget all the rules and regulations about ethics and morality. Unfortunately, not too long after his death, his epigram was used as a justification for persecution by the Catholic church.

10
biological factors in
the creation of altruism

At the inception of the preparation of material for this book, there seemed no reason to expect that the study of ethology would be involved, but as the work progressed it became apparent that whether or not man is born with an instinct towards aggression is an important question in determining how best to increase in him qualities of altruism. About that time the donnybrook among the behavioral scientists over this question came out of the ivory towers and into public prominence. If man is innately aggressive, we have two strikes against us at the very start of our effort to educate him away from aggression and towards altruism. On the other hand, if he has no such instinct at birth, or perhaps even has an innate tendency towards altruistic cooperation with his fellowmen, we are already on first base.*

---

*I have greatly shortened this chapter since the first draft for this book was written. At that time there was much difference of opinion as to whether

114 LOVE, ALTRUISM, AND WORLD CRISIS

Just what *is* "ethology"? In 1951 Tinbergen called it "the objective study of behavior." A definition more expressive of the meaning currently given the word is "the scientific study of animal behavior, especially in relation to habitat," and Hess suggests simply "behavioral physiology."[1]

After as complete knowledge as possible of the behaviors of an animal species has been obtained, the ethologist classifies the behaviors, compares them with those of other species, and analyzes the influencing factors, including particularly physiological bases. Hess says the ethologist tends to concentrate on behaviors that are normally performed by animals, rather than on learning processes. Some psychologists, viewing this emphasis on innate behavior, have mistakenly assumed that the ethologists do not feel learning to be very important, but that is not true. The ethologist would say that a given behavior is not either wholly learned or innate—both factors are important. Ethological methods have now penetrated a few areas of psychological research, and ethologists have evolved their discipline to the point where they feel able to begin making some judgments about the function of learning processes. The idea of imprinting, to be discussed later, originated with the ethologists. Ethology is beginning to make inroads into psychology; this may be in part the cause of the donnybrook among the behavioral scientists mentioned above.

man is born with an innate tendency towards aggression, and it seemed worthwhile to go into the pros and cons at length. Now, however, there is more general unanimity of opinion, and the arguments and conclusions can be considerably condensed.

The controversy about whether, or how much of, our aggression is genetically determined is part of what is sometimes called the nature-nurture problem: is aggression innate in our natures at birth or does it result from our subsequent environment and education? Some scientists answer that no part of man's aggression is innate, while others claim that all behavior is genetically determined. These scientists base their conclusions on the study of animal behavior, overlooking the fact that animal behavior studies are not necessarily applicable to the human race. It has been suggested that if aggression is innate a mutation that would produce a peaceful citizen is improbable, because too many genes are involved. More than a single mutation would be needed, and we have no assurance that the human race is to be given sufficient time for these mutations before the final nuclear or ecological cataclysm strikes.[2]

The psychologists ask a good question: "What does it mean to say a man is naturally aggressive? Does it mean that whatever he does he does from an aggressive motive, or only that he acts aggressively under certain conditions?" The answer should be that it means he has a tendency to act aggressively for the sheer satisfaction of being aggressive, rather than to achieve some desired objective—certainly not that his every act is prompted by an instinct towards aggression. Two or three commonly accepted definitions may be helpful. *Aggression* is frequently defined as behavior whose goal is the injury of some object, and is sometimes used as synonymous with hostility. *Frustration* may mean any interference with some goal-directed activity of the individual. Frustration may sometimes produce anger, and *anger* is an internal condition making aggressive responses relatively likely to occur.[3]

One more preliminary word about aggression. Most of us would consider the killing of a deer by a hungry lioness an aggressive act. Biologically, however, it is not, since the killing involves no malice, but only hunger. Strictly speaking, aggressiveness is expressed between two members *of the same species* when both want the same thing.[4]

Even though writing as recently as 1962, when his *Aggression: A Social Psychological Analysis* was published, Leonard Berkowitz was one of the earliest psychologists to give the subject of aggression extensive study in the light of the new claims of the ethologists. To Berkowitz, social psychology is the study of human behavior in response to stimuli associated with other people. Investigations of animal behavior are helpful, but not alone sufficient. Man, possessing language, is greatly susceptible to symbolic influence; he can inhibit his aggressive tendencies when overt hostilities would be a serious departure from his own moral code or the behavioral standards of other people important to him. He can also engage in aggressive actions in order to win the approval of others.[5]

Instinct as a motivational construct lost much of its favor in American psychology with the advent of behaviorism. Some scientists have attempted to make a distinction between an aggressive instinct in animals which acts spontaneously and an aggressive instinct which is activated by outside stimulation, but the distinction seems unimportant from our viewpoint. However, Berkowitz draws one important lesson from these studies: namely, that man has no instinctive drive towards war. Theoretically at least, it is possible to lessen the likelihood of interpersonal conflict by decreasing the occurrence of frustrations and minimizing the gains to be won through aggression. Social rather than biological characteristics determine the aggressiveness and warlikeness of nations or other groups.[6]

In any discussion on a matter of this kind, there is sure to come up the question of what Adler and Freud thought about it. Ernest Jones has said that as early as 1908 Adler suggested that there might be a primary aggressive instinct, but that he later changed the expression to "a will to power," and finally to simply "upward striving." Freud is frequently cited as maintaining that aggression is innate in man. True, his formulation was one of the few attempts to provide a theoretic underpinning for the assertion, but when finally he came to recognize that there may be something like an aggressive instinct in man he concluded, according to Storr, that it was primarily directed at self-destruction rather than towards mastering the external world. Freud thought man's aggression to be a secondary phenomenon, a diversion of the energy of the "death instinct" away from the self against which it was initially directed. His final view came to be that there are simply two groups of instincts: erotic instincts, which are always trying to collect living substances into even larger unities, and the death instincts, which act against that tendency and try to bring living matter back into an inorganic condition. The cooperation and opposition of these two forces produce the phenomena of life to which death puts an end. Predicated on this view, some Freudians have continued to hold that man is born with innate and enduring antisocial drives and have included criminal instincts as one of them, but sociological criminology is now an established scientific discipline and enjoys general agreement that crime, like most normative forms of conduct, is a social rather than biological phenomenon.

In July, 1971, there was held in Vienna a Psychoanalytical Congress at which some 3,000 psychoanalysts from 32 countries were present. Anna Freud, Sigmund Freud's 75-year-old daughter, who worked closely with him throughout their joint careers, was the guest of honor and gave a paper on the theme of the Congress: The World's Biggest Problem—Aggression. Miss Freud scolded those present for the poverty of their thinking about aggression and proposed a revision in what has been accepted as her father's theory. Opposing any formulation of a theory of aggression until we know much more from our clinical studies about it, she reexamined her father's belief on its nature and said that, although we do not yet know the source of aggression, she personally finds it impossible to disregard what seems to her an elemental fact—that aggression is an impulse or urge whose aim may be directed by environmental necessities. She did not speculate on the implications of her remarks, one of which implications a journalist attending the Congress thought to be that cultural and societal structures may be responsible for such manifestations of aggression as genocide, war and group brutality. As to her father's theory of aggression, Miss Freud said, "I think our study of the sexual instinct resulted in a straitjacket into which our study of aggression is being pressed." In support of her statement she cited a number of examples from her own work with children.[7]

Most authorities today probably regard aggression

as originating ultimately in response to some frustration, but Berkowitz notes that criticisms have been directed against this hypothesis; not all aggression is the result of frustration. Frustrations produce an emotional state, *anger*, which heightens the possibility of the occurrence of aggression, but whether aggressive responses actually are performed—even in the absence of restraints against hostility—depends upon other factors.[8]

In Konrad Lorenz we have not a psychologist, but one of the outstanding naturalists of our day. In his *On Aggression*, Lorenz loses no time in making his beliefs clear, and in a paper read by him at a symposium held in London he told the meeting: "There cannot be any doubt, in the opinion of any biologically-minded scientist, that intraspecific fighting is, in Man, just as much of a spontaneous instinctive drive as in most other higher vertebrates."[9]

Out of his immensely broad experience with animals, in *On Aggression* Lorenz gives case upon case to demonstrate the natural history of aggression and to make evident the means by which nature ritualizes (redirects) and inhibits actual fighting so that the individual may benefit by aggression's values while the species is saved from aggression's toll. In support of his belief, he relates in fascinating detail the story of his life-long experience in studying the behavior of birds, fish and animals. All that he says about animals may be true, but it need not necessarily follow that aggression in man is an innate, and not an acquired trait.

Lewis Mumford's succinct analysis of the Lorenz book probably sums it up well: "Excellent zoology: careless sociology."[10]

Despite its immense popularity at the time of its

120 LOVE, ALTRUISM, AND WORLD CRISIS

publication and the captivating manner in which it is written, we can make short shrift of Robert Ardrey's *The Territorial Imperative*. Ardrey is not a professional or even a serious amateur in the field of ethology; the pros have given him a really bad time, and that only in part because he asserts unequivocally that antagonism is an instinct innate in man at his birth. Ardrey's examples of animal behavior used to support his theory are devoted principally to what he calls "the territorial imperative," that is, an instinct in animals (and he says also in man) causing them to fight to protect their territory. This quotation is typical of both his reasoning and his style: "The territorial nature of man is genetic and ineradicable. . . . The territorial imperative is as blind as a cave fish, as consuming as a furnace, and it commands beyond logic, opposes all reason, suborns all moralities, strives for no goal more sublime than survival. Today's American may give thanks that on December 7, 1941, this was so. But today's American must also bear in mind that the territorial principle motivates all of the human species. It is not something that the American thought up, like the skyscraper or the Chevrolet. Whether we approve or we disapprove, whether we like it or we do not, it is a power as much an ally of our enemies as it is of ourselves and our friends."[11] It is unfortunate that Ardrey's reasoning was not as good as his style.

Ashley Montagu is one of the many behavioral scientists who deny the existence of an innate aggressive instinct in man. In *Man: His First Two Million Years*, he says:

> Evolutionary change in all animals proceeds by mutation and the storage of the adaptively valu-

able mutations in the genes. In man evolutionary change has also proceeded in this way, but with the addition of a great many nongenetic changes which also represent social evolutionary changes. These nongenetic behavioral or cultural changes are stored not in genes, but in the man-made, the learned, part of the environment, in the culture, in the tools, customs, institutions, laws, ballads, and the like, and in the memories of men as well as in other extragenetic devices for the storage and retrieval of information.

Human nature is what one learns from the man-made environment; it is not something with which one is born. What one is born with are the potentialities for learning which, by suitable teaching, are capable of being transformed into the uniquely human abilities.[12]

The first two sentences quoted should not be taken as an acceptance by Montagu of the theory that aggression is instinctive in man. In reading the conflicting material on the subject of aggression one tends to become convinced that semantic failure is the cause of much of the disagreement; if all the scholars participating in the verbal warfare about the nature of aggression could get together and agree on the ground rules and the definitions of their terms, they would probably find themselves less in disagreement than they think.

Montagu says man differs from all other creatures in the possession of five characteristics which at the same time constitute the conditions for the development of human culture: freedom from the instinctive, automatic reactions to environment that characterize much of animal behavior; extraordinary plastic potentialities for the development of a complex intelligence (educability); a highly developed capacity for symbolic thought; speech; and a highly developed capacity for innovation. A creature so endowed can interact in a creative manner with its environment, and that is what human beings have always done. Montagu's emphasis on the relationship between culture and the individual is, of course, Sorokin's "socio-cultural" factor, accepted by most sociologists. Montagu says:

> Every individual is born with a unique biological endowment of *potentialities* [emphasis added] which are like those of his fellows, but not exactly the same. This is the biological heredity of the individual. The culture into which the person is born constitutes his social heredity. The interaction between the individual's biological and social heredities is, in fact, what constitutes the person's *heredity.* There is no heredity without the interaction between one's biological equipment of potentialities and the environment or environments in which they undergo development. A man's nature is not what he is born with, but what he becomes under the organizing influence of the socializing environment into which he is born.
> Thus human nature is largely the expression of human nurture—the product of the interaction of genetic potentialities with the culturalizing factors which work upon them to give their general nature its particular form.
> It is principally through the agency of the stimulation of the cultural environment that the individual becomes a person.[13]

Montagu continues by saying that a human baby is born not only wanting and needing to be loved, but also wanting and needing to love others. On its face, the statement might seem inconsistent with his beliefs quoted above, but again the difficulty is with semantics and not consistency. He adds that for too long we have erroneously believed that babies are born rather selfish, aggressive little creatures who need to be disciplined and repressed, and that this belief has done a great deal of damage to human beings and to society. However, his concluding words on the subject cannot be criticized for lacking finality: "If man has no instincts such aggressiveness as he sometimes displays must be otherwise accounted for. The answer is simple—man *learns* to be aggressive. Men are not born with aggressive drives except possibly in some chromosomally abnormal individuals. There is no more evidence for an 'instinct of aggression' than there is for an 'instinct of territoriality'."[14]

By 1968 Montagu was becoming worried over the then increasing popularity and harmful influence of what he was convinced were the erroneous assumptions of Lorenz and Ardrey; to counteract them he edited and published *Man and Aggression*, comprising reviews of Lorenz and Ardrey by 13 scholars in the field. They are of course too long even to summarize here; probably it is sufficient to say that in a review of the book appearing in the London *Times Literary Supplement*, the TLS reviewer (always anonymous but always well qualified) commented that the popular success of the Lorenz and Ardrey books rested on Ardrey's journalistic skill and Lorenz's charm and distinction, but that they had little scientific foundation and that experts in the relative fields of knowledge had said so, their strictures being damning whether directed at the evidence or at the use made of it. The aggregate impact of the criticisms in the book is devastating. One can understand why Lewis Mumford called *Man and Aggression* "a useful emetic for those who have swallowed Ardrey's fantasies."[15]

A final comment on the Lorenz-Ardrey work is supplied in *The Human Imperative*, a recently published book by anthropologist Alexander Alland, Jr. reviewed in *Time* for May 22, 1972. In it Alland says that based on very extensive investigations of human and animal life, he is definitely convinced that Ardrey's territorial imperative argument could be proved to be innate in man only if it were universal, automatic and imperative, none of which is true. He is satisfied that a territoriality is determined by the culture rather than genes, and that since neither territoriality nor aggression is instinctive, war is not inevitable. Since culture is the major determinant in human existence, the "human imperative" is to develop a kind of culture in which war is impossible.

In an interview in the *Los Angeles Times*, Montagu emphasized the importance of love. "To be able to love," he said, "one must learn to do so. Love's failure to be so humanized during the first half dozen years of one's childhood results in a progressive dehumanization which leads to every kind of destructive behavior, all of it learned in a disordered and misguided attempt to adjust to a disordered and disordering man-made world. The fault lies not in our nature but in our nurture—and it is in the latter that the remedy also lies." This view is supported by London and Bryan[16] in a study in which they say that altruistic behavior in man is primarily learned by children and taught to them.

Anthony Storr, a London psychoanalyst, while saying that the question whether aggression is an instinct is one which we cannot yet fully answer and which may be the wrong one to ask,[17] discusses the pros and cons in his book *Human Aggression* and seems sometimes to lean towards the "innate" theory. He contributes valuable suggestions for psychiatric methods of controlling that impulse, whatever it may be, and channeling it into useful directions. In attempting to determine whether aggression is an instinct, Storr considers the possible existence of a sexual instinct and a similarity between it and the aggressive instinct, suggesting in support of this possibility an interesting example: "It is rare for the defeated animal [defeated in a battle for a female] to be seriously damaged physically, although he may suffer psychologically. It has been shown, for example, that a snake who has been vanquished by a rival will crawl away and remain sexually inactive for some weeks, whereas his triumphant adversary will, on achieving victory, immediately mate. One cannot fail to be reminded of the Duchess of Marlborough who wrote in her diary that 'My Lord returned from the war today and pleasured me twice in his top-boots.'"[18] Here again, however, we have an analogy between instincts in animals carried into the study of human behavior, which now seems to most social scientists unconvincing.

One of the most satisfactory treatments of the question, perhaps in part because it was published late in 1969 and the authors had the benefit of everything written to that time, is a book by the English scholars Lewis and Towers, entitled *Naked Ape or Homo Sapiens?* Their book could not be better designed to conclude our ethological discussion. David Holbrook says in the foreword that he cannot accept the view expressed in

William Golding's *Lord of the Flies* that, once civilized restraints were withdrawn, children would revert to savage ruthlessness; he praises the Lewis and Towers book for rescuing science itself from the damage done to its reputation by false analogies between animal and man in the works the authors attack, and credits them for showing that science does not endorse the social and political pessimism of those who proclaim that man is inescapably hostile and competitive.[19]

In summing up, the authors say they have concluded that: (1) The chief determinants of human behavior are neither anatomical nor genetical, and there is no evidence for unalterable drives for ownership or dominance or to kill; (2) All that man inherits from his animal ancestors is transformed and penetrated by intelligence and knowledge and does not exist as an instinctive force exerting an irrational compulsion upon his conduct; that is why in man stereotyped behavior patterns are not inherited; (3) We are thus brought to see the uniqueness of man in spite of his development from the animal level. In nothing is this difference and this uniqueness more clearly manifested than in man's recognition and formulation of principles of value and ethical standards.[20]

As was to be expected, Lewis and Towers disagree with Lorenz, Ardrey and Morris, although they are more polite about it; they comment on those authors' failure to cite authorities in their texts, lack of familiarity with modern theories of evolution, or genetics, on which their whole case rests, or the fossil history of early man and his precursors—a highly specialized study—or the study of comparative psychology.

In discussing the ethological approach, Lewis and Towers say the basic fallacy, which vitiates the whole approach, is the attempt to dissipate the fundamental difference between man and animals; any argument which ignores the gulf in anatomical structure, intelligence and social organization between ourselves and the anthropoids and is based on comparisons between man and fighting fish, or Graylag geese, or even between man and baboons and chimpanzees, carries no conviction. The theory of evolution now accepted does not identify man with the apes, but rather reveals a sharp break, which establishes what Julian Huxley calls the uniqueness of man.

Among other scientists they cite in support of their argument, the authors quote Huxley, who said that in man reason takes the place of instinct, and Marx, who once said that what distinguishes the most incompetent architect from the best of bees is that the architect raises his structure in imagination before he constructs it in reality. Man alone is capable of making his own history and, in doing so, making and remaking his patterns of behavior—himself.[21]

In discussing man's level of conceptual thought, Lewis and Towers say that once the leap to the potentialities of modern man was effected, as seen first in Cromagnon man about 40,000 years ago, a level was reached which offers possibilities by no means realized even yet. Man's mental powers have not changed since then by reason of any further development of the brain, though he has changed himself immensely by successive advances in technology, social organization and political structure. Dobzhansky, the leading geneticist of human evolution, is referred to for a complete endorsement of the views they have been discussing.[22]

Turning to Dobzhansky, as suggested, we do not

find him agreeing with the Lewis and Towers conclusions in so many words, but he does recognize the possibility that altruism and egotism are not products of some kind of special genes, but rather products of cultural developments transmitted not by genes but by learning. Particularly in childhood but also during his entire life, a person is able and even eager to acquire, from his parents or from other persons, ideas about what is good and what is evil and to accept instruction or counsel concerning the desirable ways of living in a society with other human beings. According to this view, man is not born virtuous or vicious but with a *capacity* for both virtue and vice. Biological evolution does not make man ethically better or worse, but it does promote intellectual alacrity and perhaps a sensitivity to ethical issues.

In *Reconstruction* Sorokin discusses "The Biological Nature of Man" and its relation to altruism. Because of the importance of the extent, if any, to which altruism and its opposite, antagonism, are controlled by man's genes (and hence are biologically innate), it has been emphasized in this chapter. In reading Sorokin's treatment of the subject it must be remembered that he was looking at biological factors in the light of the knowledge of man's biology as such knowledge existed at that time, and that he was not considering the possibility that innate altruism or antagonism could be *created* through artificial manipulation of genes. The intensive experimental work on the manipulation of genes, which suggests the awesome possibilities we shall discuss later, was yet in its infancy.

In his treatment of the biological nature of man, Sorokin dealt primarily with somatic factors (factors arising within the bodily organism). He doubted the possibility of an innate biological tendency towards aggression but, recognizing that the human organism seems to contain both altruistic and egoistic forces, regardless of how created, said our problem is to control such forces and direct them into beneficial channels, one of which could be altruistic behavior.

Since intelligence (as distinguished from learning) might be a factor in altruism, Sorokin, after conducting pertinent experiments and studies, concluded that intelligence of itself is not a factor, and this seems to meet with general agreement.

Mentioning that "emotional stability" had been much in vogue during the preceding few decades and was regarded as a factor making for integrity, altruism and other desirable social traits, Sorokin also conducted studies and experiments to determine the importance of that factor. Asking and answering three questions he himself propounded, he concluded that emotional stability is not a force operating in favor of altruism, that the great altruists of history were not "unemotional calculating machines," and that emotional stability in this sense does not really eliminate or decrease egoism (antagonism). In view of the wording of his questions, he might be right, but many believe that persons who are not emotionally disturbed are more apt to be altruistic than those who are.[23]

"Having failed to find significant factors of altruism among various somatic and psychological traits," Sorokin says, "many thinkers of the past and present have sought for them not in this or that single somatic or psychological characteristic but in the similarity or dissimilarity of the interacting individuals and groups." His studies and experiments convinced him that such similarity or dissimilarity is not a factor, or at least is not helpful, in increasing altruism. Strangely enough, however, even some writers who deny an aggression instinct believe in the possibility of an instinctive tendency towards cooperation.

Desmond Morris, for example, calls it the miracle of civilized survival that the human cooperative urge reasserts itself so strongly and so repeatedly and suggests that if we did not carry in us the basic biological urge to cooperate with our fellow-men we would never have survived as a species.[24]

Montagu says, "Far from being born with a disposition towards aggression, the evidence indicates man is born with a highly organized system of drives which are all oriented in the direction of growth and development in cooperation"; the impulses towards cooperative behavior are already present in man at birth and he has only to develop them.[25]

Some studies by Dennis Krebs deal with this possibility that altruistic cooperation may be innate. Krebs reports a study by Campbell in 1965 which caused Campbell to believe that altruistic motives are not only acquired but also have a basis in biological evolution—are innate. Experiments with rats produced no real evidence of innate altruism, but the contrary may be true of higher animals. Hebb and Thompson, researching on primates, said there is definite evidence of a phylogenetic development of something we call altruism, defined as intrinsically motivated concern for others.

Several other scholars who have debated *innate* as against *learned* altruistic cooperation, while rejecting the innate theory for individuals, have suspected that it might be valid as to social groups. Darwin's theory is today referred to as adaptive fitness, meaning that variations or mutations arise and if beneficial to an organism tend through the action of the environment to be preserved and to preserve the organism, so that such organisms are more likely to leave a larger progeny than organisms lacking similar adaptive traits (Darwinian fitness).[26] Russell and some of the other scientists who worked with and followed Darwin first suggested the possibility that "Darwinian fitness" might be applicable to a social or cultural group or species as well as to individual organisms.

In preparing for a course he was to give at Harvard on *The Social Development of the Person*, Montagu went to biological data, studying first the nature of social life among the unicellular organisms, then the multicellular, then man. He found that in various types of plant and animal life studied, groups were more immune from hostile forces (radiation, etc.) and more responsive to favorable factors, than isolated individuals (a "psychochemical" advantage in numbers). This was an earlier stage in the development of social life among the higher animals. Only after Darwinism and Spencerian sociology began to die down did mutual aid come to be discussed as a factor in evolution. Now the principal of cooperation may well become established as the most important factor in the survival of animal groups. Survival is determined more by cooperation than by individual fitness. Montagu says that the "individual" is a myth; the person is a set of social relationships and (quoting Leo Loeb) "separation between individuality and environment, especially the social environment, becomes impossible." Montagu says the belief that man is *essentially* a function of his genes is a pathetic fallacy. To bind cell to cell for cooperation—that is the essence of social life. No cell is more intimately bound to another than man is to his fellows and his social group. "Love thy neighbor as thyself" is not simply a good text for Sunday morning sermons; it is perfectly sound biology.[27]

S. J. Holmes has said that in the light of comparative psychology genuine altruism may be regarded not as something concocted out of one's individual experience but as a deep-seated trait resting upon basic instincts that go far down in the animal kingdom, and that for all social animals altruism has a very real value in the struggle for existence.[28]

W. D. Hamilton concurs, but with certain reservations, saying, "It is generally accepted that the behavior characteristics of a species is just as much the product of evolution as the morphology." He mentions that Haldane in 1932 supposed an increment to group fitness proportional to its content of altruistic members and showed that there could be an initial numerical increase of a gene for altruism, provided the starting gene frequency was high enough and the individual disadvantage low enough compared to the group advantage conferred. Haldane concluded that genetical altruism can show some advantage in population split into tribes, but Hamilton is willing to concur only if there is a periodic reassortment of the tribes such that, by chance or otherwise, the altruists become reconcentrated in some of them. Obviously much work on this theory remains to be done.[29]

Two books even more entertaining than Lorenz and Ardrey, but with one exception even less important for our purpose, are *The Naked Ape* and *The Human Zoo* by Desmond Morris. If we want to liken humans to animals, these are the books. However, in *The Human Zoo*

Morris makes a reference to imprinting which may be important in our determining what methods will be most effective in building altruism into the human animal. Imprinting can be defined as "learning, occurring rapidly and early in life, characterized chiefly by resistance to extinction or forgetfulness." Hess of the University of Chicago is perhaps the leading authority on imprinting. He calls imprinting an early experience during which a young animal forms a strong social attachment to a mother-object (which may be even a wire structure not at all resembling its real mother). It is no longer thought to fit into the usual association learning framework, but is rather one of the behaviors so persistent in character and resistant to modification by reinforcement that it cannot be satisfactorily explained by conventional laws of learning. Imprinting refers to an early experience that has a profound influence on the later adult social and sexual behavior of an animal with respect to the choice of objects for these behaviors. It occurs only at a critical period early in the animal's life.

It is now believed that imprinting or processes very like imprinting exist in every social species, particularly those in which there are parent-young relationships. Dogs, for example, cannot be made into pets if they have not had contact with human beings during the period of primary socialization. One experimenter has imprinted some waterfowl on such mother-objects as a football or a green box. Imprinting must be distinguished from association learning which, unlike imprinting, can occur later than the critical period and can be later erased, whereas the effects of imprinting are relatively permanent even when it has taken place in quite a brief period of time.[30]

Applying imprinting to the human animal, Morris

says: "During the early months of its life a human baby passes through a sensitive socialization phase when it develops a profound and long-lasting attachment to its species and especially to its mother; the attachment is not totally dependent on physical rewards obtained from the mother, such as feeding and cleaning. The exposure learning typical of imprinting also takes place. The young baby cannot keep close to the mother by following her like a duckling, but it can achieve the same end by the use of the smiling pattern. Smiling is attractive to the mother and encourages her to stay with the infant and play with it. These playful, smiling interludes help to cement the bond between the child and its mother. Each becomes imprinted on the other and a powerful reciprocal attachment develops, a persistent bond that is extremely important for the later life of the child.... A strong bond cemented during the first year of life will mean a capacity for making strong bonds during the adult life that follows.

Good early imprinting opens a large emotional bank account for the child. If expenses are heavy later on, it will have plenty to draw upon."[31] We shall consider this in more detail in discussing infant care as a means of increasing love.

Had this book been written a very few years ago, this final portion on the biological factors bearing on altruism would not have been here, and it is regrettable that things could not have remained so. It has to do with the manipulation of genes and the use of chemicals to alter traits and character.

An excellent simple explanation of genes is that given by Nobel Prize winner Beadle in a talk made in 1969. As he put it, in the nucleus of the fertilized egg

biological factors in the creation of altruism 135

cell of man there are many thousands of kinds of genes, each a long thread-like molecule of an acid with an unpronounceable name we call DNA. Collectively, they all add up to some 6 billion DNA subunits. These subunits are of four kinds, and the order in which they are arranged is a molecular code or language spelling out the directions for making a person and his individual characteristics out of that tiny cell. The alphabet of the DNA language thus consists of but four units analagous to letters; these instructions in a single cell are the equivalent of more than 1000 six-hundred-page books. Incredibly, the genes are so minute that the DNA of all the egg cells that gave rise to the 3.5 billion persons on earth today could be put in a cube one-eighth of an inch on a side.

It is only rather recently that serious consideration has been given to the feasibility of altering genes or artificially changing the "directions" they contain. Once started, the research has snowballed, as evidenced by many press releases and comments, some of which, much abbreviated, are as follows:

November, 1969. "Cloning" treated as feasible; question raised as to what would happen to the process of evolution if each new generation were identical to the last. (Cloning is a method of replacing the nucleus of an ovum with the nucleus of some specified cell from a donor's body, thus making the offspring an identical genetic duplicate of the donor and making it possible for parents to have children who would be genetic duplicates of people of famous brilliance or ability, or if they so desired exact duplicates of themselves).[32]

November 23, 1969. A team of Harvard scientists has isolated a pure gene from a living organism for the first time, thereby advancing the day when man will be able to manipulate his own genetic makeup. These scientists fear the long-run result may be to loose more evil than good on mankind. One scientist foresees the day when the tool they have explored might be used to engineer human beings according to some government's specifications. Nobel Prize winner Luria warns that that day might be closer than we think; the problem is a political one and very, very dangerous.[33]

December 19, 1969. An article in *Science*, subtitled "Expression of mammalian genes may be controlled by repressors acting on the translation of messenger RNA," explains in detail how genetic engineering might be accomplished, pointing out the difficulties involved but by no means considering it impossible.[34]

March 30, 1970. Scientists at Princeton announce that, by injecting drugs into the hypothalamus of a rat's brain, they can turn a killer rat into a pacifist and a pacifist rat into a killer. Will humans be next? Apparently at least one sponsor of the experiment foresees such a possibility—the United States Arms Control and Disarmament Agency!

May, 1970. Delgado of Yale reports to a Unesco meeting about monkeys with tiny radios attached to their brains "whose mischievous thoughts are 'corrected' by computer before the monkeys can put them into action." Delgado says that through such techniques the next five years will see "a revolution in the medical treatment of aggressive behavior as important as the appearance of antibiotics in the treatment of infectious diseases; if a person is behaving antisocially, there are chemical and electrical mechanisms that we can know and modify."[35]

June, 1970. A University of Wisconsin team headed

by Nobel prize winner Khorana has created a man-made gene—perhaps a "profound step towards genetic 'engineering' of improved humans and animals." One scientist says: "It is the beginning of the end. . . . If you can make genes, you can eventually make new viruses for which there are no cures. Any little country with good biochemists could make such biological weapons. It would take only a small laboratory. If it can be done, someone will do it."[36]

September 5, 1970. Nobel prize winner Lederberg calls for the establishment of a National Genetics Task Force to increase the momentum of efforts aimed at unlocking the genetic code of man. Etzioni says such a task force must be accompanied by a task force on the social and moral consequences of genetic manipulation and point out its dangers.[37]

January 7, 1971. The synthesizing of a human growth hormone for the first time is announced by California scientists, marking a major advance in scientific efforts to make proteins (the structural material for life) from nonliving chemicals.[38]

January 8, 1971. Announcement by research teams of the creation of the first man-made gene and the creation of a living cell made up from parts of other cells; that such knowledge can be used for harm if misapplied was acknowledged.[39]

January 11, 1971. The synthesizing of a chemical that produced a specific memory in rats and mice (fear of the dark) was announced. The method involves the alteration of RNA molecules in the brain cells and is thought to be also usable in the brains of higher animals, including man.[40]

March 7, 1971. A Veteran's Administration scientist

claims improved memories of aging patients through feeding them RNA, as well as by the use of a drug named Cylert; while pointing out what a change the discovery might make in our educational system if much of what man must learn during his too-short lifetime can be injected into him chemically, it was added that Huxley, Orwell and others have pointed out the dangers of technological mind control.[41]

November 12, 1971. A noted geneticist yesterday told how he has produced changes in the behavior of fruit flies by manipulating their genes.[42]

May, 1972. *Chicago Magazine* reports on a study by Arnold Ravin, a highly regarded geneticist, who says man has certainly gained power to make the bearers of certain genotypes more successful in survival and reproduction, making it difficult to imagine how man, given his present powers of acquiring and transmitting knowledge, can possibly avoid intervening in future evolution. After outlining what modern genetics makes possible, he says there appear to be only few, although important, technical difficulties to bar the road to such control; two methods for separating genes are already available and in utilization. Concluding, Ravin presents sound genetic reasons why such tampering with human heredity may well be disastrous.

December 29, 1972. *United Press International* announces that Harold B. Green of George Washington University recently told the American Association for the Advancement of Science that we are now only a very short step from knowing how to control the sex of an infant and only somewhat farther away from developing ways to produce clones—identical humans.

Lewis Mumford in *The Pentagon of Power* fears

what he calls "the new megamachine" and accuses it of having already produced a formidable and still growing ruling caste in the United States and Russia: a caste which he compares to the Janissaries in the heyday of Turkish despotism. The next logical step, he says, as with the Janissaries, would be to select the "elite" in their cradles and deliberately mold them for the purpose in hand so that no inconvenient human attributes would lessen their unconditional loyalty to the megamachine. Mumford refers to Hersey's *The Child Buyer* as deserving more serious discussion on this subject than it received, but says already a step well beyond this is in view: nothing less than the selection of the elite from a bank of spermatozoa and ova for gestation under control in an artificial womb. The first bold theoretic steps towards this consummation, he adds, have already been put forward. And it might be added that Huxley's *Brave New World* and Orwell's *1984* no longer seem impossible fancies as they did when they were written. The sources of power and control portrayed in those books are already practically within the grasp of government.[43]

A year or so ago there was held at the Center for the Study of Democratic Institutions at Santa Barbara a conference participated in by many nationally known scientists, at which a major subject was whether contemporary biological developments actually amount to a revolution. Among the biological advances—present and prospective—thought by the participants to have the most profound implications—ethical, ecological and social—were these: control of the sex of foetuses ("probably 10 or 20 years away"); designed genetic change to alter presently inherited and programmed physiological and/or psychological processes ("The very nature of the species seems potentially susceptible to change"); control, through genetic engineering, of human instincts, drives and emotions, indeed all physical and psychological characteristics ("For example, aggressiveness has a considerable hereditary component and is, therefore, susceptible to genetic manipulation"). One of the Junior Fellows at the Center noted that there must be discussion about the "ought," which is ethical, as well as the "can," which is technical. The horrifying thing is that this conference was dealing entirely with the "ought"—the "can" was taken for granted.[44] And even more recently, the Yale University Press has published a book called *Fabricated Man: The Ethics of Genetic Control*, in which Paul Ramsey examines the ethics of such things as the asexual reproduction of man and the breeding of human beings for special purposes, taking the "can" for granted.[45]

No doubt, even by the time this book is published the scientists will have brought us still farther along the road towards planned, controlled and robot-like birth, living and death. Review of these possibilities, unpleasant and frightening though it may have been, has seemed necessary because they do indeed open one available, although unlikely, road to creating altruistic people. Men would have to be persuaded or forced to give the necessary cooperation, although if babies conceived and born in the normal way were to be replaced by "test-tube" babies even that cooperation would not be needed. Unless altruization could be accomplished throughout the world at the same time, the survival of the peaceful part against conquest by the other would seem problematical. Even though such powers are perfected to the point which now seems possible and even if we dared and were incautious enough to place those powers into the hands of government in the hope that they would be properly used and could create a nation or world of people overflowing with altruistic love, the possibility is no answer to our present problem.

That problem—the one we have already considered at length and which prompted the writing of this book—is urgent and immediate and is not one we may happily forget in the hope that several decades from now a genetical solution may be achieved. For one thing, even if such time should arrive, there is no reason to be optimistically certain that all governments in the world could be persuaded to transform their subjects into peaceful nonaggressive world citizens. For another, with atomic capabilities being developed by more and more nations, a solution involving years rather than decades must be sought. If increase in altruistic love is a possible answer, the methods available to us for the bringing about of such increase become even more important now that the threat of perfected genetic manipulation and its misuse is becoming more and more real. These things involve questions that sooner or later must be faced by man as a species—by societies as a whole. Accordingly, let us continue our examination of more feasible and nongenetic solutions.

11
altruistic love and
the supraconscious

In *Reconstruction*, Sorokin reports on methods and techniques of the "Great Masters of Creative Altruism." Since the book was published in 1948, it must be regarded as to some extent introductory to his later works on the subject. Although acknowledging the fragmentary character of our knowledge of these techniques, he suggests that even this knowledge discloses several things common to the methods of the oriental and occidental masters of self-altruization, men who were responsible for the moral education of millions and for the cultivation of the supraconscious in man. Of what he calls the techniques of contemporary psychotherapy, Sorokin says the methods and techniques of Yoga, of the founders of the great Christian monastic orders at the beginning of the Middle Ages, of the great mystics and altruists living in the midst of the busy world and of the founders of the great religions contain in themselves nearly all the sound techniques of modern psychoanalysis, psychotherapy, and moral education.[1]

As we shall see, he says, the ancient systems employed many techniques scarcely known to today's sciences that aim at the transfiguration of man. His "few facts in support of this assertion" are gone into in more detail in his later books, which we shall examine in subsequent chapters. It may be said here, however, that the assertion enjoys considerable independent support from, among others, Jung. Jung has said that when he began his life-work in the practice of psychiatry and psychotherapy he was completely ignorant of Chinese philosophy, and it was only later that his professional experiences showed him that in his technique he had been unconsciously led along that secret way which for centuries has been the preoccupation of the best minds of the East.

Further corroboration is offered by a UPI release appearing in the press on October 28, 1971, saying that the technique of transcendental meditation is gaining in popularity throughout the world and that Stanford Research Institute is conducting a study of it, particularly because of reports that the technique has been helpful in reducing drug abuse.

In attempting to determine the methods of self-altruization used by the great altruists of the past in both the East and the West, Sorokin studied everything he could find about their lives. According to Vexliard, in this study Sorokin found five factors favorable to the specific development of their personalities: (1) a biologically favorable heredity; (2) a pressing need impelling individuals or groups to a research, invention or discovery; (3) the individual or group finding themselves

altruistic love and the supraconscious

at the crossroads of different ideas, beliefs and values, or in a stream that impels them towards new creations; (4) a certain freedom at social and cultural levels; and (5) a sort of "luck"—for example, in the form of an event able to serve as a springboard for the development of the creative process.[2]

Further, and to him of great importance, an essential process for the formation of a superior personality is that of self-identification with the supraconscious. The individual becomes progressively aware that his real *me* is neither his body, nor his unconscious, nor the bioconscious, nor the socioconscious, but rather the supraconscious, to which various names have been given. Sorokin singles out, from the psychological point of view, those favorable conditions conducive to self-identification with the supraconscious in the cases of the altruists he examines, avoiding less well-known and doubtful or inadequate factors such as agape, divine grace, spiritual inheritance, and even geographic and biological factors.[3]

The ultimate task of his studies of altruistic love, Sorokin says, is to find out the efficient ways of making persons more creative and altruistic. To do this, we must have an adequate theory of the mental structure of human personality and of the energies generated in and operating through the human organism. He regards the prevalent theories in this field as grossly defective. One blunder, he says, is merging into the category of the "unconscious" or "subconscious" two radically different energies of man: the *biologically unconscious* that lies below the level of the conscious state of mind, and the *supraconscious* that lies above the level of any conscious or subconscious and rational thought or energy. The "depth psychology" of the prevalent theories of personality he thinks faulty because it either flattens the mental structure almost exclusively to the level of the unconscious (or subconscious), with a sort of epiphenomenal and vague "ego" and "superego," or just depicts it as a "two-story building"—the unconscious (subconscious) and the conscious (rational). He says that, on the contrary, an adequate theory of personality must emphasize the highest aspect of its mental structure no less than its lower region, and must emphasize the supraconscious energy operating in human beings no less than the unconscious energy.

He mentions, as other defects of the prevalent theories of personality, an oversimplification of the "conscious" and "unconscious" energies of man, and their vagueness in spelling out the relationships between the structure and energies of the individual and those of the groups and culture the individual lives in.[4]

Since, he continues, besides the complexity of mental phenomena, the main reasons for our helplessness in rendering man creatively altruistic are the neglect of these phenomena by science during the past four centuries, the wrong conception of man and the sociocultural universe entertained by science, and the disregard of the existing body of oriental and occidental experience in the field of the supraconscious, the first remedial steps must consist in the correction of these defects. An incomparably greater proportion of scientific research and cognitive effort must be devoted from now on to the study of the superorganic "energies of man," as William James called them, in all their personal, cultural, and social manifestations. If during the next 50 years no important discovery should be made in the field of natural science, this would not seriously matter. But if our knowledge and control of man's highest energies are not markedly expanded, this will mean a real catastrophe. For the sake of man's very survival, the governments, foundations, universities, private endowers of research funds and science itself must shift the bulk of their resources and activities to this field. A series of research institutions should be established. The most productive minds should be dedicated to this purpose. With such a concentration of resources and cognitive activities, a rapid multiplication of our knowledge and control of the phenomena in question would result.[5]

Vexliard says: "Sorokin criticizes contemporary theories which make personality merely a result of conflict between the conscious and unconscious, placing greater emphasis upon the unconscious. Sorokin himself distinguished four levels of total personality, of mental life and of behavior: (1) the biological unconscious; (2) the biological conscious; (3) the socio-cultural conscious; and (4) the supraconscious. In his theory of personality, Sorokin places emphasis upon the higher levels of mental structure, the supraconscious levels, in contrast to contemporary theories stressing the lower levels of unconscious energy.... The 'biological unconscious' represents the inferior part, the animal, the instinctive, reflexological part of man's mental apparatus. The unconscious ... cannot be identified with the id of Freud.... Sorokin does not admit, as do Freud and his disciples, that the higher psychic phenomena, the creative conscious and supraconscious, can be explained in terms of the sublimation of the lower, obscure, unconscious, instinctive forces."[6]

Sorokin's term "biological (or bio) conscious" is plain enough, and his "supraconscious level" we are about to examine. The "socioconscious" is formed by way of interaction with others, by personal experiences in contact with others, by way of the collective life, its demands and recurrent testing. These collective and accumulated experiences, Vexliard understands Sorokin to say, are transmitted from individual to individual, from group to group, and from generation to generation. It is in this way that traditions, norms, moral values, philosophical and religious values, knowledge, artistic tastes, political attitudes, technological processes, institutional forms and, in a general way, socio-cultural novelties are transmitted. As each individual belongs, simultaneously or successively, to a variety of socio-cultural groups, some voluntary and others involuntary, he is assigned a variety of roles, activities and egos, corresponding perceptibly in number and character to these various groups. Thus, in our societies, nearly all men possess one or more family egos (son, husband, father, etc.) and a national, religious or professional ego, which corresponds to the diversity of roles in these different groups. Each of these egos is replete with its own values, its ideas, its volitions and its feelings. Roles corresponding to these egos include, in their turn, definite forms consisting, for example, of attitudes which at times imply a particular language, a manner of being towards another person and in certain cases even special clothing. The totality of our social groups and their cultures defines most of our conscious egos and their cultures; these socio-cultural egos occupy the major part of our conscious mentality and behavior. Every marked modification of the socio-cultural group is reflected in the structure of individual egos and, conversely, notable changes in ego structures among members of a group will have their impact upon the social groups of which they are a part.[7]

Sorokin believed firmly in the existence of the supraconscious and its power. With examples to support him, he shows the supraconscious manifests itself in most realms—natural sciences, art, literature, ethics, religion, philosophy, law, economics and, in general, all realms of truth, beauty and goodness. He readily recognizes that while the existence of the first three levels of personality structure (as just analyzed above) is hardly questioned, the existence of the supraconscious mentality, energy and activities is either denied or seriously questioned by many scholars of both the social sciences and the humanities. He thinks this is because the admission of the supraconscious goes against the dominant materialistic and mechanistic metaphysics still prevalent in contemporary psychology and social disciplines.

For this reason, he says, and also because of the exceptional importance of the supraconscious for creative altruization, it is advisable to stop at this problem somewhat longer than at the elucidation of the unconscious, the biological and the socio-cultural consciousness in man. "The supraconscious creates and discovers through supraconscious intuition. It is different from all sensory intuitions—perception, observation—and from logical, mathematical and syllogistic reasoning."[8]

When first faced with the question whether he believed in the supraconscious, Sorokin was in the same position of uncertainty as many other scientists. Roger Godel visited India many times for scientific investigations in cardiology and other fields, including Yoga. Recognizing the problem confronting physical scientists (including himself!) as new discovery after new discovery shakes their past beliefs and their world of sense experiences, Godel explained the dilemma in this way:

While the oriental truth seeker makes his way toward the interior of his own being, the occidental savant is endeavoring to question the world outside.... The "real" for him is the object, the thing (*res*), circumambient phenomenology. To know reality he must penetrate into the intimate structure of surrounding matter by process of analysis.... But now suddenly—around a bend of quantum mechanics—exploration of the objective field brings the theorist of the physical sciences to a most disquieting position; before him appears an ambiguous universe where the observer and the phenomenon observed are inextricably commingled....

In this realm of indetermination, all the symbols and formulas familiar to our experience of things vanish. Notions of energy and of matter require so profound a transformation as to lose their original meaning; energy condenses into matter, matter dematerializes into radiation. The waves associated with the propagation of light quanta need no substratum in order to propagate in space-time; they undulate neither in a fluid, nor in a solid, nor yet in a gas. Only the unreal thread of analogy links them to the image of a wave rippling the surface of water....

On this advanced horizon of the scientific spirit, the play of phenomena is still graspable under the aspect of complementary terms. But the reign of duality is here only an appearance.... This we

altruistic love and the supraconscious 151

should know; that neither the synthesizing spirit nor analysis can provide access to cognizance of the Real. This final end of the search requires for its accomplishment another mode of realization irreducible to the dynamisms of informational thought.

Yet the gains of the contemporary sciences, limited as they are, teach us one valuable lesson. They break down the fictive barrier that our corporeal *I* has improperly established between the "objective" world and "subjectivity". . . . Seen in the light of wave mechanics and the matrix calculus, the electron dissipates into a vague metaphysical nebula. In the light of this sane and ruthless examination by scientific criticism, notions of the concrete, of objective reality, indeed vanish. Similarly, the concept of "existence" reveals its factitious character and collapses when once subjected to serious epistemological examination, as Eddington has very well demonstrated. . . . In sum, the world of sense appearances has been wiped out to give place to an aspect of the universe irreducibly different.[9]

After quoting the above to strengthen his thesis that modern science can and does no longer fail to recognize the truth of the existence of supraconscious forces of great utility, Sorokin says in *Ways and Power* that the role of the supraconscious is overwhelmingly decisive in religious and moral creativity. "The greatest religious creators—the founders of great religions, the great prophets and apostles—all explicitly state that either they themselves are an incarnation of the supraconscious (God, Brahma . . . and their equivalents) or that they are revealing the suprarational, supraconscious, suprasensory Truth or Gospel. . . . Even when ordinary persons become religiously and morally inspired, they consider themselves emptied of their egos and turned into the instrumentality of the supraconscious or God. . . . We see here the same transmutation of man into an instrument of the supraconscious which we saw in all fields of creativity."

Sorokin suggests our "whiz-kid" prodigies in mathematics as an example of supraconscious intuition, but this may be a weak example, particularly since his chart of the best-known arithmetical prodigies shows that in most cases their power lasted only a few years. Perhaps better is his suggestion that in the principal mathematical *discoveries* the role of the supraconscious intuition has been enormous and indispensable, giving as examples nine eminent mathematicians and four eminent psychologists, all of whom explicitly admitted the intuitional foundations of their theories. He continues: "In the opinion of many mathematicians the supraconscious does not originate in the mathematicians but comes from the cosmos and connects the inventor with the supraconscious cosmic mind. Aristotle, Leibnitz, Schelling and Fichte called it 'participation in divinity.' . . . It is not surprising, therefore, that a large number of great scientists—like Pascal, Kepler, Newton, Galileo to some extent and others—were not only intuitionists, but mystics in the narrow sense of this term."[10]

Sorokin next turns to philosophy for examples, beginning with the Upanishads in India and Taoism in China, passing through all the mystic philosophers of the East and West, up to the more modern philosophers——even such apparent rationalists as Descartes and

Spinoza and such skeptical philosophers and objective idealists as Hume, Kant and a bewildering number of others. All of these, he says, and many other philosophers —practically an overwhelming majority—recognize some sort of intuitional axioms, "forms of mind," or intuitional truths as the basis of all the mathematical, logical and sensory-observational verities in all fields of human cognition and creativity.[11]

We must note, however, that Sorokin's only definite claim for the list as a whole is that the men on it were blessed with above-average intuition. While many of them attributed their flashes of revelation to activity of the supraconscious and some were avowed mystics, we cannot accept it as proved that all great intuition is dependent on the supraconscious. While many examples of existence of a supraconscious power are most convincing, our belief in it must still be largely a matter of faith rather than positive proof. Since Sorokin's following examples in the fields of invention and the fine arts are subject to the same comment, we can omit them here. He also cites extrasensory perception and psychokinetics as examples; perhaps, but the nature and even the existence of these things are still too much in dispute to permit us to accept them as convincing evidence.

A chapter of Sorokin's called *Supreme Love and the Supraconscious*[12] need not detain us for long; although we need as great leaders of altruism men possessing the supreme love that occurs so seldom and which Sorokin says can hardly be achieved without direct participation of the supraconscious, we have perhaps more practical interest in love of lower intensity and shorter duration, which he calls inadequate ego-centered amity. Such love, he tells us, can be easily developed in persons and groups without participation of the supraconscious, through purely bioconscious and socioconscious motivations that can be effected through the ego-centered techniques of conditioned reflexes, mechanical drilling and reward and punishment. Without doubting that supreme love acquired through the supraconscious can be of inestimable help in achieving the spread of universal love, individuals who have achieved that magnitude of love will doubtless continue to appear from time to time, if the time remains. Our present interest must be concerned rather with developing means of creating and disseminating the lower degrees of unegoistic love while time does remain; it is with these possibilities and means we must be most concerned in studying Sorokin's work and conclusions.

Before leaving the supraconscious for now, we might well glance briefly at what three or four other authorities have written about its relationship to altruistic love. Bradford Smith, writing in his *Inward Art of Meditation*, calls love a necessary factor in attaining the supraconscious, saying that "anyone who has met a practicing mystic has sensed the outflowing of light and love, childlike yet deeply mature, from the inner springs of his personality. It is by love that the mystic reaches God, and it is God's love that irradiates him. One of the surest signs of the essentially mystic nature of the religion Jesus taught is its centering on love."[13]

Chaudhuri says of meditation as an avenue to the supraconscious that, although those who find life in this world meaningless are inclined to magnify transcendental consciousness as the acme of wisdom, transcendental consciousness is awareness of only one aspect of Being.

Being is also, among many other things, the individual self as a unique creative center. By virtue of total enlightenment an individual experiences transcendent peace within himself and at the same time resolves to offer his best for the good of all and spontaneously breaks forth into altruistic action. His enlightenment attains fruition in a spirit of dedication to the collective good of man.[14]

W. T. Stace quotes two famous mystics on the subject—Meister Eckhart and Jan Ruysbroeck. Eckhart said, "What a man takes in contemplation [meditation] he must pour out in love." Ruysbroeck expressed the same certainty that the highest mystical experience must overflow in love into the world. He wrote: "The man who is sent down by God from those heights [the man who acquires supraconsciousness] . . . possesses a rich and generous ground, which is set in the richness of God: and therefore he must always spend himself on those who have need of him. . . . And by this he possesses a universal life, for he is ready alike for contemplation and for action and is perfect in both of them."[15]

Sri Aurobindo concludes a discussion of supermind (supraconsciousness) with a fairly down-to-earth passage that may serve well as a conclusion to this chapter: "It might be suggested also that until something clearly recognizable like supermind manifests itself with some definiteness and fullness or until it descends and takes possession of our earth-consciousness, we cannot be certain that it exists; till then mind holds the place as a general arbiter or field of reference for all knowledge and mind is incapable of any certain or absolute knowledge; it has to doubt all, to test all and yet to achieve all, but cannot be secure in its knowledge or its achievement. That, incidentally, establishes the necessity of such a principle as the supermind or Truth-Consciousness in any intelligible universe, for without it there is no issue, no goal for either life or knowledge."[16]

12
self-help, polarization, and avatars

Sorokin titles Chapter 11 of *Ways and Power*, *Factors in the Early Integration of the Fortunate Altruists*, but since those factors are equally applicable to the development of altruistic character in others, the chapter might better have been titled *Certain Factors in the Development of Altruism*. He starts his discussion by saying, "In our elucidation of this problem, let us first eliminate the factors which are unprovable or improbable or very doubtful"—an excellent approach.

Under "unprovable" theories, without denying their existence, he lists and briefly examines divine grace (agape), spiritual heredity, karmic influence, effects of the constellation of planets, and mysterious influence coming from interplanetary regions. As "doubtful factors" he includes "geographic" theories (those holding that certain geographic areas are, for various reasons, more conducive to the development of altruistic persons than are others, which he does not believe), and somatic traits (those pertaining to the body rather than the mind or central nervous system), which some persons think are an index to personality and mental abilities; an example would be the contention that people who are fat, with round, broad hips and narrow shoulders, tend to be sociable, tolerant and amiable. "Biological heredity" he regarded as a factor insufficiently known to justify reliance on it to establish altruism as an innate inherited trait. As we have seen, this factor has come in for much intensive study since Sorokin wrote 20 years ago, and is still in dispute.[1] In taking up his *Known, Verified and Verifiable Factors*, Sorokin deals mainly with the family factor, and this is so important a factor that we shall reserve its discussion for Chapter Nineteen, to whose subject it is more pertinent.

Sorokin recognized that in spite of its superior importance, the family is only one of numerous agencies that affect the growth of altruism. Others, he says, are the groups, persons, and forces with whom a child or youth directly interacts and to whose influence he is directly exposed. Of human groups and individuals, the most important of these agencies are the playmates, the school, sport and entertainment agencies, including movies and television, the church, and specific persons such as playmates, friends, sweethearts, counselors, doctors, spiritual leaders, and worshiped heroes, if the child interacts with such persons. At a later age the occupational and economic groups are especially important. Sometimes, under specific conditions, their effects are as strong as, or even stronger than, the influence of the family.[2]

Another and important factor is the snowballing effect of the retroactive influence of the first good deeds.

self-help, polarization, and avatars 159

Sorokin says that once started by these agencies in performance of altruistic and creative actions, the child puts himself under the influence of the retroactive effects of his first good deeds. These leave strong positive traces upon the child's physical, mental, and moral personality and begin to shape his behavior altruistically. With each additional performance of an unselfish deed, his altruistic behavior and mentality become increasingly habitual, deeper and deeper grounded in his whole personality, until the habit turns into a second nature.

Sorokin adds that an increase in habituation of creatively altruistic actions means an accumulation of the energy of creative love in the individual. The more this supreme energy accumulates, the more the altruistic children quietly grow in their altruism and overcome "road blocks" on their royal highway to the kingdom of creative love.[3] Supplementing these findings of Sorokin's, Dennis Krebs, citing his own and experiments by many others, reports that when children are taught by observation of altruistic models rather than through verbal instructions, their altruism as evidenced by their actions is generally greater.

A chapter in *Ways and Power*[4] deals with "tribal egoism," by which Sorokin means egoistic tendencies of all groups, regardless of the classification on which the groups are based. He warns us that if unselfish love is confined within only one group, be it family, tribe, nation, religion, trade union or what have you, in-group *altruism* will tend to generate out-group *antagonism*, and the more exclusive it is the more unavoidable will be clashes between the group and the rest of humanity. The member of "my group, right or wrong" cannot help treating the rest of humanity as a mere means for their group. Sorokin's examples over a wide range of history to support his thesis are hardly needed—all of us can think of many such competing groups in our own experience.

One example of the ill effects of intergroup hostility may be enough. Berkowitz begins his discussion of the subject by relating a Civil War incident in which, when the war broke out, President Lincoln offered Robert E. Lee the command of the Federal armies. Lee could not turn against his home state and, resigning his commission in the United States Army, went on to lead the Southern military forces in Virginia. He did not believe in the dismemberment of the Union, but did his best to tear it apart violently. Lee fought, not out of adherence to the ideological principles of the Confederacy, but because of his loyalty to a region. He was responsible for the death and injury of hundreds of thousands of Northern soldiers, not because he hated them and what they symbolized, but for love of the state in which he had grown to manhood.[5]

Sorokin believed there is no remedy for this intergroup antagonism and its disastrous bearing on the solution of our problems except the "extension of everybody's altruistic conduct far beyond the membership of his own groups, eventually over the whole of mankind, or over everybody and all." Recognizing that extending altruistic love over the whole of humanity may seem to us an impossible dream, he admits that taken literally the prescription is impossible for most human beings, but says that the extension of love over the whole of mankind neither means nor requires an equal distribution of love among all human beings. In its initial stage it is enough if everyone loves the members of his family and the

self-help, polarization, and avatars 161

limited circle of his friends. If this is done, everyone will find himself loving and loved by someone. In addition, everyone must abstain from all actions harmful to any human being; there would then be nobody hated, harmed or seriously mistreated by other human beings. Next, everyone, within his capacity, must extend his loving hand beyond his special group to everybody in need of help or sympathy. If each community does the same in regard to other communities, the whole human population will be blessed by at least the minimum love and help needed. What he calls the practical prescriptions for the first steps towards this program will be outlined and briefly analyzed in Chapter Seventeen.

Sorokin believed firmly that no discussion of group behavior can be fruitful unless it recognizes three inseparable socio-cultural aspects of the group: cultural, social and personal. Whatever social group we take, whether the family, the state, the church, a labor union, a business firm or a scientific society, in every such group we find these three aspects. Morever, every group exhibits a social aspect made up of all the social relationships occurring among its members; these relationships define the members' rights, duties, functions and position in the group, and their status. In our problem, he says, this means that altruistic individuals cannot be reared in a milieu of egoistic culture and social institutions, and conversely an altruistic culture and altruistic social institutions are incompatible with egoistic members. Thus, we must try to modify simultaneously our culture, our social institutions, and the personality of our citizenry in an altruistic direction; it is not enough to change only a segment.

If we want to change our personality structure, for

instance, we have to change our cultural values and our group affiliations in the same direction, and if we want to change radically our group affiliations we must change correspondingly our cultural values and our personality structure.

When a person begins to perform this triple reorganization of his ego, values, and group affiliations, he makes the first decisive step towards unity of his personality and conduct. His ultimate results are peace of mind and freedom from inner conflicts, a clear understanding of his duty, quiet happiness and self-confidence, kindness and love towards all human beings.

This triple reintegration of ego, values, and group affiliations, Sorokin admits, is not simple or easy. In its actual realization, it is a long and difficult process, requiring constant effort, undivided attention, determination, courage, and ability to solve the hundreds of secondary problems involved. After presenting a chart of some of the operations to be performed in each of the three fields —personal, cultural and social—in order that the triple reintegration may be successfully achieved, Sorokin concludes his discussion by warning that a fully successful performance of these triple operations is a tremendous undertaking for any individual and for mankind as a whole, the complete realization of which can be achieved only in the remote future, if at all, but that this must not discourage us from making the attempt.

The sociologists Sturzo and Timasheff agree with Sorokin, saying the thesis that society and its individuals are inseparable—that society is not something superimposed upon the individuals and that the individual taken out of society is an unrealistic abstraction—is dominant in sociology.[6] To the same effect, William Golding has said that he learned in the Second World War that a correct structure of society alone cannot produce good will and that you cannot remove all social ills by a reorganization of society; in looking at the system rather than the people, men are putting the cart before the horse. The social system cannot be separated from its individual members; to reform the system, both must be reformed.[7]

Northrop in seeking for a solution of the world's problems, concludes that four things are necessary: the relating of the East and West; the similar merging of the Latin and the Anglo-Saxon cultures; the mutual reinforcement of democratic and communistic values; and the reconciliation of the true and valuable portions of the western, medieval and modern worlds. He accepts as a basic premise that the cultures and the individuals will have to share equally in the amalgamation.[8]

There has, however, been some dissent to the foregoing view. The Hindu mystic Krishnamurti believes that the natural laws which govern society and the individual are not the same; society has evolved but the individual has not. If, as, and when a mutation in the individual is possible, the problems of society will be solved.[9] Jung lends some support to Krishnamurti's dissent, saying that since collectivities are mere accumulations of individuals, their problems are accumulations of individual problems, to be solved only by a general change of attitude which must begin with a change in individuals; only the accumulation of these individual changes will produce a collective solution.[10] Nevertheless, as a practical working program, we may take as the accepted view Sorokin's conviction that to solve our problem our culture and its social units and individuals must be changed at or near the same time.

164   LOVE, ALTRUISM, AND WORLD CRISIS

Realizing that at this point we may have become overly discouraged of a solution, Sorokin has suggested two possible sources of aid in our task. One is what he calls the law of polarization in times of crisis or frustration; the other, for those of us who believe in an unseen power of some kind interested in our world and its people, assistance from that source.

Sorokin's law of polarization has considerable support from sociologists and historians. In generalized form, the law states that a crisis, calamity, or frustration tends to make explicit and open the implicit and hidden contradictions, whether in one's mind and conduct, or in a social group and institution, or in a given culture. If there is a covert split in the mind or in the conduct of a person, under the conditions of calamity or crisis this becomes overt. Under the conditions of catastrophe, a hitherto hidden contradiction between meaningful cultural values or phenomena becomes explicit. Becoming open, the contradiction leads to an open fight for survival or domination among the contradictory values and the factions supporting them. Sorokin says that for persons and groups that are in a state of this inner warfare, a precipitant (an extraordinary person, a book or play, an injustice or unexpected kindness, a war, and many other things) can push the participant to a solution. Beyond this, he does not really tell us how we can make use of his law, even though it may be valid, except perhaps that in the crisis which is now here or is approaching there may occur a polarization which will bring out in the open the differences between our individuals, groups and cultures and hence make easier their healing.[11]

Somewhat along the same line, Lewis Mumford fears that only a miracle can save us, but by "miracle" he means not something outside the order of nature, but something occurring so infrequently, operating through such insignificant forces, and bringing about such a radical change that one cannot include it in any scientific prediction. He points to Maxwell's doctrine that even in the simplest physical systems at rare intervals there are moments which Maxwell called singular points. At these points an infinitesimally small force, through its character and position in the whole constellation of events, is able to bring about a change of almost unbelievable magnitude, as with a pebble starting a landslide. This doctrine allows for the direct impact of the human personality in history, not only by mass movements but by individuals and small groups who are sufficiently alert to intervene at the right time and the right place for the right purposes (Buddha, Jesus, Mohammed?). Happily, as Maxwell pointed out, the higher and more complex the system, the more often do singular points occur —there are more in biological systems than in physical systems, more in man's life than in an ant's. This theory differs somewhat from Sorokin's law of polarization, but can perhaps afford us a ray of hope even though the odds against a beneficent world-transforming miracle are huge. Nevertheless, Mumford says, if man begins with many small steps a move toward the fabrication of a world culture (many of these steps have already been made), they could form a basis, the ripple from which the new design might emerge. Mumford asks us to make one basic assumption: The destiny of mankind, after its long preparatory period of separation and differentiation, is at last to become one.[12]

Ardrey, seeing another aspect of the polarization law, asks us before giving up the reform of mankind as hopeless to recall those experiences of fire and flood and sudden storm, natural emergencies which as if by spontaneous combustion produce mutual aid, unthinking sacrifice, smiles on the faces of strangers, intimacies exchanged which have never changed hands before, a gladness and trust that leave us sorry when the emergency has passed. Radhakrishnan too says that great movements of spirit arise when despair at the breakdown of civilization makes the mind susceptible to the recognition of the insufficiency of the existing order and the need for rethinking its foundations; the contemporary situation is pregnant with great possibilities: it may be the end or a new beginning—the human race may end by destroying itself or its spiritual vitality may revive and a new age may dawn when this earth will become a real home for humanity.[14]

The second possibility of aid suggested by Sorokin lies in the theory that in times of sufficient crisis great leaders or avatars (the incarnation of a deity descended to earth) appear to guide men through to a brighter beyond.

Although he recognizes that in some measure his metarational views are based primarily on faith and not integrated wholly with his system of sociology, we cannot read Sorokin's later works without seeing that faith peek through. A proposition derived from faith might have confirmation from other sources, but in this case he does not appear to assert that it has, and, according to Ford, Sorokin expressed considerable doubt regarding philosophies that seek to trace the course of God's hand in the empirical data of history.[15] This might cause us to doubt his belief in avatars as such, but we must remember that great leaders, even those whose accomplishments seem miraculous, need not necessarily be divinely sent.

If it were for their words alone, the influence of the great prophets would be hard to understand; no mere examination of the new doctrine can fully account for their impact. It has been asserted, and probably correctly, that leaders of humanity like Christ, Buddha, Mohammed and Gandhi can change the nature of men to such an extent that after a few generations their followers may show quite different traits of character. Mumford thinks it is the greatness of the charismatic personality of such leaders that is the decisive step in making a closed society capable of entering into a more universal pattern. By loving and imitating the parental, life-nurturing image of the new leader, by bowing to his wisdom, by following in his footsteps, by accepting his ideal figure as a true and central image of man, towards which all smaller figures should tend, peoples of the most diverse backgrounds and histories achieve a common bond and pursue a common goal.[16]

Belief in avatars has been long and wide-spread, although as we have noted a great leader does not necessarily have to enjoy divine origin. The missions of Buddha, Christ and Mohammed were sudden interventions. They did not follow smoothly in the wake of events which preceded them, but were in opposition to the general trend of events. In each case a small nucleus of humanity was snatched up and placed on a spiritual summit to act as an ideal and a guiding light for future generations.[17]

The Hindu is taught that through the ages the downward trend has been interrupted by eight sudden redresses, each brought about by the incarnation on earth of an aspect of the Divinity. The ninth avatar was Gautama Buddha, the destined scope of whose mission lay outside the frontiers of Hinduism. The tenth descent, to come in the future, will be for the entire world.[18]

The Tibetan Buddhists believe there are members of the human race who have reached—as their saint, Milarepa, is believed to have done—the height of such spiritual and physical evolution as this planet admits; such people have reached the goal of enlightenment but remain on earth as Arhants. Perhaps one in 10,000 aspirants to Arhantship reaches or at least nearly reaches the goal. The Tibetans believe it quite as feasible to attain Arhantship today as it has been in any past age and that others in addition to Milarepa are men now living. Evans-Wentz examined these claims in great detail and became convinced that they ought not to be lightly set aside; after five years of Tibetan and Indian research, he believes he has good reason to think that among the Himalayan hermits with whom he has conversed there are possibly some—if perchance but two or three—who have reached the goal.[19]

All of us would of course like to believe that a divinely inspired avatar may at any moment come into our midst and solve our problems for us, but we had better accept as more certain the self-help principle of the little girl in India whose brother had set a trap to catch birds. She thought it was wrong and cruel. First she wept, but after some time became cheerful again. The mother asking her the cause, the girl said: "First I wept. Then I prayed for my brother to be a better boy. I also prayed that the trap would not catch any birds. Then I went out and kicked the old trap to pieces." Faith in divine intervention is fine and should be encouraged, but hard work at solving our own problems while we are waiting may be more effective.[20]

13
brotherly love for mankind

Unlike some of the preceding chapters, this can be a happy one. So much has been written about brotherly love—most of it patently written from the heart—that just to read it tends to create in one a warm and happy internal glow.* The difficulties in creating a world in which all men love their brothers are many and obvious. It is easy to say it can't be done, but the world's greatest thinkers have been almost unanimous in saying that it must be done; many have suggested means which will appear in a later chapter, for which this chapter may perhaps serve as an introduction.

---

*The literature on this subject is almost limitless, and it has been difficult to select from so rich a field the few excerpts which space permits me to use here; the sentiment for the brotherhood of all men has been timeless and universal. I have not attempted to put the excerpts used in the order of their date or origin, but have set them forth as I have culled them from my notes. Where a selection was too long to repeat in full, the language used in the synopsis is in part mine and in part that of the original writer.

The following excerpts on the subject have been taken from the writings of many philosophies and religions of all times and all parts of the world, yet the conclusions differ little in basic thought. They will be set out in successive capsule form without introduction.

George Harrison, explaining the philosophy of Sir Francis Younghusband (England, twentieth century): Fellowship is of divine origin. Every man is bound up with every other man and creature and is unceasingly influenced and shaped by the whole universe. If he is sensitive enough he has a glowing sense of kinship with every other living thing and a desire that all shall share the joy he feels. Men of different faiths need to be brought together for the better appreciation of one another so that in the end human fellowship may be sublimated into divine fellowship. To create this fellowship is the one great need of the world at this—and at every other—time: the one final solution of all our problems.[1]

W. W. Wagar (United States, twentieth century): People today are so irrevocably a part of and influenced by the Establishment that reasonable men hesitate to recommend courses of action that seem impractical or utopian. The seductions of affluence have brought, perhaps for the first time, nearly all available Western exceptional intelligence and wisdom into the power structure of corporate business, government, church, and higher education. Civilization's largest problems can probably not be solved through "normal" channels. We are bound by chains of gold. The Unity of Man is the warmest and noblest of all world-conceptions. Its failure to catch fire in modern times is astonishing. But now that the old loyalties to theism, nationalism, class and race are at last falling into eclipse, perhaps the idea of mankind has a chance. The only continuing existential reality in the human experience is man himself. No matter in what we believe our existence is grounded, we all share in the brotherhood of mankind and have to invest our lives in the family of man.[2]

Nanak (founder of the Sikh religion, India, fifteenth century): God will not ask man of what race he is. He will ask him, "What have you done? . . . As thou deemest thyself, so deem others; then shalt thou become a partner in Heaven."[3]

Confucius (China, fifth century B.C.): Wisdom is to know men; virtue is to love men.[4]

Erich Fromm (German-American, twentieth century): Love is not primarily a relationship to a specific person; it is an attitude which determines the relatedness of one person to the world as a whole. If I *truly* love one person, I love all persons, I love the world, I love life. I must be able to say, "I love in you everybody. I love through you the world. I love in you also myself."[5] The primitive forms of ties to soil, race, etc., can disappear only when man comes to feel at home in the world and overcomes his sense of frightening loneliness. To do this requires full development of his capacity to love and to share his humanity with all his fellow-men. Buddhism, Judaism and Christianity proclaimed this new vision of the harmonious bond of brotherhood in which solidarity and human ties are not vitiated by restriction of freedom: to be closely related and at the same time to be free; to be a part of a whole, yet independent.[6]

Sri Aurobindo (India, twentieth century): The unity of the human race, even if achieved, can only become secure if the religion of humanity spiritualizes itself and becomes the general inner law of human life; it already has the idea of the race and yet at the same time respects the individual, but its present intellectual form seems hardly sufficient. It must not be a creed or dogma or rite—mankind has tried that unity and it has failed, because there can be no universal religious system, identical everywhere in form and mental creed. A religion of humanity must mean the realization that there is a divine Reality in which we are all one. It will progressively reveal itself here; by its growth within us, oneness with our fellow-men will become the leading principle of the life of each of us—not merely a principle of cooperation but a deeper brotherhood. The individual must realize that only in the life of his fellow-men is his own life complete. Could this realization develop rapidly in man, we might solve the problem of unification in a truer and deeper way, but until then the attempt to bring it about by mechanical means must proceed. Our hope lies in the growing number of men who will realize this truth and seek to develop it in themselves....[7] Help and service to our fellow-man must be given without attachment, and without the conceit that we have helped him. It must be the selfless action so highly esteemed in Buddhism.... The enemy of all real religion is human egoism, the egoism of class and nation.[8]

Lewis Mumford (United States, twentieth century): In reestablishing ethical values in our civilization, the first essential change in attitude must be an increase in fellow-feeling. We must not be *hard*, as Nietzsche advocated, but tender and sensitive. We must feel sorrow when our fellows are in grief, joy when they are uplifted, even sympathize with their hostility and aggression to the extent of being able to recognize how far one's own conduct shows similar traits and is in fact partly responsible for producing it. The most deadly sin is that of cutting one's self off from other men.[9]

Lew Ayres (United States, twentieth century): With Moslems brotherhood is the outstanding characteristic of the religion. Brotherhood is demonstrated at the Mosque, where no reserved places exist. During the religious fasts, love of men is expressed again by the dropping of quarrels and forgiveness of wrongs.[10]

R. L. Stevenson (Scotland, twentieth century): So long as we love, we serve. So long as we are loved by others, I would almost say we are indispensable.

Christmas Humphreys (English Buddhist leader, twentieth century): From brotherhood is born love, friendship and compassion. The key to compassion in action is to concern ourselves with Self in others and to ignore ourselves. We all have mental clothes and habits of which we are ashamed; we are in process of shedding them. If we see but the best in others they may come to overlook our worst—hence the evil of gossip, which is solely concerned with the worst in all of us. Why do we take such pleasure in stabbing at the faults in others, thereby making them more sore? Why, when we wish to be better, do we maliciously hinder the total progress of us all? I know not, but we do.[11]

Clifton Fadiman (United States, twentieth century): George Bernard Shaw said, "The worst sin towards our fellow creatures is not to hate them, but to be indifferent to them: that's the essence of inhumanity." Alone, no man can find himself. Alone on his island, Robinson Crusoe was merely a highly ingenious animal. With the arrival of Friday, he became a man. We perhaps can only love our fellow-men in an abstract way, but at least we need not be indifferent to them. Civilization is the bridge one man throws up to connect himself with another man. Look at the next strange face you see—*really* look at it. Behind it is a life as mysterious as your own. If for only an instant you can feel the pressure of that life, you have hailed in passing that unique miracle—the other fellow.[12]

Simons Roof (Great Britain, twentieth century): How to do it: Whether you must break down barriers with your will or melt them away with your love, resolve to identify yourself with the whole of humanity. No longer have in your consciousness walls between nations, races and religions. See every man as a brother and not as a member of a particular country, race or faith. Recognize yourself not as a lone worker, but as one of the growing group of world servers.[13]

Teilhard de Chardin (France, twentieth century): A watchword to the nations: "Remain on your own line, but move upwards towards greater consciousness and greater love. At the summit you will find yourselves united with all those who, from every direction, have made the same ascent. For everything that rises must converge.... The Age of Nations is past. The task before us now, if we would not perish, is to build the *Earth.*"[14] In other words, if the world is to survive we must forget distinctions of nationality, race and religion, and actually get to work on the brotherhood of man, which has for too long been regarded as a reality only by mystics and idealists.

Kahlil Gibran (Lebanon, twentieth century): Ere my soul preached to me, I looked upon humanity as two men: One weak, whom I pitied, and the other strong, whom I followed or resisted in defiance. But now I have learned that I was as both are and made from the same elements. My origin is their origin, my conscience is their conscience, my contention is their contention, and my pilgrimage is their pilgrimage. If they sin, I am also a sinner. If they do well, I take pride in their well-doing. If they rise, I rise with them. If they stay inert, I share their slothfulness.[15]

Marcus Aurelius (Rome, third century A.D.): It is a man's peculiar distinction to love even those who err and go astray. Such love is born as soon as you realize that they are your brothers; that they are stumbling in ignorance, and not wilfully; that in a short while both of you will be no more; and, above all, that you yourself have taken no hurt, for your master-reason has not been made a jot worse than it was before. A branch severed from an adjoining branch necessarily becomes severed from the whole tree. A man, likewise, who has been divided from any of his fellows has thereby fallen away from the whole community. But whereas the branch is lopped by some other hand, the man by his feelings of hatred or aversion brings about his own estrangement from his neighbor and does not see that at the same time he has cut himself off from the whole framework of society. Nevertheless it is in our power, by grace of Zeus the author of all fellowship, to grow back and become one with our neighbor again, so playing our part once more in the integration of the whole.[16]

Tagore (India, twentieth century): All evils are simply indicative of want of adjustment of our individual self to our universal self. The spirit of unity of the self with nature and with all human beings prompts us to rise above narrow-mindedness and selfishness, and to demolish artificial barriers between man and man. One can obtain endless joy the moment one adjusts one's

176 LOVE, ALTRUISM, AND WORLD CRISIS

individual self to the universal spirit. This is made practical by the inculcation of love for all human beings. Narrow nationalism must be forgotten. The sages of India have taught us from the time of the Upanishads that wealth and material things should not be considered ends in themselves. They must be enjoyed and utilized as the means to the final end of the adjustment of the individual self with the universal self, which is equally present in all human beings and which is the strongest bond of unity between men in spite of artificial differences unnecessarily imagined.[17]

Charles Peirce (United States, nineteenth century): Most theology, instead of advancing the gospel of love, busies itself with abstract questions. Nevertheless, my doctrine of evolutionary love is in agreement with the teaching of the great religions—the gospel of Christ says that progress comes from every individual merging his individuality in sympathy with his neighbors. This is not a mere theory but a passionate belief which is a rule for action.[18]

Aristotle (Greece, fourth century B.C.): The human community is an association of people who need each other, and they need each other for two reasons: spiritually in order to find themselves in the full dimensions of the group, practically to take advantage of their differences.[19]

Walt Whitman (United States, nineteenth century):
I dream'd in a dream I saw a city invincible to
   the attacks of the whole of the
   rest of the earth,
I dream'd that was the new city of Friends,
Nothing was greater there than the quality
   of robust love, it led the rest,

It was seen every hour in the actions of
   the men of that city,
And in all their looks and words.[20]

Kierkegaard (Denmark, nineteenth century): Go, then and do this—take away distinctions and similarities of distinctions—so that you can love your neighbor. But you are not to cease loving the beloved because of this— far from it. If this were so, the word "neighbor" would be the greatest fraud ever discovered—if you, in order to love your neighbor, must begin by ceasing to love those for whom you have a preference. Moreover, it would also be a contradiction, for if one's neighbor is all men, then no one can be excluded—shall we now say, least of all the beloved? Love to one's neighbor has the very perfection of the eternal.[21]

Chaudhuri (United States, twentieth century): An ancient Chinese aphorism still known by everyone says that all men within the four seas are brothers. This statement is by no means viewed as a platitude; its meaning is both practical and profound. It overrides ethnic, cultural or temporal considerations and holds that men indeed may live, as individuals or as groups, in integrated understanding and fellowship.[22] Illustrative of the point is a long Chinese novel, the title to which has been translated *All Men are Brothers*, written many centuries ago and still a widely read classic in China.

Antiphon (Greece, fifth century B.C.): Different traditions that prevail in different countries divide them from one another and force them to do many things which are against nature. An educated man should rather act in accordance with nature, which has made all men alike and akin.[23]

W. H. Lecky (Ireland, nineteenth century, writing

on the Greek and Roman Stoics): The stoical philosophy recognized from the very first the fraternity of mankind. Virtue alone is a good, and all other things indifferent— birth, rank, country, wealth, are mere accidents. All men are fellow-members of a single body, united by participation in the same divine spirit. Cicero, a later Roman stoic, maintained the doctrine of universal brotherhood as distinctly as it was afterwards maintained by the Christian church. He said: "Men were born for the sake of men, that each should assist the others. . . . Nature ordains that a man should wish the good of every man, whoever he may be, for this very reason, that he is a man. . . . Nature has inclined us to love men, and this is the foundation of the law." Meander wrote that man should deem nothing human foreign to his interest. Lucan expatiated with all the fervor of a Christian poet upon the time when "the human race will cast aside its weapons, and when all nations will learn to love." Seneca said: "The whole universe which you see around you, comprising all things, both divine and human, is one. . . . Nature has made us relatives when it begat us from the same materials and for the same destinies. . . . I know that my country is the world." "You are a citizen," said Epictetus, "and a part of the world. . . . The duty of a citizen is in nothing to consider his own interest distinct from that of others, as the hand or foot, if they possessed reason and understood the law of nature, would do and wish nothing that had not some relation to the rest of the body."[24]

Haji Abdu (Ancient Persia):

> How with a heart that would through love to
>   universal Love aspire; . . .

Hardly we find the path of love, to sink the
  self, forget the "I,"
When sad suspicion grips the heart, when Man,
  the man begins to die. . . .
Survey thy kind as One whose wants in the great
  Human Whole unite; . . .
And hold Humanity one man, whose universal
  agony
Still strains and strives to gain the goal,
  where agonies shall cease to be.[25]

Radhakrishnan (India, twentieth century): All the primary spiritual data of the wide world of mankind have their foundation in the recognition of the real, spiritual unity of mankind, a unity to which the individual belongs in a stratum of his nature lying more deeply than that in which he belongs to any empirical community. If we are centered in the spiritual reality, we shall be freed from the greed and fear which are the basis of our society, which is anarchic and competitive. We must enlarge our consciousness, increase our awareness, recognize life's purpose and accept it in our work.[26]

Browne, Sir Thomas (England, twentieth century):

Boethius (Roman, sixth century A.D.): [There are two or three frames of mind which if we could persuade ourselves to remember and to practice, would clearly ease our problems in loving our fellow-men. The first will require us to convince ourselves that to become angry at others and to blame others for their faults and misdeeds makes no sense at all.] No man can justly censure or condemn another, because indeed no man truly knows another.[27]

Nietzsche (Germany, nineteenth century): Nothing

consumes a man more quickly than the emotion of resentment.[28]

Winston Churchill (England, twentieth century): [Talking about the effects of scientific invention on the human race.] Science will do all humans can wish for if they behave in a peaceful and helpful way towards one another, but of course, if they wish to be quarrelsome and bite one another all the time, there is no doubt that they can kill each other in a quicker and more wholesale manner than ever before. The choice is theirs and ours.[29]

14
altruistic love in
organized brotherhoods

In Chapter Twelve we noted the conviction of Sorokin and others that alteration of a culture, its social institutions, and its individual members must proceed simultaneously; we have also noted that he has found the growth of altruism to progress more rapidly within established brotherhoods than outside them. So that we can see the actual working of this principle, and perhaps apply it in modified form to create altruism in other groups, Sorokin has reported on clinical studies made into the history and activities of a number of well-established brotherhoods; we will look at four.

To aid in the making of studies of this kind, Sorokin originated a "model" so widely utilized by sociologists since that it is now known as the PAS model. In the understanding and appraisal of various social systems, the analyses must be based upon common denominators that will insure categorical treatment of comparable phenomena: hence this model. It is not necessary for our purposes here to go into the structure of the model itself.

Charles Loomis says that social change is the most constant aspect of group existence; once in existence a social system cannot help changing, even if all its external conditions are constant. Accordingly, since organized brotherhoods are social groups, change in them is inevitable, even though external conditions do not interfere. Two things influence change—the external pattern which establishes relationships necessary for the group's adjustment to its environment, and the internal pattern which focuses on the relationship of group members towards one another. Feeling and sentiment, including love and altruism, are primary elements in this internal pattern.[1]

Using the PAS model, Loomis made a study of the Amish, choosing them because they constitute a social system which has strongly resisted change, thus making the changes which have occurred in the group particularly significant. The community he studied covers about 150 square miles in Pennsylvania and is composed of some 6,000 persons within 33 church districts. The Amish are Protestants; they believe that each individual is responsible for his own salvation in afterlife, that the Amish are a chosen people, and in the necessity to live and worship as prescribed by the Bible as they themselves interpret it. The husband and father is the chief authority figure. As a rule only farm magazines, religious literature and newspapers are permitted in the home.

Loomis reports that although eternal life is the highest goal of the Amishman, income and success in farming being only secondary goals, nevertheless—since they consider that thrift, industry, and careful stewardship are activities which give proof of goodness—the average income and property values of these Amish farmers were for a time the highest in the nation.[2]

According to the PAS model, "systemic linkage" is the process whereby the elements of at least two social systems come to be articulated, so that in some ways they may be viewed as a single system. The Amish attempt to minimize systemic linkages with other systems cannot maintain complete isolation. Compulsory school-attendance laws, draft laws in time of war, tax laws, various governmental agricultural programs, and medical and legal services are examples of inevitable systemic linkages through which most Amish changes have come about; Loomis regards this concept of systemic linkage of great importance in understanding social change.[3]

Loomis also studied extensively the Spanish-speaking village of El Cerrito in New Mexico, pretty much isolated in an otherwise Western area. His report goes into the effectiveness of the use of a "change-agent" organization, such as a rural extension service, for instance, to purposefully bring about systemic linkage through peaceful involvement rather than disruption and violence. This suggests a technique which might be useful in increasing altruism. One Loomis conclusion worth noting is that human beings in most societies react more favorably to having things done *with* them rather than *to* or *for* them.[4]

In Chapter Twelve mention was made of charismatic leaders as agents of socio-cultural change. Sorokin and Max Weber are in agreement that a charismatic or personal leader and his followers may constitute a movement which may destroy or reorganize a traditional order. If they persist through the generations they must eventually "routinize the charisma," a process known as institutionalization, through which the elements and processes necessary for maintenance of the system through time are structured. Charismatic leaders arise in various arenas of human activity. Many students of Weber noted the charismatic character of Adolph Hitler. Talcott Parsons suggested, in terms of routinization, a parallel between Marx and Jesus, Lenin and St. Paul, and Stalin and Constantine.[5]

Change is an essential feature in Sorokin's system. As we have already noted, for him war, crime, family disorganization, slums, juvenile delinquency, and many other phenomena are inherent in our sensory and materialistic culture and are not accidents. They will not be solved by minor remedies when surgery is indicated. Loomis says that basic to the belief is the assumption, logically derived, that a crisis period will usually terminate a given development, such as that which has produced the supersensate culture of our time. This crisis, a revolutionary, stressful and bloody period, would intercede as the next development towards the idealistic culture.[6] Query: Are we now in that period?

Sorokin believed a valuable system of techniques for altruistic socialization is found in contemporary communal brotherhoods. He chose for another study and report the Society of Brothers in Paraguay (now located in the United States). He also studied the Mennonite and the Hutterite Brotherhoods, because—in contrast to the multitude of short-lived, abortive, or miscarried experiments in total communal living—the Mennonite and Hutterite Brotherhoods have existed for centuries. Since to do so they have had to modify many secondary points of their organization during their existence without much change in the essential characteristics of their way of life and organization, these brotherhoods must be accepted as efficient in the techniques they use to maintain the spirit of brotherhood in their communities.[7]

The Mennonites originated in Switzerland and the Netherlands in the early sixteenth century as an Anabaptist sect, and were long persecuted. Their resulting "theology of martyrdom" must be taken into account in finding the roots of Mennonite altruism.[8] Menno Simons, for whom this sect was named, expressed the Mennonite belief when he said that, since all Christians are baptized by one spirit into one body and are thus one, it is Christian and reasonable that they divinely love one another and that the one member be solicitous for the welfare of the other, for thus both the Scriptures and nature teach.[9]

The Hutterites established the practice of community of goods; the majority of Anabaptists did not follow this principle, but did retain a very strong sense of responsibility towards both members and non-members. During the period of suffering after the Second World War a small group of Amish Mennonites contributed over $12 million to relieve suffering and dispatch helpers to all corners of the earth. It has always been a good Mennonite tradition to relieve the sufferings of mankind in times of distress and emergency. Their history as given in a study by Krahn, Fretz and Kreider in *Forms and Techniques* contains many examples. The term commonly used to describe altruism in Mennonite communities is "mutual aid"; characterized by its religious quality, as practiced by them, it has resulted in an attempt to establish a community based on the principle of Christian love. The study contains many striking examples of Mennonite mutual aid given "regardless of the recipient's race, class or political sympathies." Formal educational techniques have been employed to perpetuate their tradition of altruism from generation to generation.[10]

The Hutterite group arose in the sixteenth century in Europe and has both spiritual and historical connections with the early Mennonites. There are in this country and Canada about 9,000 Hutterian descendants practicing community, in large part much like the Mennonites. They are noted for good mental health and are almost free from the mental difficulties which incapacitate one out of every ten Americans at one or more times and put one out of twenty in a mental hospital. Their reputation for possessing an unusual degree of peace of mind is excellent, and, according to the study by Eaton, Weil & Kaplan, since their coming to North America there have been only one suicide, one divorce, two separations, no parental abandonment of children, no incidents of arson, personal violence or attempted homocide, and no known sex crimes!

After the age of two and one-half years, Hutterite boys and girls attend a communal kindergarten. Later when they go to school they also spend many of their waking hours in the company of one another under supervision of a religious teacher. Older siblings assume much responsibility for care of their younger brothers and sisters. All members eat together in the communal dining room. All homes are furnished with standardized and simple equipment. The Hutterites have become integrated in much of the American culture, but are trying hard to assimilate selectively controlled acculturation. Some phases of Hutterite community life will be men-

altruistic love in organized brotherhoods   **187**

tioned in our following discussion of the Society of Brothers.[11]

In turning now to the Hutterite group known in Germany as the *Bruderhof* and since removal to this country as the *Society of Brothers*, we have available Sorokin's own report on his study of the group. The society was organized in Germany shortly after the end of World War I by a young married couple who had been active in the Christian student movement of their time, Eberhard and Emmy Arnold. Eberhard died in 1935. In 1964, Emmy completed an account of the life of the colony in Germany up to 1937. It is a simple but beautifully written and touching story called *Torches Together* which well repays reading.[12] Unable to survive Nazi persecution, the group emigrated to England, but when World War II began, internment as enemy aliens faced the members of the community and it moved to Paraguay. The society was still in Paraguay at the time Sorokin studied it and wrote his report. Later, for several reasons, it moved again, this time to the United States. The society today consists of three communities: one near Rifton, New York; one near Farmington, Pennsylvania; and one near Norfolk, Connecticut.*

Sorokin refers to the society as a new branch of the Hutterite movement. Although the society actually is independent today, it does operate and its members do live much as do the Hutterian groups described above, except that the Society of Brothers appears to have integrated with its environment to a greater extent than have

---

*Much of the following account is gathered from a visit I made to the Rifton colony in 1969. I was cordially received, given all information I requested, and was very favorably impressed.

the Hutterites. Sorokin says that the society originated spontaneously from the modern world in an attempt to demonstrate that peaceful and creative community is possible today on the basis of the early Christian way of life. Persons joining the group surrender all their property and use their energies in the service of God and men for the rest of their lives without seeking a reward. Their guidance in practical conduct is the Sermon on the Mount, and they have found that the pattern of a new order of justice and love among men arises out of the free dedication of each individual, and of the group as a whole, to the needs of their fellow-men.[13]

Eberhard Arnold said of his colony: "Basically this [life in the colony] is something so simple, so clear and so plain. It is joy in everything that lives. Anyone who can rejoice in his fellow living beings, who can have joy in people, in their spirit and in their lives, ... anyone who feels joy in the mutual living relationships of trust and inner fellowship—he experiences what love is.... Here there is no sourness of mien, no moping in sham holiness; here people proclaim with radiant, happy and lively eyes that the essence of love is joy."[14]

Education in the colony is for and in community, the family unit being regarded as an organic and highly important part of the whole. The children live with their parents, but join their respective age groups during the greater part of the day. The baby house, toddler house, kindergarten and school are important parts of every Bruderhof community. Breakfast and afternoon tea are taken in the families, but dinner and supper are taken in the communal dining room (each village has only one kitchen, as it has only one common purse, one communal storehouse, one laundry for all, and so on). Young people after leaving school are given opportunity for college or other outside training, which enables them, apart from the knowledge and skill acquired, to get to know other people and different ideas. They are thus encouraged to make an independent decision whether they want to join the community at the age of discretion, or live as other people do. Practically all of them choose the brotherly way of life.

There are good times as well as the communal work. Outings and picnics, celebrations of special events like engagements, weddings, and the return of travellers, folk-dancing, singing, an orchestra, dramatic productions, arts and crafts and the walks which bring the children into close contact with Nature lighten the daily grind.

One of the rules formulated in the half-century since the brotherhood was founded is that no one shall speak evil about another: he promises to go direct to the person involved if he finds anything wrong, and he promises to accept reproof by another.

Except for some profit from agriculture, the operating income for the community is derived principally from a flourishing publishing house and from the manufacture and sale of simple furniture and a well-known line of children's playthings and recreational items sold under the brand name *Community Playthings*. The shops in which these things are made are well equipped with the most up-to-date machinery. School equipment seems adequate, although well-used. The school art department has all essentials, including a kiln for the firing of pottery and statuary. The youngsters are polite and well mannered. While obviously a good deal of money could be spent on the school facilities if it were available, it is evident that the children are being well educated and are coming out far more loving, altruistic and fitted for good citizenship than the average child graduating from our public grade schools. The high school children attend school outside the community.

There are about 800 in the three communities today —roughly equivalent to the number living in the colonies in Peru before migration here. All property is still held in common. There is no affiliation with any outside church. Although the state does not exercise jurisdiction over the school, it conforms to the state requirements applicable to other schools. No resident of the colony has ever been on state or federal relief. The colony and its members are subject to the same state and federal taxation as are other residents of the state. The men do not accept military service, but are subject to nonmilitary service as conscientious objectors. Marriage is confined to members of the group, which might eventually result in harmful inbreeding. Periodicals are available, but visits with outsiders are supervised, and there is no radio or television.*

Sorokin feels that his study of these brotherhoods brings out clearly the main factors of altruism. Each

---

*The restriction requiring in-group marriage may be harmful. A very recent ten-year study of the Amish made by a Johns Hopkins geneticist and reported in *Liberty* discovered that they suffer from a congenital six-finger dwarfism, a malady found one or more times in each of 37 families studied, as against only 60 cases theretofore documented in the entire world. Victims of this malady are usually less than five feet in height and, in addition to other defects, have six fingers on each hand. All 37 families were descended from a single family settling in Pennsylvania in 1774. Nearly all descendants of the original family married persons related as second cousins or more closely. The warning against inbreeding is obvious.

member is fully "identified" with Supreme Love (God) and the precepts of the Sermon on the Mount; every member wholly surrenders his ego to the supreme value and the brotherhood; all members have thus the basic values of the brotherhood; each identifies himself with the brotherhood community, thus becoming free from all conflicting loyalties and group affiliations; the members are at peace with themselves, with one another, and with the world at large; the children freely grow into altruists and spontaneously perpetuate the brotherly way of life of their parents; and the freedom to leave the community by those who wish to do so serves as the safety valve for the community. In these respects the basic principles of the brotherhoods are similar to those of the monastic orders.[15]

15
earlier studies and experiments

In this and these next chapters we shall be dealing with specific studies and experiments made by Sorokin or under his direction. There will be frequent references to *Forms and Techniques* and to *Ways and Power* for the principal reports on those studies and experiments. In his preface to *Ways and Power* Sorokin freely recognizes that the contribution represented by those books "is very modest in comparison with the total sum of the necessary studies." His regret is that "the better brains" are too busy with less urgent problems to study "the miracle of love."

Many scholars have commented on Sorokin's use of statistics and the methods of science in investigating so theoretical matters as altruistic love and other sociological problems. Some are critical, but many go along with him and very few take his work lightly. Moore and Riley open a paper entitled *Sorokin's Use of Sociological Measurement* with the question of how the historian of the future will assess Sorokin's attempts to classify and quantify socio-cultural phenomena, and in answering predicted that he will look upon this work as well ahead of its time in two respects: focusing on total systems as they change over the entire course of history, and adapting the procedures of scientific research to these peculiarly sociological problems.[1]

Two of Sorokin's earliest studies, made before the Center had begun its work, are titled *American "Good Neighbors"* and *Christian-Catholic Saints*, and with an appendix comprise the entire book *Altruistic Love*.

In the late forties Tom Breneman's "Breakfast in Hollywood" radio program centered in part on selecting outstanding "good neighbors" through letters of recommendation sent from all over the country. About a thousand winners were so selected from the letters sent in, and from those letters Sorokin chose 500 persons who seemed to have performed more genuine good deeds than the others; these 500 persons made up his first group of "good neighbors." They were not notable altruists, but were above average in their altruistic activities. From this group each of 93 members was requested to write his autobiography and to answer a questionnaire designed to bring to light the factors that might have helped make him a good neighbor. Sorokin also collected another group of 112 good neighbors independently chosen by Harvard students and some social workers as the most altruistic persons they knew. These persons also answered questionnaires.

Examples culled from the questionnaires appear in the appendix to *Altruistic Love*. The altruism evidenced is fairly ordinary but real. Each good neighbor had helped his fellow-men and had done so freely without any legal duty or moral obligation. Most of the helpful activities were carried on for some time, occasionally for years. When asked to define "good neighborliness," most of the winners defined it as acts and attitudes that realized the Golden Rule (41 percent), love of humanity and friendliness (19 percent), unselfish interest in others (17 percent); the remainder varied.

Other factors brought out in the study may be significant. Almost half of the good neighbors came from families with six or more children and only 6 percent from one-child families; 84 percent were married or widowed; the largest number came from middle-class groups; 74 percent of the good neighbors had been born in rural areas, and about 40 percent still lived there. Division as to elementary education, high school education and college education ran fairly even, but the test results indicated that there is no close relationship between altruism or good neighborliness and school *intelligence* as measured by the usual tests.

As to religious attitudes, 61 percent attended church occasionally, 30 percent frequently, and 9 percent not at all. Most found religion helpful to them in being good neighbors. In later studies Sorokin found this union of high religiosity with altruism to be typical of a large majority of altruists in the history of other countries and periods. This may give us a hint as to the value religion could be made to have in the increase of altruism.

When asked the principal factor in making him a good neighbor, about 29 percent named parental and family training, 21 percent religion, 28 percent universal life experience, 11 percent personal life experience, and 8 percent school education. Less than 1 percent mentioned books—very humiliating to a writer. As to happiness and peace of mind, the good neighbors, although having the same sorrows and hardships as the social groups to which they belonged, felt themselves at peace with themselves, others and the world at large and their lives fruitful and worth living—one of the incidental by-products of altruistic conduct.[2]

In a 1969 paper by Dennis Krebs reviewing the history of modern investigations of altruism, we have confirmation of Sorokin's own findings that there appears to be a relationship between attributes of parents and altruism in children, that there appears to be little difference in altruistic tendencies between the two sexes, that altruism (especially in children) increases with their ages, that children from large families are apt to be more altruistic than children from small families, and that intelligence is not a factor (here intelligence must be distinguished from education, since altruism can be increased with education). Although not specifically mentioned, a factor perhaps unfavorable to some of Sorokin's studies is suggested by Krebs; he says that, in his opinion, in most cases pencil-and-paper tests are thinly disguised self-rating measures with no check for validity.[3]

Sorokin then moves on to altruists of a higher degree: Christian-Catholic saints. He says at the start of his report that up to then there had been hardly any statistical census of the saints and that we hence know little about their age, sex, nationality, race and the like, to say nothing of their less tangible characteristics. This study he hoped would help fill the gap. It investigates from certain standpoints the Catholic saints found in Butler's *Lives of the Saints*. Many of the biographies in Butler are admittedly brief and totally inadequate as relevant material. Over 3,000 saints were dealt with individually in the study and something less than 30,000 others were dealt with as groups. Sorokin gathered all of the pertinent material he could find in available biographies, then had it coded, punched and run through an IBM counter and sorter to obtain his results.[4]

About all we can say for these results is that they make interesting reading. So little is really known about the early saints, so few were made saints for purely saintly reasons, monastic life is so different from secular life in its aspects, and there is so much question about what a "saint" actually is that this half of *Altruistic Love* seems to have little value in solving our problem of how to make altruists. It may even occur to the reader that many saints became so as a reward for services rendered the church and were not necessarily altruists at all.

As a whole, the saints enjoyed extraordinary longevity; of the saints of known parentage, about half were encouraged by their parents and very few were relentlessly opposed. As to why the individuals became saints (information available on about two-thirds), 43 percent were what Sorokin calls "fortunate altruists," meaning that hereditary character and favorable environment were of advantage; 37 percent were martyrs; 11 percent were persons converted to saintly life through catastrophe and about 9 percent through other external events. The marital status of about one-third is known; of these 75 percent were unmarried but probably enjoying a rather high percentage of unchastity. About 87 percent of the saints were members of the church and monastic hierarchy, of which over half were martyrs or confessors; about 10 percent of the saints were virgins, matrons and widows. There was apparently small chance for a commoner to become a saint outside the church.

Of the two-thirds of the saints as to whom the facts

are known, almost half remained in society, 31 percent in institutional environment and only 9 percent in eremetic retirement. "Obviously," remarks Sorokin, "one need not escape the world to be saintly," and we might have expected him to bring up the doctrine of Yoga that directs yogins to remain in society and work for the improvement of others. Today's environment, he says, is not propitious for saintliness; the place of the saints are being taken by good neighbors and altruists.[5]

Sorokin was apt to give his groups of studies and experiments somewhat more grandiose and confusing captions than are really required by the context. *"Dynamics of Interpersonal Friendship and Enmity"*[6] in *Forms and Techniques* reports a study based on autobiographical sketches submitted by 50 Harvard and Radcliffe students in his classes. Each student, after a briefing on pertinent factors, was asked to describe how he happened to develop friendly relationships with a good friend and unfriendly relationships with an enemy or deeply disliked person.

The reported and classified factors of enmity or dislike are of less interest to us here than are those of friendship. In 24 percent, friendship was generated by direct acts of kindness, help and other unselfish actions, and in an additional 39 percent by desirable personal traits and values common to the two individuals, usually revealed in actions of kindness, generosity, cooperation and solidarity. Sorokin had made a similar study some years before; the results of the two studies were much alike. To him, the studies show that the most effective technique for creating friendship is that of friendly or good deeds. The same conclusion had been reached in an experimental study by J. Mark Thompson and in several other studies reported in *Ways and Power*.

A study by Lunden deals with what Sorokin calls socio-legal norms of delinquents and non-delinquents.[7] By "socio-legal norms" Sorokin means normal behavior as determined by both applicable laws and by the customs and mores of the majority of the people in the community. Because the socio-legal norms of an individual or a group constitute an important basis for patterns of interaction they are significant fields of research in human relationships.

This study involved three groups of children (12 to 19 years old) of different social positions and family backgrounds: delinquent boys and girls in two Iowa state training schools; students in a public high school in a smallish Iowa city; and students in an Iowa church academy. The purpose was to determine if there were any significant differences in the socio-legal norms of these three groups and to explain the variations in the socio-legal norms in terms of factors other than education, intelligence, or age level, the hypothesis being that variations in socio-legal norms among young people are due to the differences in family and socio-ethical backgrounds of their youth.

Twenty fictitious situations were outlined to students, each with reference to specific time, place, people, and the attached relationships. In each situation there were afforded motives either for obeying or disobeying the law involved and the consequent results as sacrifices or no rewards at all for either course of action. Each student had an opportunity to evaluate the law in terms of its worth, approval or disapproval of the action taken, and the punishment for the action. The motives for violating the law by the characters in the fictitious situations (10 of which were violated and 10 obeyed) ranged from saving a life to no motive. In each situation the student was asked to approve or disapprove the action taken, the law involved, and the consequent results.

Lunden reports that the academy students ranked highest in the scores, high school students second and the state training school students lowest, but the scores were surprisingly close. Lunden does not explain what standard was used to determine which answers were "correct." The girls scored higher than the boys, and no significant relationship was discovered between the scores and the IQ ratings of the students. Lunden felt that the difference in the scores of the training school inmates and the academy students simply evidenced the difference in the ethico-religious backgrounds of the two groups. The principal thing to be learned from the study is the importance of family training and early exposure to religion in shaping the future altruistic nature of children.

A chapter by Northrop in *Forms and Techniques* points up the principle, involved in the foregoing Lunden study and others of like kind, that if a law is to be enforceable it must conform to the socio-cultural norms of the people it is to govern. The principle, Northrop says, has highly important implications in the international sphere: No positive legal rules or institutions for bringing the settlement of disputes between nations under the rule of law, rather than of force, can be successful unless they are rooted in the living law of all the peoples and cultures affected. Disregard of this principle explains why attempts at a world legal order have been so disheartening. The positive law on which these attempts have been based corresponded at most only to the living law ethos of but one culture in the world—the modern French and Anglo-American Western culture. This is but Sorokin's point, Northrop adds, proved over again quite independently in the science of anthropology. The way to an effective world law is through philosophical anthropology. He then outlines the steps to be taken to make it possible for the first time for the international lawyer to construct an effective world law.[8]

Another study involves altruism in psychiatric nursing and is reported by Hyde and Kandler.[9] They have no doubt that empathy (the imaginative projection of one's own consciousness into another being) is a key factor in altruism and may be a prerequisite of altruistic behavior. We must identify ourselves with our fellowman if we are to feel that his goals and satisfactions are as important as our own. Hence, this study of the ways in which antipathies are resolved and empathy developed is a fundamental study in altruism.

Forty-five nurses sent to a psychiatric hospital from general hospitals for a three months experience in psychiatric nursing were asked at the end of their affiliation to talk about the means they had used to overcome antipathies in their relationship with patients. The methods recommended to and used by the nurses are described in the report.

The ways in which antipathies are resolved in this clinical setting are applicable elsewhere as well. Perhaps the most important finding of the study is that when the nurse responds to the patient according to her real feelings, rather than through the suppression and repression of her hostility or affection, improved relations develop. This was by far the most frequent method of resolution of antipathies; even an angry response is a more personal, intimate and giving response than cool aloofness. This does not, of course, endorse unconditional hostile responses.

A study by Thompson[10] was one of several made

at the Center to test Sorokin's tentative conclusion that the technique of good deeds is more efficacious than most other techniques in turning animosity into an altruistic relationship. The experimentation consists in actual performance of good deeds by one of the inimical parties to the other, or by both antagonistic interactors in regard to each other, and then in registering the main observable changes in the overt actions of the parties involved. There are many variations of this sort of experimentation with this method of altruization. The church has told men *what* to do but not *how*. Techniques of accomplishing the "how" have been detailed with great completeness in writings about Yoga and religious mysticism, but those techniques are long, arduous and difficult for many of those who would attempt it. This study was made in the search for a technique that would be more readily available for use in everyday human relationships.

Five of Thompson's close friends agreed to act as informants in the study. Each informant had to have definite negative feelings towards a person with whom he associated frequently. Each informant agreed to try to come to like this person and to make the person like him if this were not already the case, but the primary objective was for the informant to grow to like the disliked. All five persons succeeded in changing their attitudes in the direction of greater friendliness towards the persons they at first disliked. Three factors seem to stand out as important in the cases—adequate motivation for getting to like the disliked person, friendly action on the part of the informant and persistence. The technique for bringing about a friendly relationship is to act towards the person disliked as one would act towards one's friends. Altruistic behavior towards the disliked persons serves to make the actors feel more friendly towards those persons.

Jean Mandler comments on this Thompson study: "This is highly important. More study should be devoted to it. It says that you may achieve love through 'artificial' acts or behavior. This may be more valid than altruistic behavior resulting from a supraconscious infusion of love. It again raises a question of cause and effect. Does the altruistic behavior produce love or does love produce altruistic behavior?" Probably the answer should be "both." Her point is that unfelt and "artificial" kind behavior towards another, however prompted, can produce love in both giver and recipient and that hence the behavior does not require "pure" altruism or love as a motivation in order to be effective.

Perhaps the most entertaining chapter in *Forms and Techniques* has to with psychodramatic techniques and is entitled *"The Technique of Role Reversal, the Mirror Technique, the Double Technique, and the Technique of Acting Out Dreams.*[11]" The study was conducted and the report made by J. L. Moreno, founder of what Sorokin refers to as the sociometric, psychodramatic, sociodramatic and group therapy school of thought and research in sociology, psychology and psychiatry.

The chapter reports a session held at the Moreno Institute in New York City at which Moreno explained and illustrated several of his psychotherapeutic techniques. Although the report is fascinating to read, the techniques involved are too complicated and involve too much explanation to discuss here, and the reader must be referred to the book itself. In general, the patient is asked to identify himself with another person to the extent that he recognizes the double as himself; the person serving as the double has been trained to reproduce the same patterns of behavior as the patient typically produces, the theory being that this will aid the patient in recognizing and solving his own problem. The mirror technique is based upon somewhat the same principle, in this case helping the patient to recognize himself as an individual separated from others.

The technique of role reversal is a more mature technique in which the patient, instead of watching another take the role of the patient, himself takes the role of the other. Role reversal is often used in matrimonial problems. By taking the role of the other, one is better able to understand the behavior of the other in relation to his own behavior.

It is difficult to explain these techniques briefly. The Moreno report gives verbatim transcriptions of the procedure which took place on a stage with the trained double taking one part and untrained persons from the audience representing the patient. The techniques are probably effective as therapy in appropriate cases, but it is hard to see just how they can be utilized in the production of altruistic love, except in so far as an increase in understanding of self and others leads to an increase in altruistic behavior.

16
what can be done: general considerations

What our problem is by now seems reasonably clear, as does the conclusion that a sufficient increase in love, altruism and brotherly amity, if widely enough disseminated, could be one and is perhaps the only solution. Before going more deeply into Sorokin's specific recommendations, it may be well to review some fairly definite suggestions made by others as to solutions and their difficulty. In our next two chapters we can then consider specific techniques. The problem tends to divide itself into two parts, one dealing with what we can do individually to increase altruism and love in ourselves, and the other with what can be done to increase altruism and love in others, and in groups and entire cultures.

Sorokin believed that the transformation of culture and institutions, of human conduct and social relationships, can be accomplished in orderly and peaceful fashion through the willing and concerted action of individuals and groups, but cannot be effected through external compulsion even if applied by a saintly minority to an unwilling sinful majority. Also, the transformation must be carried on simultaneously along personal, cultural and social fronts, although transmutation of the individual may slightly precede the others. The individual can begin to work upon himself and, in addition, can serve the same purpose as a cultural agent and socius through the responsible performance of his cultural and social functions. In *Reconstruction* Sorokin suggests ways in which persons in various callings can help. As to whether the goal can be achieved, he gives a qualified "yes," predicated on the past experience of man; humanity has always been able to mobilize its forces to meet crises, and a shift from the decadent sensate type of culture to an idealistic form has occurred several times in the past.[1]

In considering solutions we cannot disregard those advocated by Marx, Engels, the Webbs and other exponents of what is a major Western tradition; call it socialism, communism, or what you will, its stated objectives are in line with what we are seeking here, whether or not as it is now being practiced those objectives are being attained. As an example, several years ago Fromm told of a syndicalist experiment in which the owner of a watchcase factory in a French community, wanting to make it truly fraternal, employed men from all vocations except specialized industrial workers, offering to teach them the business if they would help him search for a setup in which the distinction between employer and employee would be abolished. Within three months the men were saving nine hours of each 48-hour week because of increased productivity and using those hours for education, paid for as for regular work. The principle they worked out was to start not from the technical work in the plant but from man himself; accent was put not on *acquiring* together but on *working* together for collective and personal fulfillment. The plan worked remarkably well, both from the spirit of brotherly kindness developed and from factory profitability.

Fromm suggests that some of the lessons learned in the experiment can be usefully employed here: Each worker should be kept well-informed about the entire operation of which he is a part; he should know the economic function of the enterprise and its relationship to community problems; he should be permitted to be an active, interested and responsible participant in the making of decisions which bear upon his own work and the entire enterprise; he should regard himself not as employed by capital but as a responsible *subject* who employs capital through his participation in management and decision-making; sharing of excess profits among the workers would be helpful. Whether this could be made to work successfully in other than small communities and businesses is open to doubt, yet the chairman of U.S. Steel in a 1953 address indicated his belief that these things are feasible even in a huge corporation.[2]

Julian Huxley, in his own investigation into methods of bringing out the latent capacities of the ordinary man for altruism and love, emphasized the importance of creating a more favorable environment and a concerted policy to prevent the present flood of population increase from wrecking all of our hopes for a better world. Huxley did not doubt that the human species can, if it wishes, transcend itself—not just an individual here and there, but in its entirety as humanity.[3]

If all the people in the world could communicate

with each other, we would advance tremendously towards universal love. Scott Buchanan once said he would like to see every child taught other languages at a very tender age.[4] Even better would be teaching children a simple universal language (remember "esperanto"?) as the second language in all schools. Leisure time should be increased to be devoted to travel and intercourse on a world scale, and the present system of "student exchanges" should be greatly extended.

Storr fears that the enticing vision of a universal government is utopian, unless the earth is threatened by destruction from another planet or by some cosmic catastrophe, and favors splitting the population into smaller autonomous groups. As practical measures for the increase of altruistic cooperation among men and nations, he suggests mutual agreement between governments as to what languages should be taught in schools, student exchanges, intermarriage between dissimilar populations, encouragement of competition in all possible fields, and international studies to determine what political and psychological factors have enabled certain countries to avoid war in spite of man's proclivity for engaging in it. Above all, however, he emphasizes the necessity for reducing world population, even to the point of eliminating the extension of charity and medical and financial aid to underdeveloped countries, unless we insist that birth control go hand in hand with social amelioration.[5]

Berkowitz and many others have studied the possibilities of the use of mass media to change personal attitudes for either good or bad; there is an extensive literature on the use of mass media to effect changes in attitude. Information programs have been found to improve interpersonal and intergroup relations under some circumstances, but it has been found that messages presenting views on important issues that are greatly discrepant from the beliefs held by the members of the audience meet with a great deal of resistance and that trying to frighten people into changing their behavior is usually futile.

The media can of course do harm as well as good. Berkowitz says that to deny that TV, film and printed violence and crime are a major cause of juvenile delinquency (which denial he inclines to favor) is not to say that aggressive scenes have no influence on a child's behavior; research has shown that they may cause some children to behave in a hostile fashion, particularly those who may have aggressive predispositions.[6] A report prepared for the U.S. Surgeon General was recently summarized by two psychology professors for release at a convention of the American Psychological Association. It said that increasing scientific evidence suggests that children are using violence on television as "a partial guide for their own actions" and that it may be contributing to the aggressive behavior of "many normal children, as shown in a wide variety of situations." Other reports made at the convention bore out the finding.[7] Another release (November 9, 1971) reported a Harvard pediatrician's testimony that "television's bombarding children with exhausting stimuli with no real outlet for the feelings aroused may be the forerunner of the disillusionment of present day youth, the first 'television generation.'"[8] Nonetheless, proper use of mass media as a means of decreasing aggression and increasing altruism in man cannot be disregarded. One may well wonder what might happen if we were to turn our high-pressure Madison Avenue advertising specialists loose on such a project!

Fromm's suggestions for increasing altruism include

the use of individual uplift, persistent endeavor to get people to make real contact with each other in spontaneous and genuine group life, effective use of mass media, and an attempt to make certain forms of rituals widely and meaningfully accepted. Songs like "We Shall Overcome," which are living rituals—not just songs—might be an example; communion in silence as practiced by the Friends in their religious services could be another.[9]

To create an institution not connected with the political machines and which would work for our aims, Fromm suggests in his *The Revolution of Hope* the formation of a national council comprised of perhaps 50 Americans of unquestioned integrity and capability, with local councils and subcouncils designed to get down to the grass roots. He sets forth suggested details for such an organization and examines its potentialities. Fromm does not profess much optimism about our success in converting men and government to brotherly, altruistic and cooperative effectiveness, but thinks we have no right to abstain from the effort.[10]*

The probability that scientific making of character through the pre-birth alteration of genes will be available within a relatively few years has been discussed in Chapter Ten. Most of us will hope it is never used. No adequate control of its use comes to mind, and the possibility that

---

*A card was enclosed with each copy of the book inviting each interested person to fill in the blanks and mail the card to the publishers of the book, in the hope that enough cards might be sent in to make possible the formation of an organization somewhat along the lines suggested. On November 1, 1970, he advised me that about 3,000 persons had signed and returned the cards, an encouraging response.

under the wrong kind of government control the population might be reduced to a race of subservient, walking zombies staggers the imagination. Perhaps some day means which would ensure the use of genetic control solely for the true good of civilization may be evolved, but we can hardly count on it.

The use of established religion as a means of building love and altruism is frequently advocated and has been attempted. In our discussion of the failure of religion as a remedy we have already noted its lack of effectiveness, and some of the reasons. However, the changes in religious practices which can be made and which would make religion a helpful vehicle deserve to be considered.

Two pertinent articles were published in 1970 in *Psychology Today*. In one, Milton Rokeach reported on a survey he had made, using a national polling organization, to determine how the religious values of 1,000 adult Americans are related to their social beliefs. Rokeach found that on the average the religiously devout are less humanitarian than the less devout and that Christians do not value *loving* and *being helpful* more than do nonbelievers. However, Sorokin found (See Chapter Fifteen) that his study of "good neighbors" and atheistic altruists indicated that although religion is not necessary to active altruism, perhaps it helps. The Rokeach findings are important because they, too, point to need of reforming the church as-a social institution.[11]

The other article reports on a poll of Protestant ministers from nine major denominations in California, in which 1,580 replies were received. Those making the study (Stark, Foster, Glock and Quinley) recognizing that the church is accurately likened to a sleeping giant—an institution whose vast potential for creating brotherhood, social justice, and a more human society is lying dormant —wanted to find out why the influence of the church has remained only *potential* for so long.

When the researchers analyzed their results, they found that the reason is not so much that people do not listen to sermons but rather that there is not much to hear; most sermons rarely touch on controversial moral or ethical issues. More than one-third of the ministers said that never once had they taken a stand on a political issue (as distinguished from political *candidates*, but including as political issues controversies like school prayers, racism, drug legislation, sexual conduct, divorce and pornography). Only one-fourth of the ministers had in the past year given at least five sermons dealing with controversial topics. Analysis of the returns indicated further that fear of congregational disapproval appears to be the chief deterrent.[12] It must be admitted that the pulpit appears to be out of tune with the times.

Dr. Malalasekera of Ceylon holds that the fellowship of man can best be secured through religion, because religion's sole concern is with humanity, but that to be effective it should be a world religion. He is hopeful that union (as distinguished from amalgamation) of today's world religions will come about and can be effected without destroying the distinguishing characteristics of each. This should not be difficult, since all forms of religion arise from the common life and the common ideas of humanity. The faith of men and women inspired by religious conviction, he says, has time and again shown persistence, fortitude and determination sufficient to move mountains and could do so again.[13] Hocking so agreed that he called the mere existence of religious plurality a scandal, since religion is man's hold on what is eternal and true for all men and therefore his deepest bond with his neighbor.[14] Montaigne in one of his essays reminded his countrymen that their religion is the accidental result of their birth and education, and that if they had been born in a Mohammedan country they would have been as firm believers in Mohammedanism as they were in Christianity.[15]

Josiah Royce had his feet planted more solidly on the ground than many philosophers. In *The Problems of Christianity*, he says the office of religion is to aim towards the creation on earth of the Beloved Community and the future task of religion is inventing and applying the arts which shall win man over to unity and which shall overcome their original hatefulness by the gracious love, not of mere individuals, but of communities. Since such arts are still to be discovered, he tells us to judge every social device, every proposed reform, every national and local enterprise, by the one test: Does it help towards the coming of the Universal Community? If you have a church, judge your own church by this standard, and if your church does not fully meet this standard aid towards reforming your church accordingly.[16] And Northrop adds that for the task of creating a living religion preaching is of prime importance, since it carries auditory education beyond the school and university into adult life.[17]

In his later writings August Comte seemed to think of his philosophy almost as a new religion, which might perhaps be called the religion of man and which he thought more suitable to an age of science than a religion predicated upon the aid of and belief in a Providence. He could not believe in a religion which he thought asks us to accept unscientific theological beliefs and directs our energies away from the problems of this world. His idea for a religion dedicated to the service of love and an enlightened humanity was fine, although far from unique, but he marred it somewhat when he furnished his new religion with an elaborate ritual, saints, holy days, sacraments and prayers.[18] Comte had some precedent for his idea in the ethics of the "Philosophes," the seventeenth century philosophers who for the worship of God, Mary and the saints substituted direct devotion to man, stressing humanitarianism and help for the poor, the sick and the oppressed.

All of this seems to put us back pretty much where we started, with the statement that religion can accomplish much for the growth and spread of altruism if its moral and ethical teachings are followed. There is an anecdote about Seneca according to which he was being reproached for preaching such a noble philosophy of ethical living and himself leading so slothful and dissolute a life. His reply was in substance: "I plead guilty to the accusation; I follow that which I preach only at a great distance, slowly, on my hands and knees." Nevertheless, we have in established religions a great existing organization, world-wide in its various forms, ready for use and preaching and seeking what we need. We should not write it off merely because of its past failures. It has had some successes and can have more; a serious, determined effort should be made to ascertain and work for the things which can enable religion to achieve its great potential as a force for world brotherhood and love. We are hearing constantly today about the necessity for the reform of education; why not also religion?

17
what can be done: specific techniques

In Chapter 16 of *Ways and Power* Sorokin offers 26 specific "techniques" for the altruization of individuals and society. He warns us at once that altruistic formation and transformation of human beings is an exceedingly delicate, complex, and difficult operation, and that there is no single magic procedure that can successfully perform it nor any standard set of operations equally applicable to all persons and groups. In addition, as he has already made clear, the techniques must be supported by appropriate changes in the culture and social institutions of the persons and groups undergoing the altruistic change, and by a corresponding rearrangement of one's egos, values, standards, group affiliations and environment.[1]

The techniques that are ego-transcending—like Yoga, Zen and monasticism—Sorokin recognizes are based upon control of one's bioconscious and socioconscious egos and unconscious drives that cannot be achieved by the ordinary person. For the vast majority of us, he suggests what he calls ego-centered altruism, which views one's egos and unconscious forces as positive values and their preservation as a necessary condition for altruization. One needs only to be "enlightened" about his real self-interest, to keep his egos and drives in mutual harmony, to clean them from the excesses of "unenlightened selfishness" and to train himself to cooperate with other individuals for their mutual benefit and pleasure. This ego-centered love is utilitarian, hedonistic and "rational" in its nature. It endeavors to train the self-centered individual to live and let live, respect, be friendly to, and help and not harm others and to enjoy his life fully, as long as he does not violate the enjoyment of others.

Psychologically, this form of altruization does not require a complete control of the conscious and unconscious forces by the supraconscious. Theoretically and practically, it can operate through "rational" and "self-enlightened" harmonization of one's egos and unconscious drives with one another and with those of other individuals. This harmonization, Sorokin assures us, can be achieved through: the techniques of mechanical drilling; inculcation of conditioned reflexes; habit-forming; "interiorization" of cooperative forms of behavior; and using the stimuli of pain and pleasure, punishment and reward, utilitarian advantage and disadvantage, leader's example and followers' imitation, reasonable coercion and persuasion, scientific demonstration of utility and disutility of various forms of behavior and inculcation of scientific verities and rational ideologies. Through these and similar techniques, the ego-centered "socialization" of human beings can be accomplished.[2]

As to the 26 techniques, Sorokin says each can be used for ego-centered as well as ego-transcending altruization, although the latter requires several additional techniques and more rigorous application. Though discovered long ago, he adds, many of these ego-centered techniques have been recently rediscovered through experimentation with animals and then applied to human beings. Unfortunately, they hardly ever yield the sublimest forms of creative unselfish love, but produce low-grade, but nevertheless valuable, altruism. Each of the surveyed techniques can be used singly, but more often than not they are used in various combinations with one another.

Of necessity, Sorokin's explanation of his 26 techniques appears here much abridged; however, except where other writers are referred to, his own language has been retained. The techniques not included in this chapter will appear in the next. For more detail, reference is made to *Ways and Power*.[3] The techniques follow, in the order used by Sorokin:

1. The individual should work to achieve a biological state conducive to kind and friendly behavior of the individual towards his fellow-men—a well-tempered and law-abiding satisfaction. A moderate and well-planned satisfaction which does not contradict the moral demands of one's socio-cultural egos can be practiced by most people.[4]

St. Ignatius Loyola devised for his self-improvement a series of ingenious and scientific techniques of "spiritual exercises" which involved his "biological change." Based upon his personal experimentation, they lay down detailed prescriptions for the complete subjugation of the biological impulses in man and teach him how to discipline, and put into the service of the will of God, man's sense perceptions, imagination, associations, thoughts, will, even reason—in brief, man's subconscious and conscious energies. The principal way to attain that end is the utmost concentration of man's imagination and senses upon a chosen religious or moral point (the oriental practice of "meditation"?). St. Ignatius describes in great detail how his "spiritual exercises" are to be practiced. He asserts that just as a body can be exercised by going, walking and running, so the will of man can be trained by exercise to find the will of God.

2 and 3. The technique of conditioned reflexes, based upon more or less simultaneous stimulation by conditioned or unconditioned stimuli, can build a series of desirable acquired responses in the individual. Beginning with a piece of candy or a slight spanking, a verbal approval or disapproval in our childhood, and ending with the vast arsenal of punitive measures of criminal law and biological, economic, political and social rewards, painful and pleasurable stimuli incessantly condition our behavior from the moment of birth on up to the hour of death.

To be free from disastrous consequences, the utilization of these stimuli must follow certain rules of wisdom and practical experience. For example: (a) To persons and groups influenced by finer and nobler motivation the pain-pleasure stimuli should not be applied; (b) The concrete forms of pain-pleasure stimulation must vary in accordance with the character of the individual or group and their conditions; (c) All punishments and rewards that may seriously harm the individual or group physically, biologically, mentally, morally or socially must not be used at all.[5] A few disapproving or approving words quietly and kindly spoken are quite effective for one individual, while for another much stronger painful or pleasurable measures are in order. The physical sanctions are more fit for some individuals, while for others the psychological stimuli are more effective.

This technique has proved effective in all behavior therapy. Since Sorokin wrote, there has been developed a very successful behavior modification technique predicated on reward and punishment and pain and pleasure. Books detailing the procedures have been written by Bandura, Kanfer and others. In the April, 1970, issue of *Psychology Today*, McConnell reports on his success in training even flatworms by the use of reward and punishment. Applying the principle to today's problem of how to improve human behavior, McConnell says: "Somehow we've got to learn how to *force* people to love one another, to *force* them to want to behave properly. I speak of psychological force. Punishment must be used as precisely and as dispassionately as a surgeon's scalpel if it is to be effective." The use of rewards for good behavior cannot do the job alone.

4. In a society whose members have a similar set of values, altruization by pressure of public opinion can play an important role.[6]

5. Any weakening of interindividual or intergroup hatred is a step towards altruization. Mutual animosity of two or more parties can often be mitigated by separation of the inimical individuals and groups from one another.[7]

6. Many quarrels and fights of individuals and groups are stopped abruptly, at least for the time being, by the mere appearance of a third party at the moment

of quarrel, particularly if in a mediating, pacifying and reconciling role.[8]

7. Inimical parties can be bound together into a solidary body by setting them against a common enemy or unifying them through a common friend or cause. The enemy need not be human and involve fighting and war. Although peoples otherwise antagonistic do coalesce against a common enemy in time of war, this merely creates hate. Rather, the principle should be used to unite mankind against its common enemies like disease, insanity, poverty, suffering, crime, ignorance and pollution of air, earth and water, from which all human beings and all nations suffer. Federov in his *Philosophy of Common Cause* developed a detailed plan for fraternization of all human beings into one real brotherhood on this basis and through this technique. With teaching, preaching and propaganda, everybody's patriotic ethos and pathos in this sacred war can be easily incited and maintained.[9]

Berkowitz and Storr both agree with Sorokin on this point. Faced with a common enemy, whether it be flood or fire or a human opponent, we become brothers in a way which never obtains in ordinary life. Storr recalls 1940 and the warmth Londoners showed towards and received from their fellow-men after exposure to a night's bombing.[10] As examples of today, consider how dangers of environmental pollution, only a short time ago unimportant and largely meaningless words to the average person, have now so united mankind in its insistence on remedial measures that both public and private corporations and agencies are preparing to spend many billions of dollars for the modification of industrial plants and other sources of pollution, at which they would have once scoffed; consider too the banding together of students from all areas to force social changes they consider necessary.

8. A heroic moral example will be followed by others. An extraordinary creative achievement in any field calls forth conscious or unconscious "imitation" by others, and this is true of the achievements of a creative genius of unselfish love; it always engenders a legion of followers. Even a modest example of kindness does not remain sterile; it contributes to the moral ennoblement of others.[11]

9. We can use rational persuasion, defining the rules and patterns of altruistic behavior, communicating them to persons and groups and demonstrating the benefits of altruistic behavior and the harmful consequences of selfish conduct; however, although intellectually the technique is very successful, behaviorally it falls flat, remains on the surface of the intellect and does not penetrate into the depths of our unconscious mind.[12]

10. If perception of altruistic precepts by our intellect can be made to arouse in us a strong emotional perturbation sympathetic to these precepts and through this touch the hidden springs of the unconscious drives and draft them for the service of these "intellectual precepts," then the communicated ideas do not remain merely on the surface of our intellect but penetrate into our "body and heart," our speech-reactions and overt behavior. Emotional and affective excitation breaks the barriers of the unconscious otherwise hardly penetrable for the purely intellectual ideas. The reinforcing emotions may be of different kinds, ranging through sympathy, gratitude, love, reverence, admiration, benevolence and others, all urging a fulfillment of moral precepts. Reli-

gious cults and rituals furnish us with a rich treasury of ingenious techniques serving this purpose.[13] [Sorokin then discusses the many forms of these techniques.]

11. Putting an individual into some real life condition in which he passes through a real and direct life experience of a specified kind, lets him not only learn intellectually about the subject matter of his experience but to *live* it with all his emotions and unconscious propensities. The lesson learned in such an experience is unforgettable and tangibly shapes his personality and behavior. Direct experience of being hungry, thirsty, cold or dirty, of being beaten or unjustly treated, arrested or persecuted, teaches us more effectively about these experiences than the best sermons and lectures. The same is true of the direct experience of being helped in misfortune or shown sympathy in trying conditions. However, some of these experimentations may be physically, mentally or morally harmful to the individual undergoing the direct experience, and they should be used with care. Even with this limitation it still has a field of application much wider than that of its contemporary utilization.[14]

12. The fine arts can be used for the purposes of altruization. Beauty, truth and goodness are three mutually connected supreme values, and each of these values can be transformed into one another and can contribute to a creative growth and support of the other two.[15]

13. Discussed at length in *Ways and Power* is the use of exposure to genuine friendship, love and good will of others as a very effective means of creating love and altruism. Its importance is enhanced by its accessibility to almost every individual and group and because no special talent or training is necessary to use it fruitfully except the decision to use it.[16]

14. Creative activity is one of the important techniques for making human beings less selfish and less aggressive. The creative urge is possibly one of the basic aspirations of human beings. Most of the persons who can freely display their creative urge find some satisfaction in their lives and are more friendly towards their fellow-men and the world at large. By arranging the conditions in which a given person or group can freely engage in a desirable creative activity, the individual or group is deflected from many mischiefs, squabbles, and enmities by the much more absorbing creative thoughts and deeds. The importance of this technique was understood long ago, and most eminent educators have systematically used it.[17]

15. Creative activity is more effective when done in free cooperation with others interested in the same creative problem. In such collective creative enterprises the ego-taming and the ego-transcending effects of creative work are enhanced by the factor of collectivity or group influences. If the enterprise is of intense interest for all the participants, each is stimulated, helped and taught by the other members; in this creative process the individuals' little egos are largely dissolved and merged into one creative "we," with common joys and sorrows, successes and failures. The effects of collective creativity are inestimable. Such creative group endeavors may be recreational, educational, scientific, philosophical, religious, artistic, political, economic, charitable and so on.[18]

Somewhat allied to collective activity in Sorokin's discussion is group therapy. Such therapy is of course not new, and its benefits are recognized. Lunden experimented with it at Iowa State Penitentiary and found it successful in both reducing antagonism and increasing altruism.[19] Dennis Gabor likewise finds group contacts important, thinking it a common observation that the social behavior of most people is most powerfully molded by the small number of people actually in contact with them—the group. The most encouraging example of a cell for good, he says, is in the meetings of the Quakers. Aldous Huxley has called those meetings a great psychological invention which we would be wise to imitate.

The "Encounter Groups" therapy that received so much publicity in the late sixties, although much misused, appears to have had some beneficial results. The theory is that an excellent form of therapy is bodily contact of person to person, and the giving way to bodily impulses that might otherwise be restrained by ingrained conventions. Esalen Institute in California is one of the principal centers. At Upsala, Sweden, a staff member of the Western Behavioral Sciences Institute in La Jolla, in conducting a liturgical service for delegates to a meeting of the World Council of Churches had the delegates touching, holding one another in collective embraces and expressing feelings long suppressed. Sauna bathing with the participants kneading each other's backs and necks has been effective.[20] There may be enough possibility that the movement is developing a therapy of "letting go" which could be of substantial value for our purpose as to suggest further investigation.

16. Of all the single techniques of altruization, the technique of good deeds is possibly the most effective, and the most accessible, for everyone. At the same time it is the necessary companion of all the other techniques, because if their use does not result in good deeds by the affected person or group they cannot be considered

to have been changed altruistically. When the good deeds are adequate and wisely chosen, the performance of friendly, helpful, and loving actions can be prescribed for any person and group at any stage of their altruistic education.[21] It can be recommended even when such a person or group profoundly dislikes the addressees; see as an example the Thompson experiment related in Chapter Fifteen. As Thompson showed, besides changing the doer of good deeds, the technique also changes the recipients of the good actions. This may remind us of the assertion of Kant that love is a product rather than a cause of our beneficent acts; we learn to love those we benefit because we have given to them, more often than we give because we have learned to love.[22]

17. Ego-centered and, even more, ego-transcending altruistic transformation is impossible without a corresponding change in the structure of one's egos, values and norms of conduct, as we have seen. This change has to be effected by the individual himself, by his own effortful thinking, meditation, volition and self-analysis. Other persons can help in this difficult task, but they cannot replace the active efforts of the individual himself.[23] To put in another way part of this statement of Sorokin's, the nature of loving is such that its main condition for achieving unselfish love or altruism is the overcoming of self-love. In overcoming selfish love of self one achieves humility, without which altruistic love may be impossible.[24] Fenelon said that nothing save humility can move one to love his neighbor; nothing but the consciousness of one's own weaknesses can make one indulgent and pitiful to those of others.

Sorokin continues his emphasis on the necessity for self-change, adding seven more techniques: "The main techniques for a successful performance of this operation are: (a) self-identification of the individual with unselfish love; (b) private and collective prayer; (c) examination of conscience; (d) private and public confession; (e) private and public vow; (f) meditation and contemplation; (g) psychoanalysis." We will look at each of these techniques in the next chapter.[25]

18
what can be done: additional techniques

After dealing with each of the seven additional techniques mentioned at the end of the last chapter, Sorokin discusses two more, rounding out his 26. We'll take the ten in order.

18. A requisite to self-altruization is the redoing of one's egos, values and norms as a first step. Sorokin calls this "self-identification"; what he means is that the individual must begin to think of his "true self" as generous, kind, friendly and free from rampant egotism. If he finds himself thinking or acting selfishly, he must regard such thoughts and actions as alien to his *true* self and as a moral failure imposed upon him by his lower nature which he can overcome in time. Occasionally this identification of one's self with one's highest nature will be vague, semiconscious and intellectual, without roots in the emotional, unconscious and behavioral realms of the individual. At other times it will be principally emotional, without idealogical definition. If it stops at this stage and before it becomes total, idealogical, volitional and behavioral, its influence will not tangibly penetrate the individual's unconscious drives and overt actions. He will remain what Sorokin calls a "wishful altruist," practicing little, if at all, the virtues of the unselfish love he preaches. With sufficient effort and time he can become a behavioral altruist, who actually practices what he preaches.[1] In Chapter 10 of *Ways and Power* Sorokin analyzes the factors and techniques by which eminent altruists have solved the problem.

19. Prayer is the most sincere communication of the individual with what he regards as his highest self, soul or God. It may be vocal or silent, and done privately or publicly. The prayer to be altruistic must not ask for a boon for the one praying but for all: "Give *us* this day our daily bread." One's egos must be transcended by complete surrender to the superior power: "Thy kingdom come, thy will be done." Altruistic prayer strives to free the supraconscious in man from the shackles of his little egos for union with the supraconscious, and tends to turn our unconscious and conscious mind into an instrument of the supraconscious. In this way altruistic prayer is one of the most accessible and fruitful ways for spiritualization and altruization of human beings and groups. The more of this sort of prayer, the better for all of us. Gandhi said: "I have not the slightest doubt that prayer is an unfailing means of cleansing the heart of passions. But it must be combined with the utmost humility."[2]

20. This technique consists in one's sincere and critical appraisal of his own thoughts, wishes, words and deeds experienced during a certain past period of his life: during the preceding twenty-four hours, or three days, or week, or month or just from time to time. This examination of conscience tries to bring to light especially one's hidden impulses in all their ugliness and one's reprehensible thoughts, wishes, words, and deeds in all their selfish reality. Here the higher self of the individual carefully examines and calmly registers what the individual's conscious egos and unconscious drives have done for the preceding period. Since the operation consists in face-to-face communion of a person with himself and since there are no witnesses and no public, there is no reason for the individual to be insincere, hypocritical, or secretive. Sorokin says there is hardly any doubt as to the effectiveness of this general technique when it is performed earnestly, in a humble spirit of one's failures and one's sincere hope for moral and spiritual improvement.[3]

Many psychologists would disagree with that last statement, at least in part. The technique might work for some people, but requires a degree of self-identification impossible for others; only rare persons do not lie to themselves. Nevertheless, Mumford offers a similar prescription, calling it "withdrawal and rejection." We have to devise disciplines and exercises that will confirm their detachment from the prevalent customs and restore initiative to the human soul.

As a starting point, Mumford says, we must answer the questions: What am I and where am I? Why am I doing what I do; and why, despite my many deliberate convictions, do I omit to do so much that I should do? When our detachment is once used for self-examination of this kind, we will be surprised to find out how much of our life has been covered over by conventional routine, and how little arises out of felt needs and clear convictions. There will be dismaying discoveries: that inner inspection ends all complacency, all self-righteousness. We must recognize the pragmatic importance of dream and ideal; they must be tended and minded with the care we now give only to motorcars. Goethe counted the day lost when he had not at least contemplated a beautiful print, and Gandhi, most powerful of practical men, reserved a whole day every week to a silent withdrawal, immune to outward invasion or even to self-prompted action.[4]

21. Conscience examination will be even more effective when followed by confession of one's moral and spiritual failures to somebody else or to a group—the technique of private and public confession. To be effective, the confession should be earnest, made to a person or group with moral prestige and integrity, and should be preceded by an awareness of, repentance for and an urge to be free from selfish impulses, thoughts, words and deeds. It can be used in its religious form; or a beloved member of the family, a real friend, a respected leader or a good teacher can serve the role of confessor in a secular confession. This technique has been practiced fruitfully for millennia by the rank and file, and by the wisest and greatest educators of humanity.[5]

22. Closely connected with the three foregoing techniques is the act of taking a binding vow either to abstain from certain selfish deeds or to do certain altruistic actions; such a vow serves as an additional stimulus to altruistic growth. In certain situations the vow taken by a collectivity as a body and by each of its members proves especially effective. In the collective vow, each member is stimulated to keep it by other members and by the collectivity as a whole.[6]

23. Psychoanalysis is suggested by some as an aid to self-altruization, but Sorokin says it has discovered hardly any new sound techniques for altruistic and spiritual transformation; practically all that are sound are only a reproduction or variation of the other techniques described above and practiced for centuries.[7] He is not criticizing psychoanalysis used as therapy for mental disorders; his point is that psychoanalysis as used to treat mental disorders is of little value for moral and spiritual improvement in the normal individual, but not all psychologists would agree with him. Storr quotes Melanie Klein as saying she hopes that some day child analysis will become as much a part of every person's upbringing as school education is now,[8] and Sorokin himself elsewhere accepts certain procedures of psychoanalysis as valuable in enhancing altruism.

24 and 25. Sorokin calls this technique "supraconscious meditation and creativity." Through meditation—supplemented by his techniques of good deeds, prayer and others set forth previously—a very few individuals can achieve the self-identification with the supraconscious discussed in Chapter Eleven. Even though the technique fails to result in attainment of the supraconscious, its assiduous practice can produce in lesser mortals a lower but nevertheless effective degree of altruistic love. We cannot disregard this technique as a possible path to the growth of altruism and love—it may indeed be the only one.[9]

After first again explaining the difference between conscious and supraconscious meditation and activity,

Sorokin repeats his assertion that all the great moral teachers, up to more recent charismatic religious leaders, explicitly profess this role. Even when ordinary persons become religiously and morally inspired they consider themselves emptied of their egos and turned into the instrumentality of the supraconscious.

He tells us that we must recognize that only by strenuous labor and pertinacity can man transform his purely ideological self-identification into the total self-identification with the supraconscious. It hardly ever comes by itself. For those who can use it the techniques of Yoga or of the monastic brotherhoods assisted by the techniques of voluntary respiration, postures, control of bodily processes, of conditioned responses and so on, can be very helpful. Our research bodies must concentrate their activity on a most intensive study of this ground of all real values. The chosen few that are graced by creative genius must help us in bringing its grace to distressed humanity. Using the known methods of release of the supraconscious in every person, we have a good chance to increase its fructifying circulation in the human universe. By indefatigable efforts in discovering new techniques for this purpose we may find more effective means of its multiplication in the human family.[10]

There has of course been some scholastic criticism of Sorokin's interest in the supranatural. For instance, Joseph Ford says of him, "His catholic interests, along with his integralism, have led him to find some element of value, not only in the orthodoxies, but also in the heterodoxies of each epoch," and expresses some doubt whether Sorokin satisfactorily integrates the metarational mysticisms with the rest of his philosophy.[11]

Nonetheless, since as evidenced through the centuries, effortful practice of this technique can yield substantial improvement in love and altruism even though not attaining the highest goal, it must be accepted as one of our available "tools."

26. To avoid conflict between the egos and values of the individual striving to increase his altruism and love and those of the social groups with which the individual is affiliated, the individual must cut off his affiliations with those groups whose demands contradict the love egos, love values, and love actions.[12] In earlier chapters we have learned of Sorokin's belief that if his suggested techniques are to be effective their use must be supported by an appropriate transmutation of the culture and social institutions of the persons and groups undergoing the altruistic change, involving a corresponding rearrangement of one's group affiliations and environment. Such rearrangement of one's group affiliations is one of the most powerful factors of his progress in altruization. The influence of affiliation solely with altruistic groups is of itself inestimable.

This rearrangement of one's affiliations, Sorokin says, involves: cutting off one's affiliations with all activities—individual and collective—that contradict the imperatives of universal and supratribal love; close affiliation with activities that do realize this imperative of universal love; replacement of loyalty to all tribal altruisms by loyalty to the whole humanity; and unreserved abstention from participation in and courageous opposition to all aggressive or violent interhuman strifes and mistreatments of man by man. In terms of persons and groups, this rearrangement of social affiliations means two kinds of group membership: (a) permanent affiliation with persons and groups that practice consistently the imperative of universal love towards all human beings; (b) fluid, temporary, and only partial affiliations with persons and groups of tribal character: in so far as they practice the activities of universal love, one must wholeheartedly support these and be a member of such groups; in so far as they carry on tribal or personal aggressive policies, one must oppose them and decisively disaffiliate oneself from such persons and groups in the periods of their selfish activities. Few can carry out completely this rearrangement, but each step towards it represents progress of the individual and moral progress of humanity.[13]

As a technique for altruization, as well as a supporting technique for those listed in this and the last chapter, Sorokin had firm belief in the precepts and methods of Yoga, Hinduism, Buddhism (especially Zen), Sufism and the other Eastern religions; *Forms and Techniques* has 13 of its 28 chapters devoted to them, one reaching to almost a hundred pages. To go into those subjects here is unfortunately impossible, but interested readers will find readily available, in addition to Sorokin's own books, hundreds of others, some of which are listed in the bibliography in this volume. That these techniques have proved themselves over many centuries can hardly be questioned. However, Sorokin warns us that for the rank and file of human beings the techniques of Raja Yoga, at least, exceed their physical and mental capabilities, except in the diluted form outlined in his chapters devoted to the study of single techniques. For most people, the techniques of Karma Yoga and Bhakti Yoga seem to be more suitable than those of Raja Yoga. Karma Yoga techniques consist mainly in performance of good deeds in loving spirit for their own sake and not for their results. Bhakti Yoga techniques are based mainly on deep devotion, self-surrender and love of God.

Sorokin valued Raja Yoga in part because its technique does not prescribe any particular asceticism or mortification of the flesh, as many other techniques do. Instead it prescribes a system of physical and mental exercises which aim towards a full self-mastery over the body and the bodily mind. It does this through a series of procedures, each of which tries to use scientifically the properties of the body and of the bodily mind itself in order to bring them under complete control of the self. The two Yoga techniques of particular interest to us here are, in his opinion, mind concentration and meditation. Yoga, like Zen, he says, "endeavors to achieve the liberation of man by man's own will, true knowledge, and desire for salvation, rather than through grace of God."[14]

In 1965 Chaudhuri published the book *Integral Yoga*, which in a foreword Sorokin called the best one-volume work ever written on the topic. In explaining the teachings of integral Yoga on altruistic love, Chaudhuri says that in the initial stages of spiritual unfoldment the selfless service of society appears like a stern duty, an unconditional imperative. Love of neighbor, love of humanity, is a divine commandment. But on the attainment of self-integration, one freely serves society as a matter of joyful self-expression. One then actively and spontaneously loves humanity as the diversified expression of the one cosmic self with which one is identified. . . . The more man gives himself in the spirit of love and friendship, the more he experiences the delight of self-expansion. The more he becomes vitally concerned with the welfare of fellow-beings, the more he enlarges his own being. His active interest in others is an essential means to the bursting of the ego shell.[15]

Therese Brosse, French psychologist and cardiologist, after years of use of the methods of Yoga in her practice of psychosomatic medicine, concluded that "we need scientific research providing a biological basis for the fundamental problems of ethics, including altruization. Ethical standards must henceforth rest on the bedrock of scientifically investigated and natural law." It was to further this investigation that she went to India in 1952. Her work tested Yoga techniques and claims through the use of scientific instruments. She used as subjects more than a hundred mystics, Occidentals trained in Oriental techniques and mental concentration, adolescents and patients suffering from psychosomatic afflictions. Her instruments were those designed for electrical, volumetric and polygraphic techniques. As far as one can judge from her detailed account, occupying almost a hundred pages in *Forms and Techniques*, her experiments and tests on her subjects were scientific, impartial and thorough, and support Sorokin's claims for the value of Yogic procedures.

A pertinent chapter in *Forms and Techniques* on methods for reducing group prejudice is by Gordon Allport, who at the time of its writing was Professor of Psychology at Harvard. That the chapter is valuable to us on questions other than group prejudice is evidenced by the captions he gives the sections into which he has divided his article: "Can we expect change?"; "The research approach"; "Legislation"; "Formal Educational Programs"; "Contact and Acquaintance Programs";

"Group Retraining"; "Mass Media"; "Exhortation"; "Individual Therapy"; "Catharsis." In his "Final Word" he says: "The improvement of human relations is a broad subject—considerably broader than the scope of this chapter! Our aim has been to pass in review a large variety of recent research in the area of ethnic antagonism. From it we have learned two things: (1) There is an immense amount of activity and interest in applying scientific methods to the discovery of effective techniques for reducing prejudice; (2) Present indications favor certain techniques over others, and indicate to some extent the specific conditions when we would do well to select one technique and not another. . . . Education and religion, mass media and legislation, child training and psychotherapy—these and all other channels of human effort must be followed in order to produce a race of men who will seek their individual salvation not at the expense of their fellows but in concert with them."[16]

We can close this chapter with exhortations by two well-known scientist-philosophers, lending emphasis to Sorokin's plea for more utilization of conscious scientific efforts. Bertrand Russell said that the problem is presented to the men of science to devise a method of generating friendly feelings in the mass of mankind. "Exhortation has not proved very effective," Russell said. ". . . I have no doubt whatever that methods could be devised for creating a world in which most men had friendly feelings towards other men, but I think rivers of blood will have to flow before the holders of power will allow such a world to be created, and I am doubtful whether rivers of blood are the right kind of rivers to water the tender plant of human kindness." Karl Menninger quoted Russell's statement in suggesting methods of cultivating love and increasing our capacities for it, and for diminishing our hates; in general, his suggestions are in line with the means and techniques we have been discussing.[17]

Over 40 years before his death, Russell condemned science for failing to deal with social needs. "While we alter the environment to suit ourselves," he said, "we do not much alter ourselves to suit each other," but he expressed the hope that in the end it would. He predicted that in a hundred years we would have acquired the same control over the characters of children that we have now over physical forces.[18] We have only about 50 years left in which to make good his prophecy.

Nobel prize winner Alexis Carrel in his widely read *Man the Unknown* states what he thinks science can do. "The science of man has become the most necessary of all sciences," he says, and comes up with some suggestions for remedy. For one, since we know that the evolution of humanity is very slow and that the study of its problems demands the lifetime of several generations of scientists, we should therefore have an institution capable of providing for at least a century the uninterrupted pursuit of investigations concerning man. (Unfortunately Carrel could not have suspected that the chances of our having another century in which to cure our problems is open to doubt.) This thinking center would consist, as does the Supreme Court of the United States, of a few individuals trained in the knowledge of man by many years of study, and would be self-perpetuating. The lives of its members should be dedicated to the contemplation of the economic, sociological, psychological, physiological and pathological phenomena manifested by the civilized nations and their constitutive individuals.

For the first time in the history of humanity, Carrel says, a crumbling civilization is capable of discerning the causes of its decay; for the first time, it has at its disposal the gigantic strength of science. "Will we utilize this knowledge and this power?" he asks, and adds, "It is our only hope of escaping the fate common to all great civilizations of the past. Our destiny is in our hands. On the new road we must now go forward."[19]

19
what can be done: infant and child care and education

Many students of the subject maintain with impressive plausibility that, at least for a constructive beginning today, the most practical and effective of all methods now available for the increase of love in individuals are those that pertain to the handling and education of infants and children; this chapter will be devoted to that subject.

Sorokin gives emphatic expression to his views on the subject in *Reconstruction of Humanity* and in *Ways and Power* (somewhat abridged and paraphrased here):[1]

> The family is the first and most decisive molder of the personality and conduct of children, and the school is next. A legion of social thinkers have indicated the decisive role of the family in molding the biological, mental, moral and social properties of its offspring, the reasons for and the way of such a decisive influence and what sort of family exerts a positive influence and what sort a negative influence.

The families with a set of high values preached and practiced by their members, where harmony prevails in their relationship to one another and to the world at large, where intense and especially wise or adequate love permeates the whole life of the family, where a baby in prenatal and postnatal life is welcomed and blessed with the grace of abundant and wise love—such families tend to produce well-disciplined persons with kind and happy dispositions. It is much easier to grow in the family garden a large crop of creative altruists from newborn babies than it is to transform grown-up egoists into altruists. If all parents take necessary pains to cultivate each newborn baby with all the care of a wise and adequate love, in the short span of one or two generations they can multiply many times the number of practicing altruists. So far, this is the easiest and most fruitful way of transformation of the human universe from an ugly wilderness into a magnificent Garden of Eden.

If from the moment of birth every child is treated lovingly by his parents, siblings and others who are in face-to-face interaction with him, and if he is consistently "conditioned" to treat all human beings in a friendly way as sacred end values, regardless of their sex, age, color, creed, nationality, social position and so on, and when such treatment and conditioning are done consistently, with all the necessary operations involved—this sort of utilization of the mechanisms of conditioned reflexes and of habit-formation will produce a rich harvest of human beings friendly to all human beings, compassionate, cooperative and helpful members of man-

what can be done: infant and child care and education 243

kind. There is nothing utopian in this statement. It is corroborated by numerous experimental studies of conditioned reflexes and of the mechanisms of their inculcation, reinforcement, radiation, transference, and extinction.[2] [Sorokin's terminology is somewhat old-fashioned, but modern psychological work confirms these ideas completely.]

It is true that for a success of altruistic conditioning, the most consistent inhibition of each of the child's unfriendly actions-reactions and encouragement of each of his friendly reflexes are necessary. A few other conditions for an effective inculcation of conditioned responses have to be met also. [As examples, Sorokin says that all toys like guns, tanks, bombers and soldiers and games involving killing, like "Cops and Robbers," as well as movies and "comic books" teaching lessons of murder, sex and mishandling of man by man should be tabooed.][3] But the totality of these requirements is neither too burdensome nor too intricate to be managed by intelligent parents and educators.

Storr questions the wisdom of these restrictions, thinking they may result in repressed aggression in the adult; it is the repression rather than the possession of personal aggression which is dangerous. There should not be too many "no-nos" in a child's life.[4]

There is almost complete agreement by the psychologists and sociologists on the extreme importance of love to the infant. Montagu relies on a more utilitarian theory than do most of his colleagues. He points out that the infant soon learns that in order to be satisfied, in order to be loved, he too must love, he must satisfy the requirements of others, he must cooperate. He learns that without protest he must give up or postpone satisfying certain desires if he is to retain the love of those whose love he needs. This behavior pattern provides an important means through which the infant's socialization is achieved, first through a feeling of belonging (security), and then through love as authority, the authority of the affectionate family tie.[5]

The effect on the infant of the imprinting growing out of its relationship with its mother (see Chapter Ten) obviously points up the importance of making that relationship as close and full of love as possible.

The relationships of the infant's family life condition his personal relationships throughout his life. Montagu considers this so true that he says the importance of love in the early social development of the infant cannot be overemphasized, and cites the startling fact that but 50 years ago more than half of children died during their first year of life. Many studies to determine why and to learn the effect of hospital and institutional residence on babies have been made and are reported by Montagu. Through these studies it was learned that the babies living in homes where opportunity of love was greatest were most apt to be among the survivors. Studies by Bowlby, Ribble and Bakwins show that babies living in hospitals fail to gain properly even on adequate diets, and sleep, smile and babble less, and are listless and generally unhappy in conduct. The emotional deprivation suffered by infants in hospitals may do vastly more damage than the physical condition which takes them there. The infant can suffer no greater loss than the privation of its mother's love. An old Egyptian proverb says that since God could not be everywhere he created mothers.*

Other studies seem quite conclusive in demonstrating that individuals raised from infancy in institutions, even though restored to home life in early childhood, are handicapped throughout life. A study was made by Spitz of children confined to institutions during the first year of their lives. The institutions were excellent in all respects, but in one the infants were looked after by their own mothers and in the second were looked after by nursing personnel. Spitz found that there was not a great difference in the development quotient of the two sets of babies in the first year, but that by the end of the second year that of the second group had dropped to a development quotient corresponding to a mental age of about ten months. Even more striking, the first institution did not lose a single child through death, but in the second 37 percent of the children died during the two-year observation period.[6]

A summary by J. H. Crook of studies by others indicates that over-punitive methods produce aggressive

---

*Late reports published in *Fortune* about scientists researching with monkeys strongly back up these findings. Monkeys reared in isolation attacked other animals and even the researchers with little provocation, probably because of an actual alteration in their biochemistry or the circuitry of their brains. The evidence points strongly to the conclusion that environmental influences affect the brain and can trigger violence. One neurophysicist believes that normal pathways in the brain do not fully develop in children deprived of such expressions of affection as touching, cuddling and being carried about, but instead are left with damaged central nervous systems. Studies of peoples in other lands noted for their lack of antagonistic behavior "appear to support the theory and lend weight to the belief that changing child-rearing practices is probably the most important single thing we can do as a society."

and otherwise unfortunate characteristics in children as contrasted with guidance without punishment; aggressive children are likely to come from homes where the expression of aggression is not regulated by family rules, but rather is heavily punished, although by the age of 12 such children show less aggression than those from permissive homes with neither rules nor punishment; and the least aggressive children come from homes which confront them from infancy with strong rules to prevent aggression but in which bad behavior is controlled in a non-punitive manner—praise and affection for good behavior and withdrawal of love for bad. Much work on this subject remains to be done.

Lewis and Towers concur in these conclusions, adding that a baby's experience—which they say (relying on Harlow's research?) comes through its skin—of being fondled and caressed appears to be vital for its subsequent psychological development. They do not think much of the theory prevalent a few years ago under which babies had to be handled strictly, "fed by the clock," and otherwise forced to live by rule.[7] Montagu agrees so completely that he has recently written a book on "the human significance of the skin." Reviewers of the book have tended to concur with Montagu's conclusion —that emotions aroused through skin contacts are psychologically important—but not with his supporting arguments.

Berkowitz's summation would meet with general concurrence: "The most effectively trained youngsters are those whose parents: (1) have consistently prescribed firm standards for the children's behavior; (2) have employed love-oriented disciplinary techniques, especially relying on praise and the use of reason rather than

what can be done: infant and child care and education 247

physical punishment and the deprivation of privileges; and (3) have been affectionate and nurturant to the children throughout childhood."[8]

Here is something written 40 or 50 years ago by a man who was not even a social scientist—Emil Ludwig —but who expressed so well what is being said in this chapter that it must not be omitted:

> *La Vérité est en marche.* In all countries, particularly in England and America, societies founded for the unification of lovers of peace now number millions rather than thousands. But it is obvious that the chief leaders are not those who thus instruct and dedicate themselves to the cause, that our hope must lie rather with the young who are now growing into maturity and will believe what they are taught. If we give our boys tin soldiers, take them to gaze upon the monuments erected to victorious kings, teach them the names of battles, the songs of tramping men, the renown of generals, the splendor of armies marching to the field, the glory of a uniform, the charm of decorations, the prestige of the state, the superiority of the fatherland, the pride of conquest, they will accept it all. And when they arrive at maturity, they will seek to attain the goal that has been pointed out to them as the ideal.
>
> But reveal to them the fleeting honors of martial success as compared with the enduring victories of the spirit, contrast for them the achievements of triumphant captains and the work of thinkers and inventors, compare generals sending men to death with doctors devoted to saving lives. Teach them to realize the faults of their own countries and to

appreciate the virtues of others. Show them their close kinship to children who speak an alien tongue. Emphasize the fact that they have in common mountains and streams, that national boundary lines do not mark vital differences between the people on both sides, that customs and clothing, faith and superstition present similarities throughout the world, that literatures supplement one another, and that great foreign cities are friendly neighbors which can now be reached by aeroplane in a few hours. Do this and they will believe and be governed accordingly throughout their lives. Above all, teach them what a battle really is, show them photographs—terribly true—of life in the zone of battle where human bodies are mangled beyond recognition and beautiful lives are snuffed out in smoke and flame. Teach them the mathematical terms in which a victor nation must reckon its success when war is over. Let them learn modern languages so that they can go about everywhere. And while you educate your sons to seek an outlet for their ambitions and energies in tasks that will bring success to them, give your daughters to understand that they, the natural guardians of life and hearth, must likewise realize their solidarity with one another so that, in case another "fever-fit," as Frederick termed it, attacks humanity, they may arise and extinguish it before it bursts into war. For theirs are those weaponless hands which, since primeval times, have been superior to hands bearing arms.[9]

In the "brotherhood" communities, such as those discussed in Chapter Fourteen, family education and school education are pretty much amalgamated, and profitably so; their innovations in education and child care have been remarkably successful in building loving, altruistic men and women.

The methods prevailing in the Society of Brothers are typical of most such communities.[10] Eberhard C. H. Arnold, son of the founder, says that the first, the truly golden rule of such an education for community is the example of the adults, given by their own way of life and manner of doing things. Grown-up people are able to administer effective assistance to children in their fight for the mastery of love in their actions only in so far as they themselves wage this fight honestly. Children have a very sensitive and subtle feeling for genuineness and consistency in our actions and words. They have an almost uncanny sense of detecting hypocrisy and untruthfulness manifest in the lives of adults, and they react with resentment and passive or active resistance. There can be no true education without authority, unfortunately largely lost in modern educational practice. Many children today are deprived of the loving but firm hand to guide them through turmoils, contradictions and confusion. There must be a clear "Thou shalt" and "Thou shalt not" to which both adults and children are subject in willing obedience, but which goes hand in hand with freedom and true autonomy. The imposition of one's own will on others is opposed to the spirit of altruism; creative powers inherent in children should be allowed to unfold themselves unhampered by attempt to press them into a ready-made mold of psychological or educational theory.

The daily routine of the colony children was outlined in Chapter Fourteen. The children are brought together in little groups, beginning at an early age. Social awareness is apparent in a few weeks from birth. Even the youngest children of the colony spend most of the day in a group with others their own age, and the joy and response of a young baby to another baby is apparent, even at a few months. Here they learn, in the most natural way, the qualities of group experience, such as having true regard for one another and learning to do things together. As they grow older, they learn to perform little responsible tasks for the group, such as laying the table, cleaning the rooms, the older children playing with and helping care for the younger ones; by this means a sense of responsibility for the well-being of the group is developed. Emphasis is continually placed on loving actions. In one conversation overheard between a 7-year-old boy and a 5-year-old girl who had been looking at a magazine with pictures of fighting men, the boy remarked, "You know, if I were king, I'd call all the other kings together and we would have a meeting and I would tell them to bring me all their guns. Then I would take all the guns and smash them. Just smash them against the wall!"

During the summer the children help part-time in community work—kitchen, laundry, baby house, office, shop and so on. A long camping trip is taken. When the time comes they assist in harvesting the garden crops, some of which are used in the community and the remainder sold at a roadside stand to get money for musical instruments for the school orchestra. These children are beginning to see and understand the complexity of world problems and world needs. Most respond with shock and protest to the violence and injustice which the news brings them. Many want to go to all the surrounding

what can be done: infant and child care and education 251

farms and tell them about brotherly love and community life. On one occasion the children were preparing for a trip to New York by looking at pictures of the city. One picture showed a man sleeping on the street under a newspaper, and the children's reaction was that they must find him and take him home with them.

Emphasis is placed on developing in the children a strong sense of oneness with nature and a feeling of reverence for all things living. Together with the training of intellectual and artistic gifts in the community school, the boy or girl learns to use his hands skillfully and creatively, working at such crafts as carpentry, pottery and leatherwork, thus putting into practice Sorokin's "Technique of Individual Creative Activity." In addition, the young people take part in the music activities in the community and in its stage plays.*

Another example of the rearing and education of children in community is available to us in the kibbutzim of Israel. The following account is based largely on reports made by Bettelheim,[11] Bronfenbrenner[12] and Leslie and Karen Rabkin,[13] who have at various times lived in the kibbutzim and studied their methods. Since in many respects these methods are like those followed in the Mennonite and Hutterite communities already discussed, only the variations will be mentioned here.

A kibbutz is usually a smallish agricultural settlement, sometimes with minor industries, varying in size from 100 or less to a maximum of 2,000 inhabitants. Each

---

*I was not surprised to note while I was in the community that one of the plays they produced was Tolstoy's "What Men Live By." Much of Tolstoy's philosophy is embraced in the life these children learn to live.

forms a single unit: economic, political and social. Some hold all property in common; others permit partial private ownership. Kibbutz children live from birth (usually from the fourth day after delivery) with their age group in separate children's houses, cared for by community members assigned to the task. Each room ordinarily would have four or five occupants cared for by a "metapelet" (the name given the woman substituting for the mother), except when the mother is present. During the first six months the infant is nursed there by his mother, and his father may visit. After that time the child may visit each day with his parents in their own room for periods running from a half hour to two hours. Sickness does not alter the arrangement. At between one and two years of age, the child leaves the infants' house for the toddlers' house, where he shares a common playroom and dining room. At around four he moves to the kindergarten house, which ideally would consist of about 18 children—three toddler groups. Here one metapelet and a kindergarten teacher share responsibility. Again a common class-playroom and dining room are shared. From 7 to 12 the children live in a children's house housing up to 20, and form a society enjoying some self-regulation. The only common room in the house is the dining room. There are usually four beds in each bedroom. From 13 to 18 the youngsters live in youth houses and form a single kibbutz-wide youth society, enjoying a considerable degree of responsibility. If the kibbutz is large enough, a high school is operated.

The importance of the peer group begins in the very first days of life, which is significant since, as we have seen, imprinting is an extremely important early experience. By toddler age the group feeling is fixed;

what can be done: infant and child care and education 253

the children are comrades, not competitors. Parents are one of the three centers around which the child's life revolves and whose impact will shape his personality, so are more important in the child's life than either his metapelet or teacher. The kibbutz system is still in flux. In some, infants sleep in the rooms with their parents from infancy on, spending only their days with their peers.

Kibbutz membership is growing, but still comprises only about 4 percent of the population of Israel. Significantly, the 4 percent account for some 15 percent of the members of Parliament, and in the "6-day war" provided an inordinate percentage of the officers' corps and showed great heroism, courage and devotion, suffering 25 percent of the casualties.

As to possible use of the kibbutz system of education in a non-kibbutz culture such as ours, our three reporters differ. Bettelheim suggests that since the kibbutz is so "closed" a community and has so high a degree of consensus on all essential issues, it is hard to visualize how we could duplicate it in our society, except possibly in enclaves like the Hutterite community. He does feel, however, that where in this country slum and ghetto mothers receive public aid for their dependent children, it might be better for the children not to be reared at home if they could be reared in something akin to the communal setting of the kibbutz; this, he says, would solve the problem of our slums in short order, and as to some of our other problems, such as the children who are under-achievers, dropouts and delinquents, kibbutz education might solve them all. Youngsters in the kibbutz are made to feel that they are a moral elite compared to the rest of the world, and they are steeped in the feeling that the kibbutz needs them badly and that they carry the kibbutz and its future in their hands.

Bronfenbrenner was struck by the intimacy and warmth of the parent-child relationship, particularly during the two hours in the late afternoon that parents reserve for spending with their children and in the evening time when the parents put their children to bed. He found several leading educators to be highly critical of some but not all of Bettelheim's conclusions. He also criticized Bettelheim's study for the absence of a control group of non-kibbutz families.

The Rabkins sum up their impression of the kibbutznik, saying that he is a healthy, intelligent, generous, somewhat shy but warm human being, rooted in his community and in the larger Israeli society, and showing no sign of the emotional disturbance we would expect from a violation of our ideal mother-child relationship. However, they have concluded that we cannot translate this socialization system into American terms, since to do so would need a basic overhaul of the goals of our society.

These methods of child rearing and education with so much emphasis on the group, as portrayed in the foregoing pages, must be utilized with care—too much de-emphasis on the individual could produce dedicated statists. Bronfenbrenner has spent more than 10 years studying the Russian educational system, which turns out the "new Soviet man" as "a planned product of Communist society—the result of an explicit system of character training being employed daily in Soviet families, nurseries, school and youth groups." Children in the group not only try to improve themselves, but monitor the behavior of their comrades. In the late sixties boarding

what can be done: infant and child care and education

schools were introduced, in which children are entered at the age of three months. This system may have grown, but other types of schools keep the youngsters from eight in the morning until eight in the evening.

In 1970 Bronfenbrenner brought his report up to date. He finds that the Russian system is more efficient than the American system in reaching its goals, but the children it produces—although well-mannered, industrious, attentive and rarely antisocial—tend to be "goody-goodies" and lack the spontaneity and independence of their American counterparts. Nevertheless, since he considers our own system perilously deficient, he suggests that we borrow selectively from Soviet techniques.[14]

The Communist countries in the Balkans, as would be expected, follow Russian educational methods to a large extent.[15] A typical example is the school system in force in a cooperative farm of 40,000 acres in Bulgaria, owned and worked cooperatively by about 12,500 people living in seven towns. The school is in several adjacent buildings, one of which is the children's nursery. Here tots of from 18 to 36 months of age receive their preliminary training. Children of from four to seven attend a kind of kindergarten in another building, after which the equivalent of our grade school and high school education is given to children over seven. There are two shifts of teachers for each building. The nursery and kindergarten children are there from seven in the morning until seven at night and receive all their meals at the school. They are neatly dressed in identical uniforms, and are clean, alert and rosy-cheeked. On the occasion of a visit by one small group of Americans, the nursery children rose to their feet politely and, at the teacher's suggestion, sang a welcome song. In the large bathroom and toilet each child has his own matching towel and drinking cup; in an adjoining room each has a small bed for naps. Dollhouses with furniture and other toys are amply in evidence.

The system would seem to have the advantages of the kibbutz type of schooling without the possible disadvantage of too little contact between the children and their families. However, there can be no doubt that the inflexible communist doctrine and line are instilled in the children from infancy. In the kindergarten, the four-year-olds recited for the visiting group mentioned above, speaking of course in Bulgarian. It was later learned that one poem had to do with a sobbing South Vietnamese child whose mother had been killed in the senseless American war there, and who was being cared for by others.*

As Sorokin said, the second most decisive molder of the personality and character of children, after the family, is the school. If school education is well organized, it can reinforce sound family education to such a degree that the combined effects are indelibly stamped upon the pupils for the rest of their lives. If the family education is defective, a sound school education may correct, to a considerable extent, its shortcomings, but if the school system is defective, it can do an untold amount of harm to its pupils, and, he says, our contemporary school system is grossly defective: it fails to develop character and a sense of altruism or to engender a social outlook. The schools must establish a carefully worked out system for developing altruism in their pupils, instil-

---

*This incident occurred in a visit I made to several Balkan schools in 1970.

ling in them a set of universal values and norms. Intellectual training must be reconstructed in the interest of developing logical thinking and a passionate search for the truth rather than of cramming the mind with fragments of this or that; it must imbue the students with a sense of true wisdom, supplementing specialization by a broad general education making students the inheritors, users and guardians of the immortal values of human culture in all its fields. Standardized requirements for students (especially for university students) must be freed from their rigidity, permitting the maximum of freedom for young scholars in developing their particular aptitudes. So transformed, Sorokin concludes, the school will be one of the mainsprings of the altruistic and constructive forces which make for peace, happiness and genius.[16]

Few psychologists have been better recognized as authorities on education than John Dewey, and he still makes sense today. He calls the infant "largely potentiality." Consciousness has grown, he says, "of the extent to which a future new society of changed purposes and desires may be created by a deliberate humane treatment of the impulses of youth. This is the meaning of education . . . an intelligent direction of native activities in the light of the possibilities and necessities of the social situation." As social conditions change new ways must be devised to meet the change; old impulses are directed into new channels and a new human nature is formed.[17] Dewey says, as does Sorokin, that the flexibility of the impulses of the young can be organized into almost any disposition, depending on the way it interacts with surroundings.

Dewey says further that adults have given children

training rather than education. Each new generation is modeled after the old. Youthful impulses are not allowed to exercise their reorganizing potentialities. Original modifiability has not been given a fair chance to act as a trustee for a better human life. It has been loaded with convention, biased by adult convenience. Emerson a hundred years ago put the same thought this way: "Our culture has truckled to the times.... We teach boys to be such men as we are. We do not teach them to aspire to be all they can. We do not give them a training as if we believed in their noble nature.... We exercise their understandings to the apprehension and comparison of some facts, to a skill in numbers, in words; we aim to make accountants, attorneys, engineers; but not to make able, earnest, greathearted men."[18] Dewey concludes with a priceless epigram: "Education is the art of taking advantage of the helplessness of the young."[19]

Aristotle takes us farther back than does Emerson—some 2,000 years back. He wrote that from earliest youth, parents and teachers should intervene in the life of the child, influencing him by rewards and punishments and a beneficent environment to perform virtuous acts. He must learn *why* any certain act is good, then to choose it for its own sake alone (not for some extraneous reward), and finally this mode of action must become so ingrained in him that he can perform acts of this kind at a moment's notice, and with lasting pleasure.[20]

And from a very modern educator, Robert Hutchins, writing in *The Center Magazine*: "The only education worth having in an age of rapid change is liberal education. [Certain requirements are:] It must be for all. It must lay the foundations for wise citizenship, the sensible use of leisure, and the continuous development of the highest powers of every human being. It must be the kind of education that will bind men together, not merely in this country but throughout the world. . . . An education that tried to assist the formation of the world community would seek to connect rather than divide men; it would seek to do so by drawing out the elements of their common humanity. It would be theoretical rather than practical, because, though men do different things, they can all share in understanding. It would be general rather than specialized, because, though all men are not experts in the same subject, they all ought to grasp the same principles. It would be liberal rather than vocational, because, though all men do not follow the same occupations, the minds of all men should be set free. An education that helps all men to become human by helping them gain complete possession of all their powers would seem to be the only defensible education in a world of rapid technological change; it would seem to be the best for a national community and for the world community as well."

Will Durant quotes Bertrand Russell as calling our schools the open sesame to Utopia. There is nothing that man might not do, he says, if our splendid organization of schools and universities were properly developed and properly manned and directed intelligently to the reconstruction of human character. This, and not violent revolution or paper legislation, is the way out of economic greed and international brutality.[21]

A lament written half a century ago by Everett Dean Martin contains a practical suggestion. He watched many local elections to school boards and noted that commonly petty personal interests and crowd partisanship resulted in the choice of incompetent persons, whose influence on public education everywhere is to make it not only susceptible to crowd prejudice but an actual fabricator of mob ideas. More care devoted to the selection of the men who sit on our school and university boards might well prove a giant step towards our objective. We get a bit of the flavor of Martin's time when he comments that William Jennings Bryan, arch enemy of education during his later years, did not mean to be cynical when he said that people who pay for education have the right to decide what shall be taught.[22]

Despite its length and complexity, this discussion can be concluded very briefly with the comment that there is surprising lack of disagreement about the foregoing ideas advanced for improvement in child care and education or as to the efficacy of the methods advocated; even what needs to be done is pretty much agreed upon. However, to effect the improvement is something else again. No doubt it can be done if we are given sufficient time and if we can get proper effort behind the attempts. Large foundations and perhaps even the "establishment" which is so maligned today, could do the job if the people demand it loudly enough. An example of what *can* be accomplished is the currently widespread and insistent demand for cleaning up pollution of our air, water and earth, although only a few years ago its necessity was being given little public attention.

The United Nations designated 1970 as International Education Year. In announcing it, the Director-General of UNESCO recognized that in many countries both the forms and the content of education are being seriously challenged today. "It is out of the question," he said, "for education to be confined, as in the past, to training the leaders of tomorrow's society in accordance with some predetermined scheme of structures, needs and ideas, or to preparing the young, once and for all, for a given type of existence."[23] The world community was invited to address itself to this sort of problems during the year, in order that bold and inventive solutions might be found and applied—but not much seems to have happened. Inertia is truly a powerful force.

There is no lack of studies, articles and books analyzing the flaws in our present educational system and suggesting remedies—they are coming at us from all sides. Quite recently the three-and-a-half-year study of the nation's public schools commissioned by the Carnegie Corporation has been released. It agrees unequivocally with the severest critics of American education, and tells why. Perhaps what we need now is a top drawer study and analysis of this mass of available material, and subsequent recommendations for concrete and specific changes and reforms. This is something which will require time, money and ability, as well as experimental application of the recommended procedures and techniques evolved. Probably only the government or well-heeled private foundations can undertake such a project. Its importance is plain; whether it is something we can hope to succeed in doing, is open to doubt, yet in at least a small way it is already being nibbled at by both government and foundations.

The emphasis on the importance of education in this chapter is not to detract from the value of the many other approaches to the increase of altruism that Sorokin and the other behavioral scientists have advanced. Our problem is so complex and so urgent that we must follow all possible avenues to our goal. The solution may very well turn out to be a combination of many kinds of these recommended efforts.

20
Sorokin's challenge

The preceding chapters have of course covered only a small part of Sorokin's work, even on the one subject of altruistic love. Some of what he had to say had been said before by others, often more concisely, but never more earnestly or emphatically, or with sounder scientific basis.

Just before a recent New Year's Day, many people received two items in the mail. One was from a financial advisory service and was entitled "Stocks to Choose for the Coming Year." The other was a publication by the Lucis Trust and on one of its pages was an item entitled "Values to Live by in the Coming Year." The values were put in the form of a little poem, very aptly related to what this book is about. It ran:

> The sons of men are one and I am one with them.
> I seek to love, not hate;
> I seek to serve and not exact due service;
> I seek to heal, not hurt.

> Let vision come and insight.
> Let the future stand revealed.
> Let inner union demonstrate and outer cleavages be gone.
> Let love prevail.
> Let all men love.

Many persons doubtless purchased the recommended stocks; a few persons may have resolved to adopt the "values," but whether any of those resolutions was actually put into action is open to doubt. Yet how infinitely more vital it is to the world and its people that all men love and that love prevail! To deny that a way to that end exists is defeatism at its most costly—we *must* find the way.

Great-hearted Walt Whitman *felt* this when he wrote:

> Swiftly arose and spread around me the peace and knowledge that pass all the argument of the earth,
> And I know that the hand of God is the promise of my own,
> And I know that the spirit of God is the brother of my own,
> And that all the men ever born are also my brothers, and the women my sisters and lovers,
> And that a kelson of the creation is love.

For many it was a hopeful sign for the spread of brotherly love throughout the world when, in a telecast celebrating United Nations Week, a very large group comprised of young people of all colors and races from probably 50 nations sang a song of "love, love, love," proclaiming that *all* persons in the world must love each other without regard to their nationalities. Best of all, the youngsters sang the song as though they really meant it.

Alan Isaacs, who has been quoted before in this book, lived through World War II in London and underwent all the dangers and hardships which that entailed. Near the end of his *Survival of God in the Scientific Age*, he asks us to look at some of the alternative ways in which human civilization can develop in the nuclear space age and suggests three possibilities: (1) Civilization may destroy itself by full-scale nuclear war, or so cripple itself by limited nuclear wars that the future of life on the planet would be too deplorable even to contemplate; (2) the present phase of nuclear stalemate, expanding populations and only limited increase in food production may continue, while the poverty, hunger and misery of and increased tensions between the haves and the have-nots, blacks and whites, East and West, or whatever combinations of factions happen to emerge, make a disunited, disgruntled and dangerous world; (3) cheap and plentiful energy and food, the elimination of disease and the widespread use of automation can combine to give man not only freedom from want and illness but also freedom from fear.[1]

Probably Isaac's second possibility, to which we must add the only recently emphasized dangers of pollution, overpopulation and other ecological problems, is the most likely to happen, at least for a time stretching indefinitely ahead. Should the first occur, most or all of us won't be here, and those who are probably won't care much. We can only hope—and work—to win through to Isaac's third possibility.

Lewis and Towers, whom we have frequently

quoted, end their book with the expressed hope that it may not be too fanciful to see in some of the world-wide attitudes of youth today, with their wholesale rejection of the bourgeois values of the consumer-society, the first sign of an extensive growth of man towards *more-being* rather than simply *well-being*—it is more important to live than to have. Once that lesson is learned, the fundamental inner drives of man might be channeled away from the naked aggression character of *Naked Apes*, and into those realms of experience that are the birthright of *Homo Sapiens* if only he is prepared to live up to his name.[2]

There is quoted in Chapter One the final passage from Sorokin's *Leaves from a Russian Diary*, expressing his hope in the power of love. In an interview with his widow in 1969, she was asked about her husband's final judgment of his study and writings on altruistic love and the strength of his hope that that work might prove fruitful. She replied, "He was hopeful. He realized that there is only a chance that it will work [so far as the cure of world problems is concerned] but he thought this the only chance."*

We cannot accept Sorokin's hope as a completely impossible dream; a perhaps desperate hope indeed, but one certainly possible of realization if we can muster behind it enough widely spread power and force. There is a suggestion in Chapter Nineteen of the need for the backing of the larger foundations and of the government; it should have included *all* governments throughout the

---

*This is a question I asked Mrs. Sorokin in a visit I paid her to discuss this book. She is a grand and brilliant person.

world, or at least as many as can be persuaded that their own self-interest demands their help. Moreover, the effective support that can be given by churches (including related organizations such as the World Congress of Faiths and the World Council of Churches), universities, and other organized groups must not be overlooked. Even though our personal efforts fail, perhaps those persons making a conscious effort to increase their love for others will be rewarded with greater happiness and peace of mind during whatever time we have left.

It is only fitting that, in closing this long discussion of Sorokin's belief in the ways and power of love, we let Sorokin speak for himself—these are his concluding paragraphs in *Ways and Power*,[3] his final book on the subject:

> The conclusion is clear as to the necessity of transcendence of all tribal solidarities by the universal solidarity of mankind, if interhuman warfare is to be eliminated from the human universe. An approximate realization of the ideal of pacified humanity is neither impossible nor is it a mere utopian dream. However difficult is its attainment, it must be achieved for the simple reason of survival of creative mankind itself. This attainment is not a matter of fanciful choice, but that of stern necessity. The destiny's categoric ultimatum of "to be or not to be" can be answered positively only through extension of solidarity over the whole human race and through creative ennoblement of its nature.
>
> This hopeful answer is backed up by the practical plan of how this objective can be reached. The plan demands, first, mobilization of the unconscious,

conscious and supraconscious forces of man for this "holy war" of the united mankind against its eternal and implacable enemies: death, disease, stupidity, ignorance, criminality, sterile suffering, poverty and the like. Second, the plan shows how the power of the unconscious antisocial drives, like hatred, self-preservation, egoism, competition and so on, can be redirected into the channels serving this purpose. Third, it shows how the mechanisms of the unconditioned and conditioned reflexes can be used for unification and pacification of humanity. Fourth, how the powers of the rational thought and conscious scientific activity can help in this task, and, fifth, how the supraconscious genius of humanity can render supreme guidance and creative assistance in this undertaking.

So organized and unified into one magnificent force, the existing unconscious, conscious and supraconscious powers of man are sufficient for elimination of most of the interhuman wars, as well for a splendid renaissance of man himself, of his culture and social universe. As soon as these powers are organized according to the plan, they will begin their work and in a comparatively short time will achieve the results far exceeding the best expectations. By the mysterious forces of destiny, mankind is confronted with a stern dilemma: either to continue its predatory policies of individual and tribal selfishness that lead it to its inevitable doom, or to embark upon the policies of universal solidarity that brings humanity to the aspired-for heaven on the earth. It is up to everyone of us which of the two roads we prefer to choose.

notes

introduction

1. Sorokin (Ways and Powers) p. vii
2. Fromm (Revolution) p. xvii

chapter one

1. Sorokin (Reconstruction) 3
2. Sorokin (Social Philosophies) 319
3. Sorokin (Altruistic Love) 3
4. Sorokin (Reconstruction) 101-80
5. Sorokin (Reconstruction) 129-35
6. Ross 66
7. Ouspensky (Model) 42
8. Schneider V. I, 26, 28, 33, 34
9. Beard 6
10. Storr (Introduction) 3-5
11. Sorokin (Altruistic Love) pp. v, vi
12. Allen 459-60

chapter two

The sources for the material contained in this Chapter are set out in the Chapter itself.

chapter three

1. Northrop (Meeting) 101
2. Carlyle 222
3. Sorokin (Reconstruction) 12-18
4. Radhakrishnan, (Concept) 26
5. Radhakrishnan, (Concept) 23
6. Chaudhuri (Prophet) 20
7. Sorokin (Reconstruction) 8-12
8. Dostoevski (Brothers) 303-24
9. Sakharov 27
10. Sakharov 81-89
11. Sorokin (Reconstruction) 38
12. Sorokin (Reconstruction) 44
13. Sorokin (Reconstruction) 45
14. Northrop (Meeting) 45
15. Northrop (Meeting) 54
16. Sorokin (Reconstruction) 77
17. Sorokin (Reconstruction) 53

chapter four

1. Sorokin (Ways and Power) 3
2. DeBit, 81, 92, 109
3. Schneider V. I, 17
4. Arnold (Life) 14
5. Schneider V.I, 239-43
6. Sorokin (Ways and Power) 3-6
7. Tagore (Religion) 12
8. Bryan-London
9. Tagore 30
10. Tomlin 169
11. Riley 324
12. Fromm (Loving) p. xix
13. Chaudhuri (Problems) 26

14. Schneider V.I, 24
15. Fromm (Art of Loving) 118
16. Isherwood (Western World) 6
17. Schneider V.II, 11

chapter five

1. Sorokin (Ways and Power) 6, 7
2. Sorokin (Ways and Power) 7
3. Sorokin (Ways and Power) 8
4. Boethius 40
5. Sorokin (Ways and Power) 8
6. Sorokin (Ways and Power) 9
7. Sorokin (Ways and Power) 9, 10
8. Sorokin (Ways and Power) 10, 11
9. Fromm (Art of Loving) 9, 18
10. Buber 15
11. Sorokin (Ways and Power) 13
12. Fromm (Revolution) 137
13. DeChardin 145
14. MacGregor 151
15. Hubben 83
16. Schneider V.I, 302
17. Prabhavananda and Isherwood 89
18. Sharma 83
19. Radhakrishnan (Concept) 123
20. Magill V.II, 680
21. Chaudhuri (Problems) 120
22. Sorokin (Ways and Power) 14
23. Sorokin (Ways and Power) 15-35

chapter six

1. Sorokin (Reconstruction) 41
2. Arnold (Life) 17

3. Sachar 133
4. Ballou 1322, 1337, 1341
5. Abhedananda
6. Radhakrishnan (Concept) 197 et seq.
7. Merton 52
8. For a more complete account of the theories and philosophy of this amazing man, reference is made to a short manuscript of mine, entitled *Old Rice Wine in New Bottles*, available at the Newberry Library in Chicago in the Chicago Literary Society collection.
9. Ferm (Religion) 387
10. Thomsen 15-29

chapter seven

1. World Faiths
2. Durant (Philosophy) 368
3. Sharma 87
4. Aurobindo, (Gita) 114
5. Chaudhuri and Spiegelberg 236
6. Aurobindo, (Life) 893
7. Sasaki. This paragraph about Indra's net reports a conversation I had in Japan some years ago with Mrs. Sasaki just before she was made a Buddhist Priest. The explanation is part of material she was then getting together for a book to be entitled *Zen— A Religion*, which has probably since been published.
8. Evans-Wentz (Liberation) 57
9. Govinda 43
10. Fung (Spirit) 68
11. Radhakrishnan (Concept) 200
12. Aurelius, 152, 153

13. Hocking (Types) 403
14. Ouspensky (New Model) 340
15. Watts (The Book) Chapter 1
16. Watts (The Book) 43, 44

chapter eight

1. Sorokin (Ways and Power) 36, 37
2. Sorokin (Ways and Power) 45, 46
3. Sorokin (Ways and Power) 47-60
4. Sorokin (Altruistic Love) 77-79
5. Sorokin (Altruistic Love) 199
6. Durant (Age of Faith) 293
7. Sorokin (Ways and Power) 66
8. Sorokin (Ways and Power) 66-69
9. Sorokin (Ways and Power) 77
10. Emerson 85, 87
11. Sorokin (Ways and Power) 60, 61
12. Smock
13. Sorokin (Ways and Power) 77, 78
14. Sorokin (Ways and Power) 79
15. Mumford, (The Conduct of Life) 284-88
16. Allen 327, 328

chapter nine

1. Sorokin (Reconstruction) 58, 59
2. New English Bible Luke 6:28-36
3. American Quarterly V. 8 (1956), 40-52
4. Encyclopedia of the Social Sciences V. 2, 14
5. Merrill-Palmer Quarterly of Behavior and Development, April, 1968
6. Merrill-Palmer Quarterly of Behavior and Development, July, 1963
7. Fromm (Art of Loving) 24

8. American Journal of Sociology V. LXXI, No. 4, 407-16
9. Unpublished dissertation by W. B. Uphold, Jr., U.S.C. Graduate School, June, 1951
10. Sorokin (Reconstruction) 59, 60
11. Sorokin (Reconstruction) 60, 61
12. Sorokin (Reconstruction) 183
13. Allen 62-65
14. Lecky V. I, 2, 3
15. Magill V. II, 671-76
16. Cunningham 370-77
17. Fung (History) V.I, 127
18. Brown (Chinese) 67
19. Sharma 36
20. Aurelius 18
21. Tagore 89
22. Kemp 58, 59
23. Hocking (Types) 311-13
24. Boethius (which includes also *The Imitation of Christ*, by Thomas á Kempis, and *Religio Medici*, by Sir Thomas Browne) 389
25. Watts (The Book) 125, 126
26. Aurobindo (Synthesis) 121
27. Griffis 72
28. Sansom 54
29. Psychological Review, V. LII (1945), 109-12
30. Isaacs 203, 204
31. Schneider V.I, 221, 222
32. Watts (Psychotherapy) 15
33. Yogananda 451

chapter ten
1. Brown-Galanter-Hess-Mandler 159-61
2. Stiers, writing in Volume 2, Number 2, of *The Center Magazine* (March, 1969)

notes **275**

3. Berkowitz p. xi
4. Montagu (Aggression) 39
5. Berkowitz p. ix
6. Berkowitz 25
7. This report, although taken from the International Herald Tribune for July 31-August 1, 1971, has been verified. Miss Freud's paper was also reviewed in The Guardian for July 31.
8. Berkowitz Chapter 2
9. Ardrey 301, 302
10. Mumford (Myth) 454
11. Ardrey 236
12. Montagu (Man) 117
13. Montagu (Man) 120
14. Montagu (Man) 121, 122
15. Mumford (Myth) 457
16. Bryan and London
17. Storr 11
18. Storr 24
19. Lewis and Towers pp. xi, xiii
20. Lewis and Towers 109, 110
21. Lewis and Towers 54, 55, 76
22. Lewis and Towers 90, 103
23. Sorokin (Reconstruction) 67-80
24. Morris 24
25. Montagu in a Los Angeles Times article (May 26, 1968), criticizing Lorenz, Ardrey and Morris, and maintaining the entire solution to the problem is proper treatment and education of the child during his first six years.
26. Montagu (Man) 95
27. Sorokin (Explorations) Chapter 2
28. Psychological Review V. LII, 109-12 (1945)
29. American Naturalist (1963) 354-56

30. Brown-Galanter (Hess) 224-46
31. Morris 164
32. The Center Magazine
33. Arizona Republic
34. Science V. 166, Number 3912 (December 19, 1969)
35. International Herald Tribune, May 22, 1970
36. Arizona Republic, June 3, 1970; International Herald Tribune, June 9, 1970, and *Time*, June 15, 1970
37. International Herald Tribune, September 5, 1970
38. Wall Street Journal, January 7, 1971
39. Arizona Republic, January 8, 1971
40. Time, January 11, 1971
41. Arizona Republic, March 7, 1971
42. Arizona Republic, November 12, 1971
43. Mumford (Myth) 272
44. The Center Magazine, October-November, 1969
45. Ramsey

chapter eleven

1. Sorokin (Reconstruction) 208
2. Allen 174
3. Allen 175-76
4. Sorokin (Ways and Power) 83, 84
5. Sorokin (Reconstruction) 196
6. Allen 164
7. Allen 165, 166
8. Sorokin (Ways and Power) 98, 99
9. Sorokin (Techniques) 3-5
10. Sorokin (Ways and Power) 100-03
11. Sorokin (Ways and Power) 104
12. Sorokin (Ways and Power) 125
13. Smith 182

14. Chaudhuri (Problems) 185, 186
15. Stace 338
16. Aurobindo (Mind) 98

chapter twelve

1. Sorokin (Ways and Power) 184-92
2. Sorokin (Ways and Power) 192-203
3. Sorokin (Ways and Power) 203, 204
4. Sorokin (Ways and Power) 459, etc.
5. Berkowitz 132
6. Tiryakian 271
7. Golding 86
8. Northrop (Meeting) 436
9. Taken from my notes of a television interview given by Krishnamurti on June 25, 1969.
10. Jung 79
11. Sorokin (Ways and Power) 226-30
12. Mumford (Transformation) Chapter entitled World Culture
13. Ardrey 345
14. Radhakrishnan
15. Allen 58
16. Mumford (The Conduct of Life) 105-07
17. Lings 16, 17
18. Lings 23, 24
19. Evans-Wentz (Milarepa) 20-24
20. Isherwood (Vedanta for Modern Man) 112

chapter thirteen

1. World Faiths, Number 56 (April, 1963) 3
2. The Center Magazine
3. Brown (Hindus) p. xxi

4. Creel 45
5. Fromm (Art of Loving) 46
6. Fromm (Revolution) 66, 67
7. Aurobindo, Sri (Human Unity) 317, 322-24
8. Chaudhuri and Spiegelberg 229, 318
9. Mumford (The Conduct of Life) 152
10. Ayres, Lew
11. Humphreys (Action) 108, 111
12. Fadiman in his *The Other Fellow*
13. Roof 203
14. Walker (Mind) 166
15. Gibran Book III, 31, 32
16. Aurelius 109, 168
17. Sharma 308, 309
18. Macquarrie 176
19. Mumford (Conduct of Life) 36
20. Whitman V. I, 146
21. Schneider V. I, 226, 229
22. Chaudhuri (Problems) 10
23. Radhakrishnan (Concept) 65
24. Lecky V. I, 239-41
25. Abdu, Haji
26. Radhakrishnan (Religion and Society) 48
27. Sir Thomas Browne, quoted at page 389 of Boethius
28. Nietzsche V. IV, 15
29. Excerpt from his final speech made at the Conservative Conference in 1954

chapter fourteen

1. Tiryakian 185-90
2. Tiryakian 190-97
3. Tiryakian 197-99
4. Tiryakian 199-205

5. Tiryakian 208-10
6. Tiryakian 212, 213
7. Sorokin (Ways and Power) 441
8. Sorokin (Techniques) 309
9. Sorokin (Techniques) 310-11
10. Sorokin (Techniques) 320-27
11. Sorokin (Ways and Power) 442, 448-51
12. Arnold, Emmy
13. Sorokin (Ways and Power) 442
14. Arnold (Salt and Light) 137
15. Sorokin (Ways and Power) 453

chapter fifteen

1. Allen 206
2. Sorokin (Altruistic Love) 6-79
3. Psychological Bulletin, 1969
4. Sorokin (Altruistic Love) 91-93
5. Sorokin (Altruistic Love) Parts 25-39
6. Sorokin (Techniques) 331-46
7. Sorokin (Techniques) 347-54
8. Sorokin (Techniques) 357-63
9. Sorokin (Techniques) 387-99
10. Sorokin (Techniques) 401-18
11. Sorokin (Techniques) 419-46

chapter sixteen

1. Sorokin (Reconstruction) 231-37
2. World Union V. 14, Number 3 (June, 1964)
3. An article by Huxley entitled *Man's Destiny*, in World-Union Goodwill for October, 1965
4. Wofford 157
5. Storr 114-21
6. Berkowitz 186, 231, 254-55

7. A summary by Liebert and Baron of a report for the Surgeon General's Advisory Committee on television and social behavior, made to the Convention of the American Psychological Association held in Washington in 1971.
8. Arizona Republic
9. Fromm (Revolution) 138, 139
10. Fromm (Revolution) 151-62
11. Psychology Today, April, 1970
12. Psychology Today, April, 1970
13. World Faiths, Number 67 (Autumn, 1966)
14. Hocking (Living Religions) 17
15. Buckle V. I, Part II, 376
16. Mumford, Lewis (The Conduct of Life) 116, 117
17. Northrop (Meeting) 484
18. Aiken 122, 123

chapter seventeen

1. Sorokin (Ways and Power) 287
2. Sorokin (Ways and Power) 288, 289
3. Sorokin (Ways and Power) 290
4. Sorokin (Ways and Power) 291-93
5. Sorokin (Ways and Power) 294-99
6. Sorokin (Ways and Power) 301
7. Sorokin (Ways and Power) 303
8. Sorokin (Ways and Power) 304
9. Sorokin (Ways and Power) 305, 306
10. Storr 29
11. Sorokin (Ways and Power) 307, 308
12. Sorokin (Ways and Power) 309-11
13. Sorokin (Ways and Power) 312, 313
14. Sorokin (Ways and Power) 316, 317
15. Sorokin (Ways and Power) 317, 318

16. Sorokin (Ways and Power) 321, 322
17. Sorokin (Ways and Power) 323-26
18. Sorokin (Ways and Power) 326-28
19. Sorokin (Techniques) 447-60
20. The source here is my notes taken from a PBS telecast on July 2, 1969
21. Sorokin (Ways and Power) 329-31
22. Schneider V. II 327
23. Sorokin (Ways and Power) 332
24. Fromm (Art of Loving) 118
25. Sorokin (Ways and Power) 332

chapter eighteen

1. Sorokin (Ways and Power) 332, 333
2. Sorokin (Ways and Power) 334-39
3. Sorokin (Ways and Power) 339-42
4. Mumford (The Conduct of Life) 253-56
5. Sorokin (Ways and Power) 342-44
6. Sorokin (Ways and Power) 344, 345
7. Sorokin (Ways and Power) 346
8. Storr 2, 3
9. Sorokin (Ways and Power) 347, 348
10. Sorokin (Ways and Power) 109, 482, 487
11. Allen 60
12. Sorokin (Ways and Power) 352
13. Sorokin (Ways and Power) 482, 483
14. Sorokin (Ways and Power) 359, 362, 368
15. Chaudhuri (Integral Yoga) 25, 26, 87
16. Sorokin (Techniques) 367-85
17. Schneider V. II, 27
18. Beard 71, 72
19. Carrel 29, 291, 292, 321

chapter nineteen

1. Sorokin (Reconstruction) 149: (Ways and Power) 205, 472
2. Sorokin (Ways and Power) 472
3. Sorokin (Ways and Power) 472
4. Storr 42, 46
5. Schneider V.I, 381
6. Schneider V.I, 382-91
7. Lewis and Towers 43
8. Berkowitz 300
9. Beard 184-86
10. Sorokin (Ways and Power) 444-48, as supplemented by a book published by the Society entitled *Children in Community*, and by observations made on my visit to the Colony mentioned in Chapter Fourteen.
11. Bettelheim 331, 332, 335-37
12. Saturday Review, September 20, 1969, 72, 73, 83-85
13. Psychology Today, September, 1969, 40-46
14. Bronfenbrenner, *Two Worlds of Childhood/U.S. and U.S.S.R.*
15. This and the following paragraph consist of gleanings acquired and observations made on a trip I made through the Balkans in 1970.
16. Sorokin (Reconstruction) 149-54
17. Magill V. II, 838
18. Dewey 95-97
19. Dewey 64
20. Radhakrishnan (Concept) 110
21. Durant (Philosophy) 526
22. Beard 369, 371
23. UNESCO Courier, February, 1970

chapter twenty
1. Isaacs 179, 180
2. Lewis and Towers 127
3. Sorokin (Ways and Power) 488, 489

bibliography

Subject only to several exceptions where the information was not available, all material utilized in the writing of this book is listed either below or in the text. Where there are several editions of the same work, the one listed here is usually that most available; however, except in a very few instances, all of the books listed below are in my personal library, which means that many of the editions listed are quite old and may be difficult to find.

Where any chapter note does not state the full name of the book in question, the word or words used are those appearing in parentheses after the full name of the book as it appears below; although the books are referred to by author in the chapter notes, the shorter title is sometimes used in the text and is used where more than one book by the same author appears in the bibliography; spelling is modernized, and as is customary, Roman numerals appearing in the chapter note references designate volume numbers and Arabic numerals designate page numbers.

A

Abdu, Haji. *The Kasidah*, Mt. Vernon: Peter Pauper, n.d.
Abhedananda, Swami. *Essay on Krishna*, Published only as a tract.

Adam, J. L. *Paul Tillich's Philosophy of Culture, Science and Religion*, New York: Harper & Row, 1965.

Aiken, H. D. *The Age of Ideology*, v. 5 in the 6-volume *Great Ages of Western Philosophy*. New York: George Braziller, 1957.

Alland, Alexander, Jr. *The Human Imperative*, New York: Columbia University Press, 1972.

Allen, Philip J., ed. *Pitirim A. Sorokin in Review*, Durham, North Carolina: Duke University Press, 1963.

Ardrey, Robert. *The Territorial Imperative*, New York: Atheneum, 1966.

Aristotle. *Selections*, New York: Charles Scribner's Sons, 1927.

Arnold, Eberhard. *Life and Writings*, (Life), Rifton, New York: Plough, 1964.

———. *Love and Marriage in the Spirit*, Rifton, New York, 1965.

———. *Salt and Light: Talks & Writings on the Sermon on the Mount*, Rifton, New York; Plough, 1967.

Arnold, Emmy. *Torches Together*, Rifton, New York: Plough, 1964.

Arnold, Sir Edwin. *The Book of Good Counsels*, Edinburgh: John Grant, 1924.

Aurelius, Marcus. *Meditations*, Baltimore: Penguin, 1964.

Aurobindo, Sri. *Essays on the Gita*, (Gita), New York: E. P. Dutton, 1950.

———. *The Ideal of Human Unity*, (Human Unity), New York: E. P. Dutton, 1950.

———. *The Life Divine*, (Life), New York: Greystone, 1949.

———. *The Mind of Light*, (Mind), New York: E. P. Dutton, 1953.

———. *The Synthesis of Yoga*, (Synthesis), New York: E. P. Dutton, 1950.

Au-Young, S. N. *Tao Teh King*, New York: March & Greenwood, 1938.

Ayres, Lew, *Altars of the East*, Garden City, New York: Doubleday, 1956.

B

Babcock, C. M., ed. *Wisdom of the Koran*, Mt. Vernon: Peter Pauper, 1966.

Bacon, Francis. *Essays*, New York: Carlton House, n.d.

Ballou, Robert O., ed. *The Bible of the World*, New York: Viking, 1939.

Barnett, L. D. *The Path of Light*, New York: Grove, 1959.

deBary, W. T., ed. *Introduction to Oriental Civilizations*, 3 v. New York: Columbia University Press, 1960.

Beard, Charles A. *Whither Mankind*, New York: Longmans Green, 1928.

Beck, L. Adams. *The Story of Oriental Philosophy*, New York: Cosmopolitan, 1928.

Berkowitz, Leonard. *Aggression: A Social Psychological Analysis*, New York: McGraw-Hill, 1962.

Bettelheim, Bruno. *The Children of the Dream*, London: Collier-Macmillan, 1969.

Boethius. *The Consolation of Philosophy*, New York: Random House, Modern Library, 1943.

Brown, Brian. *The Wisdom of the Chinese*, (Chinese), New York: Garden City, 1939.

———. *The Wisdom of the Hindus*, (Hindus), New York: Garden City, 1938.

Brown, Galanter, Hess, Mandler, eds. *New Directions in Psychology*, New York: Holt, Rinehart & Winston, 1962.
Brown, Peter. *Augustine of Hippo*, London : Faber & Faber, 1967.
Browne, Lewis. *This Believing World*, New York: Macmillan, 1930.
Bryan, James H. and London, Perry. *The Psychology of Altruism*. (This work was read while still in manuscript, thanks to the kindness of the authors).
Buber, Martin. *I and Thou*, New York: Charles Scribner's Sons, 1958.
———. *The Knowledge of Man*, (Knowledge), New York: Harper & Row, 1965.
Buchanan, Scott. *Embers of the World*, Santa Barbara: Center for The Study of Democratic Institutions, 1970.
Buck, Pearl, trans. *All Men Are Brothers*, New York: Grosset & Dunlap, 1939.
Buckle, Henry T. *History of Civilization in England*, 2 v., each in two parts. New York: Hearst's International Library, 1913.
Byles, Marie. *Journey into Burmese Silence*, London: Allen & Unwin, 1962.
———. *Paths to Inner Calm*, London: Allen & Unwin, 1965.
Bynner, W., trans. *The Way of Life According to Laotzu*, New York: John Day, 1944.

C

Carlyle, Thomas. *On Heroes, Hero-Worship and the Heroic in History*, London: Oxford University Press, 1965.

Carrel, Alexis. *Man the Unknown*, New York: Harper, 1939.
Center Magazine, The
Chang, Carsun. *Development of Neo-Confucian Thought*, New York: Bookman, 1957.
Chaudhuri, Haridas. *Integral Yoga*, London: Allen & Unwin, 1965.
―――. *Mastering the Problems of Living*, (Problems), New York: Citadel, 1968.
―――. *Sri Aurobindo: The Prophet of Life Divine*, (Prophet), Calcutta: Sri Aurobindo Pathamandir, 1951.
――― and Spiegelberg, eds. *The Integral Philosophy of Sri Aurobindo*, London: Allen & Unwin, 1960.
Clark, W. E. *Indian Conceptions of Immortality*, Cambridge: Harvard University Press, 1934.
Clarke, Humphrey. *Message of Milarepa*, London: John Murray, 1958.
Conze, Edward. *Buddhism: Its Essence and Development*, New York: Philosophical Library, n.d.
Conze, Edward, ed. *Buddhist Texts Through the Ages*, New York: Philosophical Library, 1954.
Conze, Edward, trans. and ed. *Buddhist Wisdom Books*, London: Allen & Unwin, 1958.
Creel, H. G. *Chinese Thought from Confucius to Mao Tse-Tung*, Chicago: University of Chicago Press, 1953.
Cunningham, G. W. *Problems of Philosophy*, New York: Holt, 1924.

D

DeBit, Ralph M. *Universal Will*, Los Angeles: Sacred Science, 1930.

DeChardin, Pierre T. *Hymn of the Universe*, London: Collins, 1965.
Dewey, John. *Human Nature and Conduct*, New York: Carlton House, 1922.
Dostoevski, Fedor. *The Brothers Karamazov*, (Brothers), New York: Random House, Modern Library, 1929.
———. *The Idiot*, (Idiot), New York: Random House, Modern Library, 1942.
Dumoulin, Heinrich. *A History of Zen Buddhism*, New York: Pantheon, 1963.
Durant, Will. *The Age of Faith*, (Faith), New York: Simon & Schuster, 1950.
———. *The Story of Philosophy*, (Philosophy), New York: Simon & Schuster, 1926.

E

Eckermann, J. P. *Works of Goethe*, New York: Classic Publishing Co., 1933.
Edgerton, Franklin. *The Bhagavad-Gita*, 2 v., Cambridge: Harvard University Press, 1952.
Eliade, Mircea, Yoga: Immortality and Freedom, New York: Pantheon, 1958.
Eliot, Sir Charles. *Hinduism and Buddhism*, 3 v., New York: Barnes & Noble, 1954.
Elwell-Sutton. *Persian Proverbs*, London: John Murray, 1954.
Emerson, R. W. *The Portable Emerson*, New York: Viking, 1965.
Encyclopedia of the Social Sciences, 8 v. New York: Macmillan, n.d.
Epictetus. *Discourses*, Mt. Vernon: Peter Pauper, n.d.
Evans-Wentz, W. Y. *The Tibetan Book of the Great*

Liberation, (Liberation), London: Oxford University Press, 1954.

———. *Tibet's Great Yogi Milarepa*, (Milarepa), London: Oxford University Press, 1951.

F

Ferm, Vergilius. *An Encyclopedia of Religion*, (Religion), New York: Philosophical Library, 1945.

———. *A History of Philosophical Systems*, (Systems), New York: Philosophical Library, 1950.

Fromm, Erich. *The Art of Loving*, (Loving), New York: Harper, 1956.

———. *The Revolution of Hope*, (Revolution), New York: Harper & Row, 1968.

———. *You Shall Be As Gods*, (Gods), London: Jonathan Cape, 1967.

Fung, Yu-Lan. *History of Chinese Philosophy*, (History), 2 v. London: Allen & Unwin, 1937 and Princeton: Princeton University Press, 1953.

———. *The Spirit of Chinese Philosophy*, (Spirit), London: Routledge & Kegan Paul, 1962.

G

Gibran, Kahlil. *A Second Treasury*, New York: Citadel, 1962.

Giles, Herbert, trans. *Chuang Tzu*, London: Allen & Unwin, 1961.

Golding, William. *The Hot Gates*, London: Faber & Faber, 1965.

Govinda, Lama Anagarika. *Foundations of Tibetan Mysticism*, London: Rider, 1959.

Gowen, H. H. *Outline History of Japan*, New York: Appleton, 1927.
Great Ages of Western Philosophy, 6 v., New York: George Braziller, 1957.
Griffis, W. E. *The Religions of Japan*, New York: Charles Scribner's Sons, 1907.

H

Hart, H. H., trans. *Seven Hundred Chinese Proverbs*, London: Oxford University Press, 1945.
Hegel, G. W. F. *Philosophy of History*, New York: Willey, 1900.
Herbert, Edward. *A Taoist Notebook*, London: John Murray, 1955.
Hocking, W. E. *Living Religions and a World Faith*, (Living Religions), London: Allen & Unwin, 1940.
———. *The Meaning of God in Human Experience* (Meaning), New Haven: Yale University Press, 1912.
———. *Types of Philosophy*, (Types), New York: Charles Scribner, 1929.
Hooke, S. H. *Babylonian and Assyrian Religion*, Oxford: Blackwell, 1962.
Hsü, L. S. *The Political Philosophy of Confucianism*, London: Routledge & Sons, 1932.
Hubben, William. *Dostoevsky, Kierkegaard, Nietzsche, and Kafka*, New York: Collier 1966.
Humphreys, Christmas. *Concentration and Meditation*, (Concentration), London: John M. Watkins, 1959.
———. *The Way of Action*, (Action), London: Allen & Unwin, 1960.
Huxley, Aldous. *The Perennial Philosophy*, New York: Harper, 1945.

I

Isaacs, Alan. *The Survival of God in the Scientific Age*, London: Penguin, 1966.

Isherwood, Christopher, ed. *Vedanta for Modern Man*, (Modern Man), New York: Harper, 1951.

———, ed. *Vedanta for the Western World*, (Western World), Hollywood: Marcel Rodd, 1945.

J

James, William. *The Varieties of Religious Experience*, New York: Collier, 1961.

Jennings, J. G. *The Vedantic Buddhism of the Buddha*, London: Oxford University Press, 1947.

Joad, C. E. M. *Philosophy and Ethics*, London: International University Society, 1958.

Jones, R. D. *Erasmus and Luther*, London: Oxford University Press, 1968.

Jung, C. G. *Psychology and Religion: West and East*, New York: Pantheon, 1958.

K

Kemp, J. *The Philosophy of Kant*, London: Oxford University Press, 1968.

Knox, G. W. *Development of Religion in Japan*, New York: G. P. Putnam, 1907.

Korzybski, Alfred. *Science and Sanity*, Lancaster: International Non-Aristotelian Library, 1941.

Krishnamurti, J. *Commentaries on Living*, New York: Harper, 1956.

L

Latourette, K. S. *The Chinese: Their History and Culture*, New York: Macmillan, 1949.

Leach, Maria, ed. *Dictionary of Folklore, Mythology and Legend*, 2 v., New York: Funk & Wagnalls, 1949.
Leary, Timothy. *The Psychedelic Experience*, New York: University Books, 1964.
Lecky, W. E. H. *History of European Morals*, 2 v. New York: Appleton, 1929.
Legge, James. *The Religions of China*, London: Hodder & Stoughton, 1880.
Lewis, John, and Towers, Bernard. *Naked Ape or Homo Sapiens?*, London: Garnstone Press, 1969.
Lin, Yutang, ed. *The Wisdom of China and India*, New York: Random House, 1942.
Lings, M. *Ancient Beliefs and Modern Superstitions*, London: Perennial, 1964.
Lorenz, Konrad. *On Aggression*, New York: Harcourt, Brace & World, 1963.

M

Macaulay and Berkowitz, eds. *Altruism and Helping Behavior*, New York: Academic Press, 1970.
MacGregor, Geddes. *Introduction to Religious Philosophy*, New York: St. Martin's Press, 1964.
Macquarrie, John. *Twentieth Century Religious Thought*, London: Student Christian Movement Press, 1903.
Magill, Frank N. *Masterpieces of World Philosophy in Summary Form*, 2 v., New York: Salem Press, 1961.
Maimonides, Moses. *The Guide for the Perplexed*, London: Routledge & Sons, 1947.
May, Rollo. *Love and Will*, New York: W. W. Norton, 1969.
Merton, Thomas. *Mystics and Zen Masters*, New York: Farrar, Straus & Giroux, 1967.

Montagu, M. F. Ashley. *Man and Aggression*, (Aggression), London: Oxford University Press, 1968.
———. *Man, His First Two Million Years*, (Man), New York: Columbia University Press, 1969.
Moore, C. A., ed. *Philosophy - East and West*, Princeton: Princeton University Press, 1946.
Morris, Desmond. *The Human Zoo*, New York: McGraw-Hill, 1969.
Muirhead, J. H. *Coleridge as Philosopher*, London: Allen & Unwin, 1954.
Mumford, Lewis. *The Conduct of Life*, London: Secker & Warburg, 1952.
———. *The Myth of the Machine*, (Myth) (also titled *The Pentagon of Power*), New York: Harcourt Brace Jovanovich, 1970.
———. *The Transformation of Man*, (Transformation), New York: Macmillan, 1956.

N

New English Bible, The, Oxford University Press and Cambridge University Press, 1970.
New York Times
Nichols, William. *Words to Live By*, New York: Simon and Schuster, 1959.
Nietzsche, Friedrich. *The Works of Nietzsche*, New York: Tudor, 1931.
Nikhilananda, Swami. *Essence of Hinduism*, Boston: Beacon Press, 1948.
Northrop, F. S. C. *The Logic of the Sciences and the Humanities*, (Logic), New York: Macmillan, 1947.
———. *The Meeting of East and West*, (Meeting), New York: Macmillan, 1946.
———. *The Taming of the Nations*, (Nations), New York: Macmillan, 1952.

O

Ouspensky, P. D. *A New Model of the Universe*, (New Model), London: Routledge & Kegan Paul, 1960.
———. *In Search of the Miraculous*, (Search), New York: Harcourt Brace, 1949.

P and Q

Parrinder, E. G. *A Book of World Religions*, London: Hulton Educational Publications, 1965.
Patanjali. *The Yoga Aphorisms of Patanjali*, London: Allen & Unwin, 1960.
Pegis, A. C., ed. *The Wisdom of Catholicism*, New York: Random House, 1949.
Peters, Fritz, *Gurdjieff Remembered*, London: Victor Gollancz, 1965.
Prabhavananda and Isherwood, Christopher, trans. and eds. *How to Know God*, London: Allen & Unwin, 1960.

R

Radhakrishnan, Sarvepalli. *East and West*, London: Allen & Unwin, 1955.
———. *The Recovery of Faith*, (Recovery), New York: Humanities Press, 1961.
———. *Religion and Society*, (Religion), London: Allen & Unwin, 1947.
Radhakrishnan, Sarvepalli and P. T. Raju, eds. *The Concept of Man*, (Concept), London: Allen & Unwin, 1966.
Ramsey, Paul. *Fabricated Man: The Ethics of Genetic Control*, New Haven: Yale University Press, 1970.
Reischauer, E. O. and Yamagiwa, J. K. *Translations from Early Japanese Literature*, Cambridge: Harvard University Press, 1951.

bibliography 297

Riley, Woodbridge. *Men and Morals*, New York: Frederick Ungar, 1960.
Roof, Simon. *Journeys on the Razor-Edged Path*, New York: Hodder & Stoughton, 1960.
Ross, Nancy W. *Three Ways of Asian Wisdom*, New York: Simon & Schuster, 1966.
Russell, Bertrand. *A History of Western Philosophy*, New York: Simon & Schuster, 1945.

S

Sachar, Abram L. *A History of the Jews*, New York: Alfred A. Knopf, 1967.
Sakharov, Andrei. *Progress, Coexistence and Intellectual Freedom*, New York: W. W. Norton, 1968.
Sansom, G. B. *Japan: A Short Cultural History*, New York: Appleton-Century-Crofts, 1943.
Schneider, Isidor. *The World of Love*, 2 v., New York: George Braziller, 1964.
Schopenhauer, Arthur. *Philosophy of Schopenhauer*, New York: Tudor, 1933.
Schroeder, Eric. *Muhammads People: A Tale by Anthology*, Portland, Maine: Bond Wheelwright Co., 1955.
Schweitzer, Albert. *An Anthology*, Joy, C. R., ed., Boston: Beacon Press, 1947.
Seneca. *The Stoic Philosophy of Seneca*, Garden City, New York: Doubleday, 1958.
Sharma, I. C. *Ethical Philosophies of India*, London: Allen & Unwin, 1965.
Skinner, B. F. *Beyond Freedom and Dignity*, New York: Alfred A. Knopf, 1971.
Skinner, B. F. *Beyond Freedom and Dignity*, New York: Alfred A. Knopf, 1971.
Smith, Bradford. *Meditation: The Inward Art*, London: Allen & Unwin, 1964.

Smock, Ruth. Title of Article, *World Faiths*, Spring-Summer, 1969.

Stace, W. T. *Mysticism and Philosophy*, Philadelphia: J. B. Lippincott, 1960.

Steinilber-Oberlin, E. *The Buddhist Sects of Japan*, London: Allen & Unwin, 1938.

Storr, Anthony. *Human Aggression*, New York: Atheneum, 1968.

Sorokin, P. T. *A Long Journey*, New Haven: College & University Press, 1963.

———. *Altruistic Love*, Boston: Beacon Press, 1950.

———. *Explorations in Altruistic Love and Behavior: A Symposium*, (Explorations), Boston: Beacon Press, 1950.

———. *Leaves From a Russian Diary*, Boston: Beacon Press, 1950.

———. *Social and Cultural Dynamics*, (Dynamics), Boston: Porter Sargent, 1957.

———. *Social Philosophies of an Age of Crisis*, (Social Philosophies), Boston: Beacon Press, 1951.

———. *Sociology of My Mental Life*, in Philip J. Allen, ed. *Pitirim A. Sorokin in Review*, Durham, North Carolina: Duke University Press, 1963.

———. *S.O.S.: The Meaning of Our Crisis* 1, (S.O.S.), Boston: Beacon Press, 1951.

———. *The Reconstruction of Humanity*, (Reconstruction), Boston: Beacon Press, 1948.

———. *The Ways and Power of Love*, (Ways and Power), Boston: Beacon Press, 1954.

———. *Forms and Techniques of Altruistic and Spiritual Growth*, (Techniques), Boston: Beacon Press, 1954.

Suzuki, D. T. *The Lankavatara Sutra*, London: Routledge & Kegan Paul, 1956.

———. *Mysticism: Christian and Buddhist*, New York: Harper & Brothers, 1957.
———. *The Zen Doctrine of No-Mind*, London: Rider, 1949.
Suzuki, Fromm and De Martino. *Zen Buddhism and Psychoanalysis*, London: Allen & Unwin, 1960.

T

Tagore, Rabindranath. *The Religion of Man*, (Religion), London: Allen & Unwin, 1961.
Taylor, G. R. *The Biological Time Bomb*, New York: World Publishing Co., 1968.
Thomsen, Harry. *The New Religions of Japan*, Tokyo: Charles E. Tuttle, 1963.
Tiryakian, Edward A., ed. *Sociological Theory, Values and Sociocultural Change*, New York: Harper & Row, 1967.
Tomlin, E. W. F. *The Eastern Philosophers, An Introduction*, London: Radius Book/Hutchinson, 1968.
Toynbee, Arnold. *A Study of History*, New York: Oxford University Press, 1947.
Tsu Chi. *A Short History of Chinese Civilization*, London: Victor Gollancz, 1942.

U and V

Vivekananda, Swami. *Karma-Yoga and Bhakti-Yoga*, New York: Ramakrichna-Vivekanando Center, 1949.

W

Waley, Arthur. *The Way and Its Power*, London: Allen & Unwin, 1949.

———. *Three Ways of Thought in Ancient China*, London: Allen & Unwin, 1946.
Walker, Kenneth. *A Study of Gurdjieff's Teaching*, London: Jonathan Cape, 1957.
———. *The Conscious Mind*, (Mind), London: Rider, 1962.
Waller and De Mauny, eds. *Middle East Anthology*, London: Lindsay Drummond, 1946.
Watts, Alan W. *The Book*, New York: Collier, 1966.
———. *Psychotherapy East and West*, (Psychotherapy), New York: Ballantine, 1970.
Wei Wu Wei. *Why Lazarus Laughed*, London: Routledge & Kegan Paul, 1960.
Werblowsky and Wigoder. *Encyclopedia of Jewish Religion*, New York: Holt, Rinehart & Winston, 1966.
Westwood, H. *There is a Psychic World*, New York: Crown, 1949.
Wheeler, P. *The Sacred Scriptures of the Japanese*, New York: Henry Schuman, 1952.
Whitehead, Henry. *The Village Gods of South India*, Calcutta: Association Press, 1921.
Whitman, Walt. *Complete Poetry and Prose*, 2 v., New York: Pellegrini & Cudahy, 1948.
Wofford, Harris, ed. *Embers of the World*, Santa Barbara: Center for the Study of Democratic Institutions, 1970.

World Faiths

Wright, Arthur F., ed. *Studies in Chinese Thought*, Chicago: University of Chicago Press, 1953.

X and Y

Yogananda, Paramhansa. *Autobiography of a Yogi*, New York: The Philosophical Library, 1946.

Z

Zaehner, R.C. *The Dawn and Twilight of Zoroastrianism*, London: Weidenfeld and Nicholson, 1961.

Zimmerman, Carle. *Sorokin, the World's Greatest Sociologist*, Saskatoon: University of Saskatchewan, 1968.

index

Abdu, Haji, 178
Abou Ben Adhem, 67
Adler, Alfred, 117
Agape, 37, 157
Aggression in Man
 aggression in children, 124
 animals in, 116, 119
 definitions, 115, 118
 innate in man, 115, 121, 124-128
 nature, 118, 119
 relationship with sexual instinct, 125
 semantic problem, 121
 TLS, 123
Agramonte, Roberto, 88
Alexandria Quartet, The, 86
Alland, Alexander, Jr., 124
All Men Are Brothers, 177
Allport, Gordon, 236
Altruism
 Christian, 107, 108, 190
 forms and gradations of, 94, 95, 108
 nature and definitions of, 89-95, 228

 somatic biological factors, 128, 140, 157-159
Altruist, The, 91
Altruistic Review, The, 91
Altruria, 91
American Academy of Asian Studies, 54
American Academy of Arts and Sciences, 17
American Association for the Advancement of Science, 138
American Psychological Association, 209
American Sociological Association, 19, 20
Amish, the, 182, 183, 185, 189n
Anabaptists, 185
Antiphon, 177
Ardrey, Robert, 120, 123, 124, 126, 132, 165
Arhants, 168
Aristotle, 84, 152, 176, 258
Arnold, Eberhard, 37, 60, 187, 188
Arnold, Eberhard, C. H., 249
Arnold, Emmy, 187
Asoka, 83, 84

303

Associates and group memberships, effects and importance of in developing one's altruism, 148, 161-163
Atman, 53
Atomic and nuclear warfare (see Introduction), 20
Augustine, Saint, 108, 111
Aurelius, Marcus, 74, 75, 102, 106, 175
Aurobindo, Sri, 26, 71, 105, 155, 171
Austria, 19
Avatars and great leaders
   Arhants, 168
   rise of in time of great need, 164, 166-168
Ayres, Lew, 173

Babson, Roger, 109
Bakwin, Harry and Ruth, 244
Balkans, the, 255
Baratynskaya, Elena, 15
Barber, B., 20
Baüls, the, 38
Beadle, George W., 134
Beard, Charles A., 7
Belgian Royal Academy, 19
Bentham, Jeremy, 98, 105
Berdyaev, Nikolai, 2
Berkowitz, Leonard, 116, 119, 160, 208, 209, 220, 246
Bernard of Clairvaux, Saint, 108
Bettelheim, Bruno, 251, 253, 254
Bhagavadgita, The, 71
Bhakti Yoga, 234, 235

Boethius, 47, 179
Bolsheviks, 15
Bowlby, John, 244
Bradley, Francis, 54
Brahman, 71
Brain surgery and selective stimulation, effects of, 136, 137
Brave New World, 139
Breakfast in Hollywood, 194
Breneman, Tom, 194
Bronfenbrenner, Urie, 251, 254, 255
Brosse, Therese, 236
Brothers Karamazov, The, 27, 46
Brothers, Society of (Bruderhof), 184, 187-189
Browne, Sir Thomas, 104, 179
Bruderhof (see Brothers, Society of)
Bryan, James H., 124
Bryan, William Jennings, 260
Buber, Martin, 49, 50n
Buchanan, Scott, 208
Budd, Louis J., 90, 91
Buddha, 62, 165, 167
Buddhism, 41, 59, 62, 66, 72, 83, 171, 172, 234
Bulgaria, 255, 256
Butler's *Lives of the Saints*, 18, 196

Campbell, D. T., 130
Carlyle, Thomas, 24
Carnegie Corporation, 261
Carrel, Alexis, 238
Center for the Study of Demo-

index **305**

cratic Institutions at Santa Barbara, 139
Center Magazine, The, 258
Chaudhuri, Haridas, 40, 54, 154, 177, 235
Chicago Magazine, 138
Chicago, University of, 133
Child Buyer, The, 139
Christian Catholic saints, factors in their making, 194, 196, 198
Christianity, 4, 14, 32, 37, 40, 59-62, 66, 67, 91, 92, 107, 109, 171, 185, 188, 211, 213
Chu, King of, 64
Churchill, Winston, 180
Cicero, Marcus T., 178
Cloning, 135
Coleridge, Samuel, 71
Community Playthings, 188
Competition, merits and demerits, 4
Comte, Auguste, 91, 213, 214
Confucius and Confucianism, 59, 63-65, 101, 171
Consciousness, the four levels of, 147
Constantine, Emperor, 184
Cousins, Norman, 76
Cro-Magnon man, 127
Crook, J. H., 245
Crusoe, Robinson, 173
Cunningham, G. W., 99, 100, 102
Cylert, 138

Danilevsky, Nikolai, 2
Dartmouth College, 31

Darwin, Charles, 81, 130
"Darwinian fitness," 131
De Bit, Ralph, 36
De Chardin, Pierre T., 51, 174
De Courcy, Reginald (*see* Introduction)
Delgado, José, 136
Democracy, essentials for, 23-26
Descartes, René, 152
Dewey, John, 91, 257, 258
Dobzhansky, T., 127
Donne, John, 75
Dostoevski, Fyodor, 27, 32, 46, 51, 87
Durant, Will, 70, 259
Durell, Lawrence, 86, 87
Dwarfism, 189n

Eaton, Joseph W., 186
Eckhart, Meister J., 155
Economic systems as factor for world peace, 29
Eddington, A. S., 151
Edison, Thomas, 86
Ego-centered altruism
  how created, 217-233
  merits of for majority of people, 215, 216
Einstein, Albert, 86
El Cerrito study, 183
Emerson, Ralph Waldo, 7, 84, 258
Empathy, experiment re its necessity to altruism, 201
Empedocles, 45, 47, 48
Empiricist theory of morals, 98
Encounter groups, 224

Energies of Men, 86
Energism, 100
Engels, Friedrich, 14, 206
England, 170, 187
Epictetus, 178
Epicures, 97
Eros, 37, 38
Esalen Institute, 224
Ethology, 113, 114, 126
Etzioni, Amitai, 137
Evans-Wentz, W. Y., 72, 168

Factory workers, effects of altruistic work program on, 206, 207
Fadiman, Clifton, 173
Family, the, and child education, child rearing in kibbutzim, 251-254
  child rearing in Russia and Bulgaria, 254-256
  child rearing in the Society of Brothers, 248-251
  importance in creating altruistic persons, 200, 241-248
  principles to be followed, 242-248
  significance of the baby's skin, 246
Family, the, as a factor in altruistic growth, 196
Farmington, Pennsylvania, 187
Fedorov, N. F., 46, 220
Fenelon, Francois, 225
Fichte, Johann, 152
Fiske, John, 91

Ford, Joseph, 96, 166, 232
Fortune, 245n
Foster, Bruce, 211
Francis of Assisi, Saint, 96
Fretz, J. W., 185
Freud, Anna, 118
Freud, Sigmund, 40, 41, 81, 117, 118, 147
Friends (Quakers), 210
Fromm, Erich *(see* Introduction), 40, 41, 49, 50, 171, 206, 207, 209, 210
Fuji, Mt., 67

Gabor, Dennis, 224
Galileo, 152
Gandhi, Mahatma, 26, 46, 167, 228, 230
Garden of Eden, 242
Genes and their manipulation, 132-141, 210
George Washington University, 138
Germany, 187
Gibran, Kahlil, 174
Glock, Charles, 211
Godel, Roger, 149, 150
Goethe, Johann, 76, 230
Golden Rule, the, 59, 61, 195
Golding, William, 126, 162
Good deeds as a factor in creating altruism, 194, 195, 201-203
Good neighbors, factors in their making, 194, 195, 201-203
Govinda, Lama, 73
Grand Inquisitor, The, 27

index **307**

Great masters of creative altruism, study of, 143
Green, Harold B., 138
Group cooperation tendency, extent to which it may be innate, 130-132
Group loyalty, bad effects of if overdone, 233

Haldane, John, 132
Hamilton, W. D., 132
Harlow, Harry, 246
Harrison, George, 170
Harvard Research Center in Creative Altruism (*see* Introduction), 9, 17, 88, 194, 202
Harvard University (*see* Introduction), 16, 17, 75, 81, 131, 194, 198, 209
Hebb, D. O., 130
Hedonism, 100
Helvetius, Claude, 106
Hersey, John, 139
Heschel, A. J., 53
Hess, Eckhard, 114, 133
Hinduism, 53, 59, 62, 70, 72, 168, 234
Hippies, 42, 60, 61
Hitler, Adolph, 184
Hocking, William, 75, 103, 212
Holbach, Paul d', 106
Holbrook, David, 125
Holmes, S. J., 106, 132
Howells, William D., 91
Hui Shi, 73

Hume, David, 153
Humphries, Christmas, 173
Hunt, Leigh, 67
Hutchins, Robert, 258
Hutterite brotherhoods, 184-188, 251, 253
Huxley, Aldous, 138, 139, 224
Huxley, Julian, 127, 207
Hyde, R. W., 201

Idealistic cultures, 3
Ideational cultures, 3
Identification with others, 38, 190
Idiot, The, 32
Illinois, University of, 15
"Imperatives," categorical and hypothetical (Kant), 103
Imprinting, 133, 134
Inbreeding, 189n
India, 5, 25, 62, 70, 72, 83, 101, 102, 149, 152, 168
Indonesia, 19
Indra's Net, 72
Inductive theory of morals, 97
Inquisition, the, 27
International corporations, 27
Intuitional or Intuitive theory of morals, 98-101, 110
Iowa State Penitentiary and Training Schools, 199, 200, 223
Isaacs, Alan, 106, 107, 265
Isherwood, Christopher, 41
Israel, 254

Jacoby, Neil, 27

308 LOVE, ALTRUISM, AND WORLD CRISIS

Jainism, 59
James, William, 86, 146
Janissaries, 139
Japan, religions in, 66, 67, 105
Jen, 63, 64, 65, 74
Jesus Christ, 27, 28, 32, 59-62, 108, 154, 165, 167, 184
Johns Hopkins, 189n
Jones, Ernest, 117
Judaism and Jews, 59, 61, 171
Jung, C. G., 144, 163
Justine (Durell novel), 87

Kandler, Harriet, 201
K'ang Yu-Wei, 64, 65
Kant, Immanuel, 4, 49, 54, 99, 101-103, 153, 225
Kaplan, B., 186
Karma Yoga, 234
Kegon Buddhism, 72
Kepler, Johann, 152
Kerensky, Alexander, 15
Khorana, H. G., 137
Khrushchev, Nikita, 18
Kibbutzim in Israel, 251-254
Kierkegaard, Søren, 177
Klein, Melanie, 231
Kojiki, the, 105
Komi peasants, 13, 18
Koran, The, 61, 62
Koussevitzky, Serge, 16
Krahn, Cornelius, 185
Krebs, Dennis, 130, 159, 196
Kreider, Robert, 185
Krishna, 62
Krishnamurti, J., 163

Kroeber, Alfred, 2

La Mettrie, Julien de, 106
Lao-Tse, 63
La Rochefoucauld, Francois, 106
Latin-American ethic, contrast with Western, 31
Law and ethics, relationship between, 30
Law, international, 31
  essential factors of, 200
League of Nations, 25
Lecky, William, 97, 98, 177
Lederberg, Joshua, 137
Lee, Robert E., 160
Leeds, Ruth, 92, 93
Legalism, 63
Leibnitz, Gottfried, 152
Lenin, Vladimir Ilyich, 15, 184
Leningrad, University of, 19
Lewis, John, 125-128, 246, 265
Liberty, 189n
Lilly, Eli (*see* Introduction), 17
Lilly Endowment (foundation) (*see* Introduction), 17
Lincoln, Abraham, 160
Littlechap (in the Broadway musical) (*see* Introduction)
Lives of the Saints, 18, 196
Locke, John, and Lockean philosophy, 31
Loeb, Leo, 131
London, Perry, 124
London Times Literary Supplement, 123
Longley, Alcander, 91

Loomis, Charles, 16, 20, 182-184
Lord of the Flies, 126
Lorenz, Konrad, 119, 123, 124, 126, 132
Los Angeles Times, 124
Love:
  aspects of, 45-55, 79, 88
  dimensions of, 55-57
  effect on length of life, 81, 82, 85
  as energy, 45-48, 79-88
  nature and definitions of, (*see* Introduction), 9, 35-39, 41, 60, 86
Loyola, Saint Ignatius, 217, 218
Lucan, M., 178
Lucis Trust, 263
Lucretius, 54
Ludwig, Emil, 247
Lunden, W. A., 199, 200, 223
Luria, Salvadore E., 136
Luther, Martin, 108

Macaulay, Thomas B., 106
Mahayana Buddhism, 62
Malalasekera, G. P., 212
Mandeville, Bernard de, 106
Mandler, Jean, 40, 110, 203
Marlborough, Duchess of, 125
Martin, Everett Dean, 259, 260
Marx, Karl, and Marxism, 2, 14, 31, 81, 127, 184, 206
Masaryk, Jan, 15
Matsya Purana, 5
"Maxwell's Doctrine," 165
Mayan handball competition, 5

McConnell, James W., 219
Meander, 178
Media, mass, effects on listeners, readers and viewers, particularly children, 208, 209
Meditation as a technique, 144
Mencius, 65, 73, 100, 101
Menninger, Karl, 237
Mennonites, 184-186, 251
Merejkovsky, Dmitri, 2
Merton, Robert K., 20, 64
Mexico, 5, 31
Michigan State University, 20
Midlarsky, Elizabeth, 92
Milarepa, 168
Minnesota, University of, 15
Mohammed and Mohammedanism (Moslemism and Islam), 59, 61, 62, 66, 165, 167, 173, 213
Mohism, 63
Montagu, M. F. Ashley, 120-124, 130, 131, 244, 246
Montaigne, Michel, 213
Moore, Mary, 193
Morals, intuitive and utilitarian theories of, 97-106
Moreno, J. L., 203, 204
Morris, Desmond, 126, 130, 132, 133
Moses, 61
Mumford, Lewis, 87, 119, 124, 138, 139, 164, 165, 167, 172, 229

Nanak, 171

Narcissism, 41
Nazi persecution, 187
Neibuhr, Reinhold, 51
Neo-Confucianism, 74
Netherlands, the, 185
New English Bible, The, 90
New Model of the Universe, The, 6
Newton, Isaac, 152
New York Times, 28
Nietzsche, Friedrich, 172, 179
1984, 139
Norfolk, Connecticut, 187
Northrop, F. S. C., 2, 24, 31, 163, 200, 213
Nygren, Anders, 37, 38

Orozco, José, 31
Orwell, George, 138, 139
Ouspensky, P. D., 6, 76

Palmer, George, 38
Paraguay, 184, 187
Parsons, Talcott, 3, 184
Pascal, Blaise, 152
PAS model, 181-183
Patanjali, 53
Paul, Saint, 36, 184
Peirce, Charles, 7, 41, 176
Peru, 31, 189
Peter and Paul, Fortress of, 15
Petronius, Arbiter, 106
Philia, 37
Philosophes, the, 214
Plato, 39, 84
"Polarization" in times of crisis, 164-166

Prabhavananda, Swami, 53
Princeton University, 136
Problems of Christianity, The, 213
Psycho-dramatic techniques for creating altruism, 203
Psychological Review, The, 106
Psychology Today, 211, 219

Quakers, 224
Quantum Mechanics, 150, 151
Quinley, Harold, 211

Rabkin, Leslie and Karen, 251, 254
Radcliffe College, 81, 198
Radhakrishnan, Sarvepalli, 25, 26, 166, 179
Raja Yoga, 234, 235
Ramsey, Paul, 140
Ravin, Arnold, 138
Religio Medici, 104
Religion, established, reasons for failure to effect its purpose, 30, 211-214
Riad (Mohammedan sect), 8
Ribble, Margaret, 244
Rifton, New York, 187
Riley, Mathilda, 193
Rokeach, Milton, 211
Roof, Simons, 174
Royce, Josiah, 213
Russell, Bertrand, 131, 237, 238, 259
Russia (*see* Introduction), 13, 254, 255
Ruysbroeck, Jan, 155

Saint Petersburg, University of, 14
Sakharov, Andrei, 28, 29
  his plan for world peace, 29
Sales, St. Francis de, 108
Sartre, Jean Paul, 75
Saskatchewan, University of, 19
Satan, 28
Sattva, 5
Saturday Review, 76
Sawyer, Jack, 93
Sawyer, Tom (Mark Twain hero), 16
Schelling, Friedrich, 152
Schneider, Isidor, 36, 37, 42
Schools, utility in creating altruism, 256-261
Schopenhauer, Arthur, 40, 70
Schubart, Walter, 2
Schweitzer, Albert, 2
Science, 136
Self-love, 41, 42
Seneca, 178, 214
Sensate cultures, 3
Sermon on the Mount, 14, 50, 59, 60, 67, 90, 95, 108, 188, 190
Sharma, I. C., 101
Shaw, Bernard, 173
Shintoism, 66, 67
Sidgwick, Henry, 98, 99
Sikh, religion, 171
Simons, Menno, 185
Smith, Bradford, 154
Society for Creative Study of Civilizations, 19
Socioconscious, the, its importance and use, 215

Solovyev, V., 46, 47, 49
Sorokin, Elena, 266
Sorokin, Pitirim (Since Sorokin's name appears on most pages of this book, references to him are not indexed)
South Vietnamese child, 256
Soviet Academy of Sciences, 28
Spain, Arabian ruler in, 82
Spencer, Herbert, 91, 131
Spengler, Oswald, 2
Spermatozoa and ova banks, 139
Spinoza, Benedict, 153
Spitz, R. A., 245
Stace, W. T., 155
Stalin, Joseph V., 184
Stanford Research Institute, 144
Stark, Rodney, 211
Steinmetz, C. P., 109
Stevenson, R. L., 173
Stoicism, 97, 178
Storr, Anthony, 8, 117, 124, 125, 208, 220, 231, 243
Stuart, H. W., 94
Sturzo, Don Luigi, 162
Sufism, 234
Supraconscious, self-identification with:
  importance of study of, 145, 232
  suggestions for such study, 146, 147
  its use in fields of endeavor, 152, 153
Sutra of the Golden Light, 62
Switzerland, 185

"Systematic linkage," 183

Tagore, Rabindranath, 38, 39, 102, 175
Taoism, 59, 63, 73, 152
Tao Te King, 63
Techniques (26 in all) for altruization of individuals and society, 215-233
Techniques of Yoga, Zen and Sufism, 215, 232-235
 value in cultivating altruism, 202
Teleological theory of morals, 99, 100
Ten Commandments, 18
Teresa, Saint, 108
Tertium Organum, 6, 76
Thompson, J. Mark, 198, 201-203, 225
Tibetans and Tibetan Buddhism, 72, 73, 168
Tillich, Paul, 36, 46
Timasheff, N. S., 162
Time, 124
Tinbergen, Niko, 114
Tolstoy, Leo, 14, 16, 51, 251n
Torah, the, 61
Towers, Bernard, 125-128, 246, 265
Toynbee, Arnold J., 2
Trotsky, Leon, 15
Tunc (Durell novel), 86
Turkey, 139
Twain, Mark, 16

Unamuno, Miguel de, 2
UNESCO, 136, 260
Union League Club of Chicago (*see* Introduction)
United Nations (*see* Introduction), 23, 25, 260, 264
United Press International, 138
United States Arms Control and Disarmament Agency, 136
United States Steel Company, Chairman of, 207
Unity of All Creation, 69-77
Upanishads, 39, 71, 152
Uppsala, Sweden, 224
Utilitarian theory of morals, 97, 98

Vassar College, 15
Vedantism, 41, 70
Vexliard, Alexandre, 144, 147
Vivekananda, Swami, 70

Wagar, W. W., 170
Wang-Ming, 101
Wars, civil and foreign, frequency of, 26
Watts, Alan, 77, 104, 109
Webb, Sidney and Beatrice, 206
Weber, Max, 183, 184
Weil, R. J., 186
Wei Wu Wei, 74
Western Behaviorial Sciences Institute, 224
What Men Live By, 51, 251n
Whitman, Walt, 176, 264

index **313**

"Whiz-kids," 152
Winchester, Massachusetts, 16
Wisconsin, University of, 15, 136
World, the (Kang's three ages through which it must pass), 64
World Congress of Faiths, 267
World Congress of Sociologists, 19
World Council of Churches, 224, 267
World government (*see* Introduction), 25, 26, 28, 29, 65

Wright, Arthur, 65

Yale University, 136
Yale University Press, 140
Yoga, 53, 108, 143, 149, 198, 202, 215, 232, 234-236
Younghusband, Sir Francis, 170

Zeitgeist, 92
Zen, 215, 234, 235
Zimmerman, Carle, 18

About the Author

Joseph Allen Matter

A lawyer, lecturer, and writer, Mr. Matter was a partner in the Chicago law firm of Chapman and Cutter until 1966. Since then he has written several books on the Tudor period of English history. For his support of literature, he received the annual literary award from the Cliff Dwellers of Chicago. Recently he was appointed a member of the Arizona State Investment Council, which is in charge of state and local pension funds. He also is a trustee of Hastings College, and founder of the Sedona Community Center.

A past president of the Union League Club, Mr. Matter is a founder and director of the Union League Civic and Arts Foundation. He also is a member of the American Bar Association and other professional and civic organizations.

Mr. Matter received his J.D. degree from Northwestern University. He also did graduate work at the University of Chicago.